ARARAT

FRANK WESTERMAN

Ararat

TRANSLATED FROM THE DUTCH
BY

Sam Garrett

Harvill *Secker*
LONDON

Published by Harvill Secker 2008

First published as *Ararat* in The Netherlands in 2007 by Uitgeverij Atlas

2 4 6 8 10 9 7 5 3 1

Copyright © Frank Westerman 2007

English translation © Sam Garrett 2008

Frank Westerman has asserted his right under the Copyright,
Designs and Patents Act 1988 to be identified as the author of this work

First published in Great Britain in 2008 by
HARVILL SECKER
Random House, 20 Vauxhall Bridge Road,
London SW1V 2SA

www.rbooks.co.uk

Addresses for companies within The Random House Group Limited can be found
at: www.randomhouse.co.uk/offices.htm

The Random House Group Limited Reg. No. 954009

A CIP catalogue record for this book
is available from the British Library

ISBN 9781846550898

Foundation for the
Production and
Translation of
Dutch Literature

The publishers are grateful for the support of the Foundation
for the Production and Translation of Dutch Literature

Typeset in Fairfield LH Light by Palimpsest Book Production Limited,
Grangemouth, Stirlingshire

The Random House Group Limited supports The Forest Stewardship
Council (FSC), the leading international forest certification organisation.
All our titles that are printed on Greenpeace approved FSC certified paper
carry the FSC logo. Our paper procurement policy can be found at
www.rbooks.co.uk/environment

Mixed Sources

Product group from well-managed
forests and other controlled sources
www.fsc.org Cert no. TT-COC-2139
© 1996 Forest Stewardship Council

Printed and bound in the UK by
CPI Mackays, Chatham ME5 8TD

For Vera

Contents

Prologue

THE WATER HAD polished the stones to eggs. Milky quartz was solid white and opaque. Granulite, greenish and spotted. Otherwise you had limestone, which felt almost brittle.

The mountain stream rolled the stones steadily towards the sea and pounded them to gravel – 'scrubbed gravel', the kind they dredged up from the lower reaches of the big rivers. Speeds of up to one kilometre per century were quite normal, but during an ice age the transport could grind to a halt.

The stones in the Ill, a wadeable stream in the Austrian Alps, had been on their way for at least a few millennia by the summer of 1976, when several hundred were temporarily waylaid and moved slightly off course. On 23 July of that year, children at play lifted the rocks with their bare hands from the dry section of the riverbed. They lugged them towards the stream, then tossed their cargo into the water, which made an extra *splash!* amid the rapids.

One of those drudges was me. Eleven years old, and probably the youngest. I remember pausing to look at the change each stone made in the current. The dam we were building raised the level of the stream three or four hand's-breadths, reined it in for a moment, then swung it abruptly to one side, like a judo move. It was a glorious sight. My raw fingertips and the tingling in my forearms added to the sensation that we were helping to alter the natural course of things. The Ill tugged at our ankles and knees but could not make us lose our footing. Along both shores the

1

wooded hills rose up darkly, but there was nothing grim about the valley floor. The nearby covered bridge on the road to the village of Gargellen, with swallows nesting beneath its eaves, lent a carefree, model-railway feel to it all.

Our game on that cloudless day had grown serious. There were three 'master-builders', gangly beanpole boys in their teens, who stood in the water handing out orders. They had their T-shirts tied piratically around their heads. Following instructions from the supreme master-builder, we raised a dam that stretched to the middle of the Ill. There, along the river's longitudinal axis, lay a bare, elongated island, little more than a pebble beach that split the stream in two at its bow. The Ill complied by flowing alongside in two roiling halves, only to entwine again agitatedly at the stern. As soon as the dam was finished we were going to set up a tent on the island and build a campfire.

Waldcamping Batmund, where we were spending the holidays with our parents, had 42 pitches; the 'Ill-Insel' on the other side of the riverine woods was to be number 43.

Somewhere around noon the causeway was finished. All it needed was one boulder to anchor it in place, and to that end the supreme master-builder had dragged a log down from the woods. As the rest of us looked on, he lifted the log on his own and slammed it in place beneath a boulder like a battering ram.

'Freitag!'

To my amazement and joy he was calling me, and gesturing that I should slide a rock beneath the lever.

Just a little further down, *genau*!

Among the common labourers building the dam there were no Austrians. Only Germans, a pair of Belgian twins, Danes and Dutchmen.

I forced a speckled rock beneath the log and jumped back. I was proud of my nickname, of having been singled out. My dripping arms poised just inches from my ribcage, I stood and watched; a boy among thousands who had no desire to grow up, who dreamed of being able to remain 11, even 12 at a pinch, for all time, because homework started at 13. Then the playing would end.

I used my elbow to push a lock of hair out of my eyes. As I stood there waiting for what the rest of life had in store, I suddenly realised that it was Thursday – *Donnerstag*! – but from fear of somehow being mistaken after all, I didn't dare say that out loud. How grand it would be if it could always remain Thursday, this Thursday! If the Earth's axis could only lock with a click – it wasn't impossible, the Lord had done it once before so the people of Israel could win a war. He had caused the sun to pause in its course above the hilltops, just like the rising moon on the other side of the battleground, and of course all those soldiers and their horses must have been knocked to the ground, all of Asia must have been thrown out of bed.

One – two – three . . . The boulder wouldn't budge at first, but when two other boys came and leaned on the lever it tipped away from the embankment. Like the molar of a prehistoric animal, the chunk of granite popped loose and pounded down the hillside with four, five deep thuds, into the stream.

The sun had already passed its zenith; it must have been around two in the afternoon.

In the year 1976, the control room of the Vorarlberger Illwerke AG was equipped with table-high panels with recessed dials. Some of the controls worked automatically, but important matters, such as the level of the five reservoirs along the upper reaches of the Ill, were still regulated manually.

The interior of the control room was sober, you could say, were it not that one wall was covered by a huge representation in relief of the peaks and valleys of the Silvrettagruppe. Some would have called it a topographical map, or a scale model – but in fact it was something in between. Five blue, backlit perspex cutouts symbolised the Illwerke's reservoirs, while the turbines of the steam generators were indicated by tiny lamps. The Ill branched and squirmed like a blue vein. Just before Sankt Gallenkirch, at a bend in the valley, was a symbol consisting of two square brackets standing back to back: the bridge on the road to Gargellen. The campsite was not on the map; you could, however, see the Illwerke utility mast that towered over the tents and caravans.

On 23 July 1976, the duty operator was keeping a worried eye on the water balance of the Silvrettasee. The reservoir, which contained 38 million cubic metres of water, was held in check behind a concrete wall 80 metres high and 38 metres thick at its base. With a storage capacity that big, there was no reason why the water balance – supply minus drainage – necessarily had to remain constant.

For weeks, however, steady summer temperatures had been causing far more meltwater than usual to pour into the reservoir, bringing the level very close to the permissible maximum. Unless action were taken, water would start spilling over the top of the dam between eight and nine o'clock that evening. Generally, surplus water was drained during the night, but the operator felt that it would be irresponsible to wait any longer. At 1.30 that afternoon, he threw the handles that opened both floodgates at the foot of the Silvrettasee.

As soon as we had inaugurated the dam, we began gathering armfuls of firewood. I remember picking wild strawberries as well, amid the stand of willow along the bank, and putting them in the front pocket of my shorts. Tottering over the stone causeway, I carried my bundle of wood to the island in the Ill. There I took the jammed strawberries out of my pocket and arranged them on a polished stone; squatting, I watched as the master-builders laid out a circle of stones for the campfire.

My sister and the other girls from the campsite had gone to the Spar supermarket to buy potatoes, foil, flour, yeast, salt, milk, cola and, if they could, a bottle of Stroh rum to go with it. I thought about how we would bake the potatoes in foil that evening, and loaves of French bread on willow sticks. Our parents, still busy with their holiday reading beside the tent, would soon come down to take a look. I already knew how that would go: my mother was afraid to walk across the loose stones in the dam, but fortunately my father wasn't.

I sat there like that for a while, deep in thought, dabbling my fingertips in the current. It struck me that even though the pebbles looked dull when dry, once in the water they turned orange or green or red, like gems.

With an eye to the growing influx of tourists, Illwerke AG had posted warning signs along the Ill. Written on them in black letters was the word LEBENSGEFAHR!, along with an explanatory paragraph. No measly little signs these, but sturdy metal constructions on both sides of the river. One of them was attached to a pylon at the edge of the woods behind Waldcamping Batmund. In practice, everyone seemed to assume – without reading it – that the warning had to do with dangerous electrical currents and the obviously sensible ban on climbing the pylon.

We were arranging the faded green canvas of an army tent when we heard the roar of an approaching plane. My job was to hold up one of the telescopic metal tent poles. As the noise grew louder we all peered up at the sky above the treetops. Looking up like that, water suddenly came rushing into my shoes before I saw it. My first thought was to keep the firewood from getting wet. Then I saw the island go under, in one flowing movement. Upstream a foaming barrier of water was racing at us, filling the riverbed from shore to shore. It was not a roller or a steep, curling wall, but a layered, wildly spattering wave. Surf pounding the beach during a north-westerly storm.

Hopping into the shallow water along with the others, my chest sticking out like a runner crossing the finish line, I saw the dam wash away. With a dull bounce, the stones beneath my feet were bowled over the bed of the stream, which turned at once into a river; behind me the sheets of canvas and piles of firewood were being dragged by the current in the direction of the Gargellen bridge.

The others reached the shore, I remember seeing that, but I was seized around the waist and pulled under.

Masis

PILE UP THE syllables of Ararat and you get a mountain:

A
R A
R A T

I love to build words from letters, and stories from words. For the sake of the sound, the cadence, the meaning. And because of the sparks. Strike two sentences together and you get fire. Ararat is Armenian. Ararat is Turkish.

If all is well (and with Ararat all is well), the story rises above the rightness of the individual sentences, its summit like the first dry land after the deluge, a clean slate for a new start – that is how Ararat is anchored in the faith of my childhood.

The first time I saw Mount Ararat with my own eyes, I was not prepared. It was November 1999, in the days when the millennium bug was on everyone's lips. On Times Square, but also – closer to home – on Moscow's Red Square, you could watch the seconds tick by on bright digital screens. The great countdown had begun, the things one did were done a little more hastily, but also more intensely. The remote possibility that a built-in computer blunder could dislocate part or all of earthly civilisation lent the days a special aura. Who could guarantee that, at 00.00 hours on 1 January 2000, a barrage of Russian nuclear missiles would not rise from their silos along with the fireworks? You could remain stoic in the face of it, you could poke fun at it, you could see it as Armageddon in the offing.

It was during that time that I travelled to Armenia. I was working as a newspaper correspondent in the former Soviet Union, but had never visited the southern boundaries of my patch. An Aeroflot Ilyushin maintained the link between Moscow and Yerevan. For the first few hours the rotund aircraft followed a single meridian, then flew in a gentle curve over the Caucasus and its wars, dormant and active. Not so very far below us lay the sparkling mountain streams of Chechnya, and all one could hope was that we were above anti-aircraft range.

Upon arrival that first time in Yerevan, there was something I overlooked: the tube between the aircraft door and the airport complex sucks the unsuspecting visitor into the heart of a volcano. The architect had designed the terminal in the shape of a flattened cone, with the control tower rising from its crater like a jet of lava. As a passenger you don't notice that, because you're looking for your suitcase, shaking off annoying porters and cab-drivers, and all you really want to do at first is to have a pee.

Having collected my bags, I hopped aboard a shuttle bus idling in its own exhaust fumes beneath a concrete viaduct. As we headed into town, I was struck by the realisation that the flat country-side with its distant vines and poplars was shielded by a cordon of rock. The little wooden and stone huts, the irrigation canals and windbreaks – all were standing in the lee of that one barrier. It was not a wall, more a climbing wattle of layers green and grey. Strangest of all was the way the slopes continued up and up, like Jacob's ladder, filling the entire window of the bus. I had to crane my neck to see whether this pile of boulders and grass ever stopped, and leaning over a little further, I saw at last a black ribbon of rock capped by a veil of ice. Only above that came the blue of the sky. It was as though Ararat had seen me before I saw her.

In Yerevan one never escapes Ararat's gaze. That made me restless; what I felt like most was sitting down at a pavement café and staring back. 'Masis' the Armenians called her, or 'The Mother Mountain' – with a perfect volcanic cone on her flank that had once sprung from her womb amid thunderous contractions. I tried to go about my business, but was distracted by the backdrop of that two-headed mountain. Drumming in my head was the sentence my Russian teacher had once made me recite like a mantra, in order to practise the rolling 'r': '*Na gore Ararat rashtot krupny vinograd*' (On Ararat there grows an enormous vineyard). I caught myself taking pleasure in saying aloud the word 'Ararat' (which would not allow itself to be whispered). You could let the two r's roll like an avalanche of stone on a distant slope.

Daily life in the city went on as usual: street merchants displayed their wares – cut flowers, newspapers, puzzle books. Elsewhere, money-changers were busy jotting down the day's new exchange rates and sliding them into their *We Buy/We Sell* panels. But what I noticed most was how the day grew increasingly hazy as it wore on, making the lower slopes of Ararat look as though they had been drenched in lakes of milk. In the afternoon a collar of cloud arose around the level of black rock, but the gleaming whiteness of the summit still thrust its way through. There was nothing pointy about Ararat; the summit was a rounded, rolling icecap.

But even if you stayed inside there was no avoiding Ararat. Her likeness was on banknotes, postage stamps and printed as a holo-gram on credit cards. Even when I wasn't paying attention, she popped up in all kinds of surprising forms.

It started with the Yerevan Cognac Distillery, a granite fortress built in the Empire style of which Stalin was so fond. Its location atop a rocky outcrop provided a clear view of the alluvial plain and the stately volcano with its two peaks (the one with an icecap, the other bareheaded). 'Ararat' was the name of the cognac liqueur produced and bottled here, and the label sported a picture of the view from the distillery itself, rendered in gold paint. On the wall of the cellar where the cognac lay ageing, the writer Gorky had once scratched out a maxim of his own:

COMRADES, RESPECT THE POWER OF ARMENIAN COGNAC! IT IS
EASIER TO CLIMB UNTO HEAVEN THAN TO SCRAMBLE UP OUT OF
HERE ONCE YOU HAVE IMBIBED TOO MUCH.

The elderly Armenian in the three-piece suit who showed me
around was called Eduard. He ran his hand over the oak barrels
and talked about the Ararat grape, which grows only at the foot of
the mountain.

'You read the Bible?' The question sounded more like an instruc-
tion, or a recommendation at the very least, and he added confidently:
'The vines from which our grapes come grow in the vineyard that
Noah planted here himself.'

And so it went, again and again. With a photographer I took a
taxi to the National Salt Works, a mining operation where even the
company buildings at ground level were on the verge of collapse.
After the extraction stopped, an asthma clinic had been set up in
one of the shafts.

In what was once the miners' changing room we were outfitted
with helmets and hung with lab coats. Anoush, a paediatrician with
the looks of a stewardess, ran through the safety instructions. She
tossed her torch, thick as a man's wrist, from one hand to the other,
and arched her plucked eyebrows: only when she was satisfied were
we allowed to descend into her hospital. We climbed into a lift cage,
the grille door closed, and we sank wobblingly into the earth. Anoush
laughed and clicked on her torch. 'If the electricity fails, we'll need
this.'

Playing with the beam of light, she drew waves on the passing
strata. I recognised boulder clay, limestone formations and then,
quite suddenly, salt.

At 234 metres beneath the surface the cage stopped. A red neon
cross hung above the door, which opened on to a corridor hacked
out of solid salt crystal, with walls of the roughest plaster imaginable.
Moisture from the lungs and sweat of the miners had melted the
walls and ceilings as in a fantasy grotto. Behind plastic curtains
hanging from metal rods were children with moist black eyes who
could barely breathe in the normal air outside.

We were invited to sit down at tables fitted with things that looked like soup bowls. This was where the young patients received their 'oxygen cocktail' three times daily. The masks that hung beside them were each marked with a child's name. Then, as though we hadn't fallen deeply enough under Dr Anoush's spell, she said: 'The layer of salt in which we find ourselves precipitated immediately after the Deluge, when the waters receded.'

Perhaps this was all nonsense, but the salt bore witness in any event to the fact that the plains at Ararat's feet had once been a sea, or an inland sea, that had since evaporated like a bowl of water. The only question was: how many millions of years had gone by since this crust was formed?

The Armenians I spoke to weren't interested in what carbon-14 or potassium-argon dating had to say. For them, only one thing mattered: they were living in the land of Noah, the place where the first rainbow had appeared in the sky. In accordance with the letter of the Bible, they believed in an Ark that had been 300 cubits long, 50 wide and 30 high, a lifeboat caulked with pitch in which man and animal had survived the flooding of the whole Earth. They could point out the grave where Noah's wife was buried: a slate ruin on a hill. And yonder, close to that triangular spot of shadow on Ararat's northern flank, was where Noah had found the stone that served as the altar on which he sacrificed 'of every clean beast, and of every clean fowl'. Looking up at the omnipresent Masis, the Armenians saw the focal point not only of their own world but of the universe.

And my, were they religious – despite (or perhaps due to) the 'scientific atheism' to which they'd paid lip service during 70 years of Soviet rule.

Long-forgotten illustrations from my children's Bible came back to me there in Armenia, on the eve of the new millennium: I saw bearded Noah kneeling beside his altar to pray; the rainbow, the sign of God's covenant with mankind; I saw the dove with the olive branch in its beak; the animals swarming out of the Ark, two by two, with orders to 'be fruitful and multiply' upon the face of the Earth. That swarming, I knew even as a child, had taken place step by step, and not by joyful leaps and bounds. The giraffes and zebras, stiff from standing still for so long, had edged their way down the mountainside on their fragile legs.

Of course I didn't really believe that the Ark had run aground up there – to me, the story of Noah's Ark was a story, first and foremost – but the fact that you could say 'up yonder' and point to it with your finger did not leave me cold. I had never paused to consider that there were Biblical locations one could actually visit: the myth of the Ark was anchored in the rock-bottom reality of an actual mountain. One with a name, an altitude (5,165 metres) that could be measured precisely, and with coordinates (39° 42' north, 44°17' east) indisputable by human standards.

The beginning (t=0)

In one of the first photographs of me, I'm wearing a white gown. The gown has a train of artificial white silk that must be at least half a metre longer than my pedalling little legs. 'Baptism, 24 January 1965' the caption says, in my father's finest handwriting.

Again I saw myself, this time with a little polar bear at the zoo in Emmen, aboard a peat ship at Barger-Compascuum, and as a toddler at a sheep-shearing festival in Exloo: '5 June 1967'. My parents had a story to go with each picture, but I had no memories of this black-and-white world.

We were at the house where I grew up, sitting around the living-room table with its moss-green kilim. My mother went to her dresser and brought back a jewellery box. Lying on its velvet cushion was one of my milk teeth. There was also an envelope with my first lock of hair. Angel-white, as she called it.

'Look,' my father said, 'this is you, doing your first circus act.'

I saw myself holding my father's hand, balancing on a pipeline along a ditch. On the next page: picking blackberries, bucket in hand, and in the background the storage tanks of the transfer station for crude oil.

There was nothing I recognised, unless it was the nodding donkey pumps lined up in the wings of my earliest memories. Of all the oil installations I had grown up among, the nodding donkeys gave off the most penetrating smell.

I asked my parents about 'the derrick at 't Haantje'. Didn't they have a picture of it, not even one – preferably in silhouette against

12

the evening sky, so you could see if it was already a few degrees out of true?

In our family, the phrase 'the derrick at 't Haantje' has a mythical ring. When talk turns to 't Haantje, my parents and my elder sister effortlessly take the cue from each other's commentary and nods, while I remain completely in the dark. As soon as they start on about it, I hear in their voices a slight, time-tempered shiver, overshadowed by the bravura of hindsight: that we had been standing right under it, that even then it was already leaning like the Tower of Pisa, that we had escaped disaster by a whisker.

'Even then' was Sunday 28 November 1965: exactly two weeks after my first birthday. But the only picture from those days is one in which, rising up out of a highchair, I'm trying to sink my fingers into a cake with one candle.

It was Easter 2002 – two and a half years after my visit to Yerevan. I had given up my job as a correspondent, and with it my post in Moscow, which put me further away than ever from Ararat – almost 1,000 kilometres further, as the crow flies.

The web-fine outlines of the two-headed volcano, however, still hung in my thoughts. I had gone back to read the passage about Ararat in the Bible. 'And the Ark rested in the seventh month, on the seventeenth day of the month, upon the mountains of Ararat,' it said in Genesis 8:4. It sounded to me like a soft landing, back on the ravished Planet Earth. In the previous verses, though, that happy ending had not been entirely guaranteed; if you read carefully, it seemed as though God had for a time forgotten Noah's rudderless ship. 'And the waters prevailed upon the earth a hundred and fifty days. And God remembered Noah, and every living thing, and all the cattle that was with him in the Ark.'

Even as a child, the story of Noah and the animals had seized me by the scruff of the neck. It had always produced the same frisson of safe-and-snugness I'd felt when we sang 'He's got the whole wo-orld, in His hands' during the Monday morning assemblies at primary school. All six classes sat together then on the assembly hall's linoleum floor, and that same rolling gospel chorus was trumpeted again and again by six-to-twelve-year-old voices, until the windowsills around us seemed like a ship's railing.

Seeing Ararat had brought back that old lifeboat feeling. And to make matters complete, it was there in Armenia, in 1999, that the desire was born to climb Biblical Ararat and walk its highest ice fields. I had undergone the same thing as the poet Osip Mandelstam, who wrote from Armenia in the 1930s: 'I have developed a sixth sense, an Ararat sense: the feeling of being drawn in by a mountain.'

Back in the Netherlands, however, it didn't happen. My mind was not on distant journeys, let alone on mountain-climbing; not surprising, perhaps, for someone who had just become a father. Our daughter, Vera, had entered the world at three minutes to three on the afternoon of 6 March 2002, without mishap, by Caesarean section.

And what do you do when your first child is born?

You go back to where you come from. If anyone had tried to tell me that beforehand, I would gladly have bet against it ('Just wait, one year from now we'll be living in Istanbul'). But fatherhood does unexpected things to you. As you're growing up you extend your operating radius step by step, you swap the garden path for the street, the street for the city, and before you know it you find yourself aboard the Hellas Express to Thessalonica. But once you have reproduced, you begin retracting that world-band aerial segment by segment, and start your sentimental journey home.

We began visiting Drenthe, where I was born, more frequently than ever. The sheets and blankets in my parents' spare room and the conifers in the garden smelled the same as ever. The ageing ladies of the neighbourhood reported striking resemblances: Vera was just as blonde as I'd once been, she had the same inquisitive look, she had my mouth. The resemblance that struck me most, however, was this: I looked like my father when he had helped me tightrope my way along that pipeline, more than 35 years ago. Before long, Vera and I would be doing precisely the same thing, me offering

14

my arm for support in that same way, bent over slightly just like him, and it was that furious turnover rate of the generations that knocked the wind out of me.

Vera was asleep in the carrycot; she fluttered a nostril but didn't wake. Eight weeks old now, and unbaptised.

My parents never said a word about my daughter's condition, but had I asked them point-blank, my mother would have said, from deep down in her heart: 'A pity.' My father would only have nodded; she was his spokesperson in all things precarious.

Among the odds and ends that landed on the table were our Austrian hiking medals, and the stamps from the Alpine lodges to which we had climbed: Lindauer Hütte, Totalp Hütte, Saarbrücker Hütte. The 1970s came back in Kodak-Technicolor tints.

I opened the holiday scrapbook labelled *Vorarlberg, 1976*, and before I even reached the photographs of Waldcamping Batmund I saw myself, aged 11. It was as though I could taste the water of the stream all over again. Clear as a bell, the moment returned at which I had been snatched away by the current. Half under, half above water, I had been dragged beneath the bridge to Gargellen, where the Ill hurled itself between a boulder and a concrete pillar. Just before the mouth of that funnel, the water roiled up, I was lifted by a rising swell and spat out to one side, into a shallow inlet where I could grab hold of the rocks. The churning water beside me retreated again, plunging into the hole beneath the bridge.

Another memory arose immediately, tangled up with that one: after that summer I had begun to pray differently, more intensely, with my hands clasped so tightly that my knuckles turned white. Before then I had prayed out of habit, before and after meals. My sister and I would rattle off a bit of jabberwocky, 'Bessy's foot twitches extended ewes', rather than 'Bless this food to its intended use.' But being dragged away by the Ill had caused me to clutch at prayer. I would thank God the Father for having heard my cry above the roaring waters. He had seized me by a wrist and an ankle and tossed me from that flood. That's the way it had happened.

15

I was amazed to see myself again as that boy in pyjamas who addressed himself to Our-Father-who-art-in-Heaven. Was that really me? It had been more than 20 years, I realised, since I had prayed; I couldn't do it any more. There had been no radical break, no real renunciation in fact. I had come to see religion, in whatever form, as a kind of theatre, a round-the-clock performance written and directed by earthlings.

To my surprise, my parents knew nothing about my narrow escape from drowning.

'What I *do* remember,' my mother said after a while, 'is that one day the stream turned into a river.'

'Into a seething rusty-brown torrent,' my father added.

Apparently I had kept my most terrifying experience from my parents, and shared it only with God.

My mother, frightened by what she had never known, began fretting in hindsight; my father made the mental leap to 't Haantje. 'All four of us were almost killed that time.'

It struck me that, for my parents, 't Haantje must have felt like the same kind of close call as my experience in the Ill. The story told within the family said that the earth at that particular spot 'had been turned inside out, like at Sodom and Gomorrah'. Our family, like Lot's, had escaped by a hair's breadth. But to me, 't Haantje remained a blank spot on the map, and that began troubling me.

I asked my parents to tell me exactly what had happened on 28 November 1965. And I didn't want to hear the myth any more, only the facts.

They gave the following account:

My father, who worked in the drafting office at the Nederlandse Aardolie Maatschappij (Dutch Petroleum Company), had read in the NAM news bulletin that colleagues were drilling for gas beside the Oranjekanaal. 'Hey, kids, that's close to Emmen,' he'd said. 'Let's go and have a look.'

My mother and sister were not particularly enthusiastic. Compared with a nodding donkey, which at least takes elegant bows for the viewer, a drilling derrick is a static and boring thing. A pylon without arms or cables.

'A replica of the Eiffel Tower, that's more like it!' My father, with his penchant for hyperbole, had won the case, and so, carrycot and all, I was loaded into the back seat of our first car, a Renault Dauphine. We drove out of Emmen in the direction of Sleen, then followed the Oranjekanaal to the former peat-cutting settlement of 't Haantje. In a pasture at the bottom of a dead-end road stood the derrick. The oilfield itself, a tarmac space the size of two football pitches, was surrounded by a concrete gutter and a fence topped with coils of barbed wire. On the closed barrier hung a sign posted by the Dutch Mining Authority: NO SMOKING.

My sister, almost six at the time, was the first to notice the strange registration plates on the parked cars.

'They're from France,' my father told her. 'What did I tell you? The builders of the Eiffel Tower are at work here.'

The drilling camp looked more like a gypsy settlement than anything else, in terms of both location (remote, a good 100 metres in this case from the last farm in 't Haantje) and accoutrements (messy, with scrap metal stacked up between the egg-shaped caravans). There were a few cement silos from the firm Halliburton, a rack of steel pipes, a pair of smoking diesel generators and three workmen's huts which my father, in his oilfield English, called 'doghouses'.

The gypsies were sun-baked Frenchmen, members of a travelling *equipe* from Forex, a drilling company based in the town of Pau at the foot of the Pyrenees.

The only car with Dutch plates, a black Volkswagen Beetle, belonged to Jan Servaas, one of my father's colleagues who had been assigned to the crew as 'mudboy'. My sister wanted to know what a mudboy was – did he really work with mud, the way my father claimed?

She never got to ask him, because no one came to the gate that afternoon. We could only watch the helmeted workmen from a distance. They wore round-tipped boots and filthy plastic aprons over their clothes, and one was standing on a platform three-quarters of the way up the tower.

'That one up there is called the "derrickman",' my father pointed out, holding me in his arm. 'His job is to thread one drill pipe on top of the other.'

Doghouse, mudboy, derrickman – those were the first English words to make it into our family circle.

What happened after we left, however, my parents knew only secondhand. My father, as it turned out, had kept a few memorable clippings in a file with the title 'Finance & Planning'. One of them was from the front page of the daily newspaper *Noord-Ooster*, dated 2 December 1965:

DERRICK 'T HAANTJE COMPLETELY DESTROYED

Large part of drilling installation disappeared into the ground.
It was as though an invisible hand tore open the earth. The
derrick buckled and collapsed with a loud noise. Machines
and drilling equipment sank deeper and deeper into the crater
caused by the explosion. It was a scene from judgement day,
worse than a bombardment.

If I really wanted to know the ins and outs, my father suggested, why not talk to Jan Servaas, the mudboy at 't Haantje? In the last few years before they retired, he and my father had worked together in the planning department.

'Jan's a staunch, strait-laced character,' he warned me. 'Fairly eccentric. When things got too noisy for him he used to crawl under his desk and work there.'

Jan Servaas' number was there in the directory. I phoned, and immediately recognised the way he talked: this was NAM-speak. The Dutch spoken by the mudboy from 't Haantje bore no trace of a regional accent, and was punctuated every few sentences by an English term such as 'toolpusher' or 'well engineer'.

I asked whether, as an eyewitness and a man of practical experience, he could tell me what had gone wrong back in 1965 during the exploratory drilling known by the name of 'Sleen II'.

'Aha, 't Haantje,' he said. 'That was a huge act of grace.'

A huge act of grace! The phrase sounded so archaic, like the seventeenth-century translation of the Bible from which my grand-father used to read aloud. I wondered whether this Jan Servaas might see God's hand at work in the disaster – and did my best to arrange a meeting.

The idea of a clean slate was what attracted me to 't Haantje. With his universal flood, God had been out to eradicate His creation and start all over again. That, on a small scale – you could almost call it 'laboratory scale' – was precisely what had happened here too. The deep geological substrata had been rolled and mixed together into a porridge that defied all attempts at dating. At the very spot where the NAM engineers had performed their engineering work, 2 December 1965 was t=0.

It reminded me of my maternal grandfather and his unshakeable faith in the Word. Year after year he would go to the Monday morning cattle market in Rotterdam, buy a cow and a pig and walk them back to his yard, where he killed them with a single shot from his butcher's pistol. Not long before he died, his old school honoured him with a great deal of pomp and circumstance as its oldest living alumnus (he was well into his nineties by that time). The press was there, the mayor, the headmaster. The conversation turned to the subject of age, and the headmaster found that a fitting moment to show my grand-father a fossil from the Cretaceous period. 'This is a petrified ammonite. It lived on the earth one hundred million years ago.'

My grandfather rested his meaty hands on the head of his cane. 'A hundred million years? That's ridiculous. The earth is six thou-sand years old. Add up the genealogies from Adam on and work it out for yourself.'

Fine. That was my grandfather, vintage 1903.

Then you had his daughter, my mother, born in 1934. Once, when I had completed a school essay on the subject of 'aggres-sion among humans and animals' and was proudly showing her the results, she had stiffened in horror. 'Although man is descended from the apes . . .' She couldn't make it past the very first sentence.

And what about me, born in 1964; where did I stand? I didn't want to burden my daughter with my own inability to believe. But exactly what I *did* want to pass on to her, I wasn't quite sure yet.

Two weeks later I met Jan Servaas at Café Wapen van Sleen. We ordered rustic omelettes on white bread.

'Just call me Jan,' Servaas said. He rearranged his knife and fork on the place mat (red-checked tablecloth pattern, with an old-fashioned village scene in the middle) in front of him.

'I have fond memories of the Wapen van Sleen,' he said. And, nodding at the owner behind the bar: 'Her mother did the catering for our crew. She used to drive out in the van and bring us salami sandwiches for lunch, goulash or schnitzel with mashed potatoes for dinner.'

Drenthe had certainly changed since 1965, but the Wapen van Sleen had not. No kitsch for the tourists here, only African violets on the windowsills. Lace curtains. Fruit machines, dartboard, antlers.

As soon as the woman of the house had put down the plates of three egg yolks in a wreath of crinkly bacon, Jan closed his eyes.

'Bon appétit,' I said.

'Amen,' he said.

It startled me for a moment, even though my father had told me that Servaas belonged to the rigidly orthodox branch of the Dutch Reformed Church. To me, faith had been an intimate thing, something you didn't parade in public. The days when I had asked God's blessing for the food in a restaurant lay far behind me. And even back then, on the rare occasions when our family had done that, I had always felt embarrassed in front of the waiters.

Even before Jan had finished tying his napkin around his neck, he told me there was one possible misconception he wanted to set straight. The mudboy, he said, is not the dogsbody of the drilling crew. When he works with lead or lye, he wears a canvas apron and a perspex mask. The mudboy mixes. Diesel oil, magnesium chloride, barite, clay. In an open tank he makes a slush of a given specific weight and viscosity. That slush – or 'mud' – is then pumped into the drill hole: a column of fluid to counteract the pressure of the gas or oil bubble which – with explosive force – is searching for release at the surface.

'We used powdered lead to keep Blijham down. Not good for the environment, that's right. But if you don't keep it down, the damage is unimaginable.'

He took off his glasses and rubbed the memories from his face. His eyebrows were those of a 67-year-old, white and thin. Above them: furrows of concentration that would no longer let themselves be massaged away.

Jan Servaas began working for NAM two years after my father did, in 1958 – at a time when production at the Schoonebeek field was reaching record levels. Because he had a way with languages, he was assigned to the press and publicity department, where he organised promotional junkets for potential employees who wanted to find out whether life really existed out on the desolate peat flats of Drenthe. He also acted as guide to delegations of dignitaries from NAM shareholders Shell and Esso, who would arrived at Emmen aboard a chartered train. 'I used to take them to Hotel Grimme. They always got coffee and pastries.' Jan would welcome them, then start the film *Deep Holland*. The film's message: after centuries of laborious peat extraction (= poverty), mineral resources (= wealth) were being drawn from the region's carbon-age strata. Then the tour bus would pass the crude oil transfer station, the switchyard where tankers were filled to the brim before going to the refinery at Pernis. Along the way, Servaas would have the bus stop beside clusters of nodding donkeys, with their air of calm and hospitality. Those pumps went with this landscape just as St Andrew's crosses went with level crossings, so naturally and completely that the citizens of Schoonebeek felt uneasy when their sonorous droning was temporarily silenced during maintenance.

The high point of these excursions was always the futuristic recreation centre De Boo, set up by the NAM at the edge of the village. De Boo was a members-only club with tennis courts and bowling alleys, exclusively for NAM employees. According to local clergymen, the heated swimming pool there was a cesspool of vice, where visitors bobbed around blithely on the Lord's Day, and in mixed company to boot. Although Servaas always remained true to his strict Reformed faith, De Boo was his ace in the hole: after each visit his charges would sit on the sunny patio and speak admiringly of such peerless company facilities.

My parents saw *Deep Holland* at the Cineac theatre in Rotterdam. They did not, however, belong to the category of doubting Thomases who had to be convinced by means of an excursion. As a young, newly engaged couple, the most important thing was finding a house to rent. My father's job as draughtsman and design engineer for railway carriages was becoming increasingly uncertain, and so in 1956 he applied for a job with Royal Dutch Shell in The Hague. He was taken on, and told that he would be transferred immediately to Venezuela. My father was horrified; he had never dreamed of moving that far away. In that case, his superiors said, they had another offer: he could go to work at Schoonebeek. That was still in the Netherlands, there was no denying that.

My parents had no choice, they were thrilled. Which is not to say that the move from a village outside Rotterdam all the way to south-eastern Drenthe did not feel like outright emigration. On the map they looked up Emmen, their future place of residence. Running your finger over the road that led there, you came across towns and villages with names like Moscou, De Krim, De Nieuwe Krim and Ballast.

The house the NAM assigned them was on Walstraat, a broad lane of shady trees close to the local zoo. Our neighbours were geologists, drilling foremen, surveyors. Young couples who played bridge at each other's houses on Saturday evenings. The NAM owned 18 houses on the street, all with thatched roofs. Another striking feature was the half-dozen black Volkswagen Beetles parked out in front, the company car for those who drove daily from well to well. Every bit as noteworthy were the identical front gardens (beech hedges, lawns and flowerbeds) maintained by a NAM gardener. Walstraat played a central role in Press & Publicity's excursions.

'Whenever we drove through there, all I had to say was: "This is how our employees live.'" Servaas himself rented a flat amongst the peat workers in the Emmermeer district. 'Walstraat was a close community. If one family bought a fridge, three more were sold the same week.'

After a few years of guiding tours and endlessly starting *Deep Holland*, Jan had a chance to sign up for the company course in General Drilling Technique. Afterwards he opted for 'mud engineering', a specialism that took him where he wanted to be: out with the real workers, at the drilling sites.

He still drove a Volkswagen. We left Sleen at the cruising speed of a tour bus and crawled across the rolling rises of the Hondsrug. A blue-and-white sign indicated the turnoff for the Continental Relaxation Centre, but we drove on. Two lever-arch files with the daily drilling logs from Sleen II were lying in readiness on the back seat.

On a little road beside the Oranjekanaal, between a kayak rental firm and a lone fisherman, Servaas turned off the engine. It was from this spot that he had seen the derrick disappear. A real spectacle, and at the same time so moving that it had brought tears to his eyes. 'We'd spent two whole weeks fighting to save the installation, but there it went, into the depths.'

Servaas leaned one of the files against the steering wheel and clicked open the metal rings. 'Here,' he said, 'on the eighteenth of November 1965, we hit gas, at a depth of one thousand eight hundred and forty-four metres.'

The manometer had read 290 bars, almost twice the anticipated pressure. The well began spilling over immediately, that is to say: the drilling fluid, with a specific gravity of 1.2 kilograms per litre, came bubbling up out of the wellhead. Along with his French colleagues, Servaas stiffened the sludge with barite (powdered *blanc fixe* from Cyprus), and only when the specific gravity reached 1.7 was the well once again 'dead'.

Schlumberger, another French company, arrived with a test vehicle full of equipment for monitoring the gas-bearing layer: its porosity, permeability and other properties of the rock. The technicians lowered a radioactive core, installed electrodes and calculated the potential yield curves.

Because Sleen II was growing so unstable, NAM issued orders to the specialists needed most urgently: do not leave the well until further notice. 'We were given a sleeping bag, an army parka and an extra pair of mittens, and that was it.'

There were further setbacks. While the drill chuck was being brought up for replacement, the shaft collapsed. An obstruction had formed one kilometre down, in the Cretaceous layer, and the drill was trapped. Servaas noted the first losses of sludge, indicating the presence of an unstable layer of mud and gas. The column of fluid, meant to act as a cork on the gas bottle, was oozing away into the surrounding limestone. To avert a disaster, a rotating 'blowout-preventer', a steel lid beneath the drilling floor, had to be installed immediately, to keep the wellhead closed while the drill was being raised and lowered. That kind of equipment was not available in the Netherlands, and had to be ordered post-haste from abroad.

For as long as the rotating lid was not fixed in place, there was no way of preventing a blowout. 'Everything would have been blown sky-high,' Jan said.

When the safety valve arrived from Germany, the crew spent Sunday 28 November installing it.

That was the afternoon that my parents, my sister and I had watched from the other side of the fence. We had walked down the little tarmac road as far as the barrier. Without our knowing it, a shaft almost two kilometres deep was burrowing its way beneath our feet, and 72 hours later would swallow up the drilling grounds, including the road and the barrier. That was the situation in which our little family found itself; no more threatening than that, but no less threatening either.

'It was a horrible, nerve-racking job,' Servaas recalled. 'The Frenchmen ran around swearing like troopers.'

His glasses sitting on the tip of his nose, he read on: '"*Monday the twenty-ninth of November. Lowered rotating bit with sludge to nine hundred and twenty-seven metres. Sludge loss: four cubic metres. Rotating blowout-preventer leaking.*"

'That was a bad sign. We told each other: I hope we can keep this thing under control. If gas and sludge started bubbling up behind the shuttering, it would all be too late.

'"*Tuesday the thirtieth. Counterpressure falls from twenty-three to four kilos per square centimetre. Sludge loss: seventy-four cubic metres.*"

'Three full tanks in a single day; you wondered where it was all going.'

That afternoon, Servaas' wife Rineke appeared at the gate. She had cycled all the way from Emmermeer with the children, the younger in a seat on the handlebars, the older of the two on the back. The reunion at the barrier was a quick one. She had come to bring Jan a basket containing shaving soap, clean socks and underwear. But also to tell him that she had a bad feeling about the whole business.

'We have to hand it over,' he had told her. 'Hand it over' was an expression that made me blink again; I had always thought that my mother was the only one who used it, in the sense of 'putting it in God's hands'. Apparently the Servaas family was more like ours than I'd been prepared to admit.

Rineke and the children were barely out of sight when it started hailing. The storm kept up all night, and the next morning the fields were covered with a white crust.

Wednesday 1 December. The melting hail and cold gusts of wind did little to improve the crew's humour. The situation at the well had become so critical that Servaas had to keep a constant eye on the manometer. 'When I whistled, Kwant, our toolpusher, stuck his head over the railing. He was on the drilling floor, a couple of metres higher. He nodded to ask what was going on. "The pressure's rising!" I shouted.'

Much higher up, almost at the top of the tower, was Jean, the derrickman.

That day's logbook was incomplete. Servaas took the last page out of the folder and eyed it carefully.

Between 12.10 and 13.40, the drilling master let the bit drop from 1,011 to 1,065 metres. That was equal to six nine-metre lengths of pipe. With the seventh, the counterpressure dropped: the blockage had been removed, and the well was once again connected to the gas-bearing layer at 1,850 metres. Servaas expected to see the pressure rise but instead the needle on the manometer began falling towards zero. 'Bad news. Somewhere, far down there, the stone had begun to split. The gas and sludge were disappearing into all kinds of cracks and cavities.'

Servaas whistled again. Kwant looked down at him. What was it now? This time the toolpusher's expression was not one of curiosity or irritation, but amazement. At the spot where his mudboy was standing, he saw the asphalt bulge. It was 15.10 hours. The ground under Jan's feet was heaving like a tarpaulin. Molehills were sprouting up. 'Well, how can I explain it? I was being lifted up by little piles of sand that were pushing their way straight through the asphalt. Miniature volcanoes.'

The mudboy leapt back, almost tripping. But behind him the asphalt was also lifting with a hiss. Someone shouted: 'Run for it!'

Kwant chased his men off the drilling floor. Jean started climbing down from the derrick but was still somewhere between heaven and earth when the rotating blowout-preventer exploded. There was the sound of shearing metal; the hissing turned to a whistle, and there was a strong smell of methane. Then, 50 metres beyond the workmen's hut, the pasture split asunder. A geyser of mud at least 15 metres high came spouting out of the ground. 'And you should have heard the noise! It was like standing beside a fighter jet at takeoff.'

The Frenchmen hopped into their cars and made off. The forklift driver from Hoogeveen drove away in his forklift truck. Kwant stayed, Servaas stayed. He turned off the auxiliary generator for the sludge basins, snatched the drilling logs from his desk and tossed them in his car. Then he phoned the chief engineer, a man named Bos, in Oldenzaal.

'Sleen II here. We have a blowout. What do you want us to do?'

But Bos couldn't hear him.

In the absence of instructions, Servaas made one final tour of inspection. He knew in theory what a blowout involved, the kinds of forces it unleashed. Nevertheless, the mudboy did not realise that a circular hole was being burrowed out beneath him and would soon reach the surface. He went into the doghouse two more times to jot down observations in the logbook.

An entry: *At approx. 15.45 hours, tower starts to lean. The casing on the scaffold is starting to move. Little geysers popping up to a height of approx. 1 metre within a 300-metre radius. Large crater blowing to approx. 5 metres. Halliburton silos listing. Substructure is collapsing. Craters spouting mud appear along western perimeter. Pipe rack collapsing.*

And then, at the end, with the sobriety of a bank draft: *16.02 hours, leaving location.*

Servaas followed Kwant's Ford Cortina up on to the dyke along the Oranjekanaal. There they climbed out and stood in silence, watching the mud spray. Before their eyes, the pastureland was being turned inside out by dozens of geysers.

At 16.27 the derrick at 't Haantje began to quiver, like a giant robot taking its first, shaky steps. But it proved unequal to the task: in fits and starts, the four-legged construction crumpled and disappeared into the ground.

The same fate lay in store for the two Badouin motors that had been driving the chuck all that time. They were simply pulled into the ground by their winch cables. The Halliburton silos followed shortly afterwards, along with the three doghouses, the sludge tanks, the diesel generators, the wastewater reservoir and hundreds of nine-metre drilling pipes.

Only the sodium lamps at the corners of the field, which had spread their orange glow over the installation by night, remained upright. The guards' caravans were not swallowed up either, but cast from their moorings. They bobbed about on the waves of mud like sailing boats in a raging storm.

Taking turns, with one foot up on the back of the car, we pulled on our boots. In the distance, down the straight road at right angles to the canal, lay the crater woods. Jan had never been back here. Why, I wanted to know, had he remained at the well for so long that day, knowing how bloody dangerous it was?

'Sense of duty,' he said decidedly. There was no fear at first, that only came later. 'You didn't have counselling for post-traumatic stress back then. It was your job, and it was up to you to do it.' That strict way of seeing things was rooted in his faith, that's right. 'The Good

Book puts it this way: "In the sweat of thy brow shalt thou eat bread, till thou return unto the ground."'

On the way we passed a bale of silage wrapped in a sheet of agricultural plastic. Then a KPN Telecom pole behind a pointy fence.

Servaas looked shaken; it wasn't easy for him to relive this. 'No one was killed and no one was injured. We were all able to save our cars. No one was punished, but we were all warned.'

I asked whether he saw God's hand in the accident.

'I see it as a reprimand. A warning against human arrogance and the pride of science. We at NAM may think we're able to do just about anything, extract gas from great depths, for example, but we're not almighty. Only the Lord is.'

But was that the lesson, then: never to drill again? To forswear fossil fuels and go back to the days of the megalith builders?

I had misunderstood him. Jan pulled out a packet of full-strength rolling tobacco. 'What it's all about is the Day of Judgement. We need to be ready for that at all times.' He quoted from Matthew, 'the sermon on the last things', in which Jesus says that the end of the world will be announced by great catastrophes. 'And there shall be famines, and pestilences, and earthquakes, in divers places. All these shall be the beginning of sorrows.' Methodically, using the earpiece of his glasses, he tamped down the tobacco in his hand-rolled cigarette, then cited another verse: 'As it was in the days of Noah, so shall it be also in the days of the Son of Man. Two men shall be in the field; the one shall be taken, and the other left.'

I looked over at Jan; the grooves in his face were set. I wanted to take him seriously, but how could I? The mere suggestion that one should passively accept the existence of such a cruel God made me angry. The recurring notion that natural disaster – in accordance with the moral of the Deluge – was a punishment from the Supreme Being I found downright appalling. That was how the God-fearing citizens of Zeeland province had explained the great flood there in 1953, but in the face of deadly hurricanes, earthquakes and volcanic eruptions in other parts of the world, you saw the same thing – with every religion. Catastrophe was a warning to the survivors that they

28

had turned from God, and that provided an immediate explanation for the resulting suffering as well: penance.

To prevent life being unbearable, it seemed that suffering had to be by design, and the absolute precondition to that was the existence of a Designer.

I thought I detected a pattern here: anyone who felt solid ground beneath his feet for a while would begin believing in himself, in mankind, but anyone who saw the bottom drop out of his life promptly began believing in God. I wondered whether I myself, perhaps when confronted by the hand of fate, would also call upon a higher power. On the face of it, that didn't seem likely. Yet when I stopped to think about it, I had to admit that I wasn't sure. I had no idea. But, in fact, I wanted to know.

At the start of the path to the crater woods, the forest service had erected a sign for visitors. Under the heading '1965: AN EXTRAORDINARY EVENT' was a brief description of the blowout that had taken place here, a disaster by which the wellhole itself had been transformed into a seething crater some 200 metres in diameter. For months afterwards, huge quantities of mud were still being launched into the air.

Jan Servaas read aloud the note under 'UNUSUAL NATURAL PHENOMENA': '"Having been brought back to the surface, seeds buried at great depths for centuries may succeed in germinating here. It will be interesting to see which plants and animals are able to gain a foothold in this 'moonscape'."'

Apparently, palaeontologists saw this scar in the earth's crust as a test plot for the return of prehistoric flora. I pondered the significance of this. As we walked into the woods past a duck pond, heading for the clearing, I imagined how at this latitude the earth had once, long ago, before the last ice age, been overgrown with magnolias and swamp cypresses. Then the glacier tongues arrived from Scandinavia, leaving behind lateral moraines and the occasional boulder. People appeared, dressed in animal skins, and rolled those boulders to a flat place where they piled them up into megaliths. Their descendants built a tarmac space and drilled a hole in the ground, but something went wrong and the old strata twisted their way back to the surface. With that eruption, man's efforts had been smothered in mud and cast back in time with a gigantic thud. That was 40 years ago. And so could we now expect the primal vegetation to start sprouting again?

My imagination boggled at the idea that nature had started all over again here, but Servaas wasn't interested at all.

'Well,' he said, 'every organism has its own orders from the Creator, that's all I know.'

How distant this view of the world was from my own. Orders from the Creator? Apparently he took Genesis 1 literally. I had been brought up with the Bible as well, but that had never made me turn off my powers of reason. I simply couldn't accept that the mudboy of this very well, who could precisely calculate for you the subtleties of pressure and counterpressure, could see God's work in a man-made disaster.

In an attempt to speak his language, I said: 'It reminds me more of Ecclesiastes.'

'Ecclesiastes?'

'You know, that all human effort ultimately leads to nothing, that everything is "vanity" and dust in the wind.'

'But even Ecclesiastes finally ends up at God,' Jan said.

He was right. What I had left out was that I was actually thinking about Ecclesiastes minus God, about the merciless way in which the King of Jerusalem had held all human ambition up to the light and let it pop, as though pricking it with a pin.

We walked down the track through the woods. With every step our shoes sank deeper into the spongy soil, leaving us no choice but to hop from one clump of grass or broken branch to another. After a few minutes we arrived at the clearing. Where I had expected to see a bowl there was instead a ridge of clay, covered in peat moss. Here, by the looks of it, was where the earth had breathed its last gasp.

Jan Servaas leaned against a tree with his tobacco pouch in his hands; I walked on. I knew that I didn't have to worry about open shafts or holes; the crater's chimney had filled with mud. A toad, listless and ugly, hopped off to one side. It was strange to stand atop a derrick that had disappeared into the earth without a trace.

Ash and lava

THE MINING FACULTY in Delft was on Mine Street, which pretty much said it all. At home, 'Delft' had always been synonymous with training for a career as a rockhound in the service of oil and gas extraction. That, more than its delft-blue porcelain or the royal crypts beneath the New Church, was what the town's name evoked. Mining at Delft was an institution, and all the streets could do was reflect that.

I had never been to this engineers' sanctum, not even on the annual 'orientation days' for secondary school pupils. My father would have loved to see me do that, though; Royal Dutch Shell offered scholarships and the prospect of a job to NAM children who chose mining. In fact, I had never been to Delft at all. Crossing the canal that divided the medieval city centre from Anthracite Square and Bauxite Lane, I looked around in amazement. Budding engineers in polo shirts were hanging out of the windows of a Catholic hall of residence, like a scene from Hogarth. VIGILATE DEO CONFIDENTES – KEEP WATCH AND TRUST IN GOD – was engraved on the plaque above their heads. When I asked for Mine Street, they pointed the way with the necks of their swing-top beer bottles.

It was a warmish afternoon in June, and Mine Street was longer than I'd imagined. At number 120, between buildings squat as cloisters, I found what I was looking for. The faculty building had its own belfry, a German-looking slate roof, a lion balancing on a ledge. Chiselled into the pediment above the entrance were the words INSTITUUT VOOR MIJNBOUWKUNDE, but my visitor's eye was caught first by the stainless-steel plaque beside the door, which read simply TECHNICAL EARTH SCIENCES.

I entered the hallway for a meeting with my former geology professor, Salomon Kroonenberg. The professor and I had recently moved to a first-name basis, which meant that I was not to call him Salomon, but just plain 'Salle'. I had written to him to ask whether he could help me, from a geologist's perspective, to dredge up Ararat's past. I'd also mentioned that I was working on a book about 'belief and knowledge, religion and science, with Ararat as its focal point'; that I wanted to get to know both the myth and the reality of that mountain, and ultimately to climb it. It was to be a sort of pilgrimage, but then again, the pilgrimage of a non-believer.

To that end, I first needed to get to grips with the hard facts about Ararat – age, composition, origin.

Salle Kroonenberg was a trained field geologist and had done his doctoral research in the Surinam interior. That he had never gone looking for extractable ore or oil-bearing strata on behalf of some multinational was down to his own interests, which were too eclectic for that. At the age of 35, as a generalist with an unconquerable urge to know as much as he could about everything, he was offered the Chair of General Geology at the Agricultural University in Wageningen; I enrolled there one year later, in 1983. Along with about 150 other freshers I had attended his lectures, which made no lasting impression on me.

Years later, though, for the elective 'Geology II', I encountered him again in a less crowded setting, and this time unforgettably. A few strands of his hair always stuck out above his crown as though blowing in an invisible sea breeze and he had the habit of pacing back and forth in front of his slide screen as though keeping time with the momentum of his words. More than once in those lectures he had touched upon the November 1985 mudslide that turned the Colombian town of Armero into a necropolis, burying alive 30,000 of its inhabitants. He talked about how the whole world had over-looked signs that the Nevado del Ruiz, the volcano that caused the catastrophe, was about to erupt. It had, as I recalled, something to do with cows that died after breathing in particles of volcanic glass.

And about the annual beauty contest at a local ski resort. Pictures had been preserved of Armero's prettiest girls, posing in scanty clothing on slopes that were no longer a pure white, but dull with ash.

The point of his lectures was always the same: man is forgetful and stubborn; the forces of the earth go their own, indifferent way, and will overwhelm him time and time again.

The door to office 225 stood ajar: Prof. Dr S.B. Kroonenberg had slid the little plaque reading 'IN' under his nameplate, but the office seemed vacant. The corridors of the mining faculty were lined with glass display cases containing chunks of gneiss, schist and feldspar, as well as unpolished crystals – some transparent as mica, others lemon yellow or ochre. The late-afternoon light made them look like poisonous flowers.

'Come in.' I heard what was definitely Salle's voice, but couldn't tell where it was coming from. On the wall of his office was a map of the primal continent of Pangaea, the accreted land mass as it had been before fissures arose and the tectonic plates were cut adrift.

'Be with you in a minute. I put a few things on the round table there. Have a look and see if it's what you're after.'

Opposite his desk were a couple of fifties-style chairs arranged around a coffee table covered with a still life of maps, computer printouts and opened books. I sat down and was just peeling off the top layer when Salle suddenly appeared beside me in his shirt-sleeves. He shook my hand, apologised for the delay, and began tying his shoelaces. 'I had to stand in rather unexpectedly for a colleague at the presentation of a degree.' He slid aside the folding screen that had concealed a sink and a microscope. He folded his bands and gown hastily and stuffed them into a checked suitcase.

Perching on the edge of a chair, he started. 'What I always consult first is *Volcanoes of the World*, from the Smithsonian Institute in Washington.'

The reference work lay open at Mount Ararat. According to the Smithsonian's classification, the volcano was number 0103-04. Country: Turkey. Altitude: 5,165 metres. Type: Stratovolcano.

'Which means?'

'That it's built up from ash and lava. Layer by layer, like baklava.' Stratovolcanoes, he said, were the most common. Mount Etna was a stratovolcano, as was Vesuvius. 'You find them in places where two tectonic plates collide.'

Then he ran his index finger over to the heading 'Status', which listed three possibilities: extinct / dormant / active. Ararat was listed as active.

'So it's a working volcano that could start spitting ash and lava any moment?'

'In principle, yes. But I wouldn't worry about it. In this case, "active" means that it has erupted at least once since the Holocene era. In other words, since the last ice age.'

I confessed I had forgotten how long ago that was.

'Ten thousand years,' he said, graciously refraining from a sigh at my ignorance.

The next publication on the pile was entitled *Вчлканцзм Армянской ССР*. It was a Soviet publication from 1971; according to the back flap, it had cost 94 kopeks.

For a moment I had a sneaky suspicion he was bluffing, that he was as incapable as I of deciphering complicated Russian texts. But then I remembered that line on his website: 'Excellent understanding, speaking, reading and writing of English, Spanish, French, Russian, German, Italian; fair knowledge of Portuguese, Finnish, Surinamese.' Behind his back his colleagues called him 'the poet among geologists', which in their book was not a compliment per se.

That Salle Kroonenberg could at least make himself understood in Russian was something I had seen first-hand. Shortly after I returned from Moscow we had bumped into each other at an Amsterdam arts cinema, at the screening of an old Soviet film. The lights in the cinema were turned down, but I knew straight away that it was my old geology professor sitting up there in the front row. After the film we spent time talking with some Russians. Salle introduced himself in Russian and said that, as a member of a research group, he had been racking his brains over the inconstant level of the Caspian Sea. I, in turn, said that I had known Salle for a long time, that he had driven a Peugeot 504 to visit the 'concrete mud' burying the town of Armero (the car had shown up repeatedly in his slides), and that, in his words, the continents moved 'with the speed at which your nails grow'.

He was surprised, pleasantly surprised, but couldn't for the life of him place me. When we exchanged addresses, he scribbled 'Salle' on his business card, between his doctor's title and his initials.

'There's a fair amount of information in this one about the fault lines of the Ararat basin in Armenia,' he said, using his sleeve to wipe the dust from the Russian cover. 'Bear in mind that the Arabian Plate and the Eurasian Plate collide there, and that there was once an ocean between them.'

Then, from beneath the pile of books, he pulled out a map. An 'aviation map' was what he called it. Aviation maps were absolutely dependable; NATO used them too. Amid the whirl of brownish tints in the upper right-hand corner of page G-4b, where the borders of Turkey, Armenia, Azerbaijan and Iran came together, one little star-shaped dot of white stood out like a barnacle on driftwood: AĞRI DAĞI (MT ARARAT).

From the contour lines you could see just how far the lava had flowed. Salle, with his cartographer's eye, used the scale to establish that Ararat covered a surface area of at least 500 square kilometres.

'I like glaciated volcanoes,' he said, sounding unbusinesslike for the first time. 'There's something about them that attracts me.'

I was seeing something very different. From behind imaginary pilot's goggles I was letting the countryside flash by below me. How long, I wondered, would it take an F-16 to fly from the oil wells of northern Iraq (at the southern edge of the map) to Ararat? Forty-five minutes? An hour? And when would that solitary icecap and the pointed cone of Little Ararat rise up in your sights? This was the landscape of the Old Testament, with the sources of the Tigris and Euphrates in the middle, and at the bottom the ruins of the city of Nineveh, marked with the symbol ∴. Aviation maps may have a reputation for accuracy, but this one also had blank spots bordered with a message: AIRCRAFT MAY BE FIRED ON WITHOUT

WARNING. Announcements to that effect were found in black-framed stickers along the line that ran around the northern edge of Ararat: the border between NATO and its traditional enemy, the USSR, which coincided today with the Turkish–Armenian frontier. Page G-4b, or at least the 1985 edition of it, reeked of the Cold War.

Ever since our unexpected reunion that evening at the arts cinema, the vertical teacher–student relationship had begun to tilt. In his emails Salle Kroonenberg had fed me new findings about the wax and wane of the Caspian. Soon he revealed that he was writing an essay on the subject, as a minor part of what was to be an all-inclusive manuscript about the state of the earth sciences. We agreed that I would read his book-in-progress and comment on it.

'Don't spare me,' was written on the package he himself posted through my letterbox. 'You're the second person to read it, after my wife Corrie.' And he added: 'I'm still nervous about your opinion. Don't think that goes away as one gets older.' Salle Kroonenberg was 58; there was 18 years between us.

Yesterday, Today Was Tomorrow: the working title was shot through with mortality. Sunken memories bubbled to the surface as I read on: Gumbel's extreme value statistics, with which you could calculate the probability of dam bursts; Seneca's words about the earthquake that had struck Pompeii 10 years before its final destruction: 'We regard nature with our eyes, and not with our understanding.' I revelled in the allusions to world literature. Salle quoted García Márquez, Nabokov, Borges, Barnes.

By way of setting the tone, he opened with a passage from García Márquez's *Memories of My Melancholy Whores*: 'He told me: the world moves on. Yes, I said, it moves on, but in a circle around the sun.'

The way he borrowed from the library of literature (which Borges said was the only real universe) did not strike me as pretentious. Salomon Kroonenberg beaded together necklaces of facts and cross-references into a geological 'Theory of Everything'. It seemed brilliant to me, but was I really able to follow it?

'As far as the degree of difficulty goes,' I wrote to him, 'anyone without a bent for science won't make it past the prologue.'

'Then so be it,' he replied by return. 'For readers who close my book when they get to the word logarithm, I can do nothing.'

I had one other objection – the corniness of his jokes – but I didn't quite know how to broach that subject. Finally I came up with a cheerful-sounding phrase: 'During your lectures, of course, that light touch of yours works quite well.'

'I appreciate your diplomatic candour,' was the reaction that plopped into my inbox.

But did he actually mean that? Sitting facing each other at the table now, talk turned to his manuscript, seemingly of its own accord. 'Sometimes I do write rather *parlando*, you're right,' he said. 'As though I were lecturing.'

I felt like agreeing, but held my tongue so as not to seem too pleased to have scored a point. In the silence that rose around us like a fogbank, a ludicrous thought came to me: we could just as well start arm-wrestling. All it would take would be for one of us to challenge the other by planting his elbow on the table.

Instead, I asked Salle what motivated him to publish this marathon lecture.

'I want to demonstrate man's insignificance,' he said instantly. 'That he's nothing but a tiny cog in the whole process. An almost negligible factor.'

I nodded; that message had found its mark. Salle Kroonenberg stood to fetch a bottle of mineral water. 'And what about you?' he asked, pouring me a glass. 'You say you're writing a book about religion and science?'

He eased himself down into listening position, leaning back, two fingers held to his temple.

I hesitated. 'I had a religious upbringing.' Casting about for the right words, I started telling him about the church, the Advent Church in Assen-across-the-Tracks, where we had made our appearance each Sunday. It hadn't seemed like a chore, it was nothing unpleasant. I described the architecture of the building, which stood like a white snail shell on the lawn beside an institution for the mentally handicapped. My mother always cycled to church 15 minutes before us, to help wheel in the bibbed, rubber-necked patients. As a child I had been taught that these were the 'poor in spirit' spoken of in the Beatitudes, and that they were blessed because 'theirs is the Kingdom of Heaven', no matter what, even if they interrupted the service with their loud yelps. They couldn't help it of course, but their lack of physical control embarrassed me. And there was something I didn't understand: why go to all the trouble of rolling them in and out of the church if they were going to inherit eternal life anyway? One Sunday – I suppose I must have about 10 – I suddenly thought I'd worked out the logic behind it: the inhabitants of the Hendrik van Boeijen Home were press-ganged into the church row by row to keep the pews from looking so empty. I had no sooner thought this than an awareness of my own sinfulness overtook me. I began shivering, and during the silent prayer I almost started sobbing for forgiveness, because I too wanted to go to heaven. When I opened my eyes, I was looking through a blur of tears straight at the enormous stained-glass window. To my relief, in that abstract jumble of colours I saw the dove, flying towards me with the olive branch in its beak.

I didn't go into all of this with Salle Kroonenberg, but I did mention the final outcome: that I had lost my old sense of faith. 'It used to be there, but I can't get to it any more. I can't summon it up.' And in the same breath I added: 'To be honest, I'm not sure whether I'm missing anything.'

My monologue grew increasingly diffuse, and Salle listened without a word. To avoid any misunderstanding, I explained that I felt no need to settle my account with the Church, that I merely wanted to understand how the religion had trickled out of my life.

I told Salle that his manuscript had perhaps given me a clue.

'Do explain,' he prompted.

'What you wrote about the early geologists. Their struggle to reconcile their findings with the Bible; I recognise myself in that.'

In *Yesterday, Today Was Tomorrow*, Salle Kroonenberg had dedicated a chapter to the founders of geological science. They were mostly Scotsmen, remarkably enough, along with a few Swiss. People from remote areas where the earth's layers came to the surface in the form of rugged mountainous formations.

One of them was Charles Lyell, a nearsighted Scotsman whose three-volume *Principles of Geology*, completed in 1833, was the first 'modern handbook of geology'. In it he contested the unshakeable tenets of his day, the same on which he himself had been raised:

– That the Earth was less than 6,000 years old. (The Irish Anglican James Usscher had calculated that Creation had begun on Sunday 22 October in the year 4004 BC, a date noted on the flyleaf of many subsequent editions of the Bible.)
– That God had taken six days to separate day from night, the waters from the earth, and to create the animals and the first man. On the seventh day he rested.
– That, 1,656 years later, he had sent his all-consuming Deluge, which had covered the entire earth.
– That, on 5 May 2348 BC, on a Wednesday, the Ark had run aground on Ararat.

In other words: the entire spectrum of landscapes, from swampy deltas to deserts, from limestone caverns to mountain lakes – in short, the Earth as it manifested itself to us – had this one history and no other. Until far into the nineteenth century, rock formations and fossils were regarded in that light. With compassion and empathy, Salle described the fallacies of thinkers like Thomas Burnet who, in his *Sacred Theory of the Earth* from 1684, had explained the origins of that inconceivable volume of Deluge waters ('eight oceans full'): according to Burnet, the Earth was originally created in the form of an egg filled with water, and God – enraged by man's depravity – had broken its shell.

Since that time, the realisation had gradually dawned that the various layers of rock were the stone pages of a book in which was written the history of the Earth. And even later still: that that history must have begun long before the appearance of man. What interested Salle was that geological timescale, which was so 'bottomless' as to make meaningless the very distinction between BC and AD.

He described the successive breakthroughs that had led to the present-day conclusion (also thought to be infallible) that the Earth is 4,550 million years old.

In the journey taken by the Earth scientists were stages that corresponded with my own. Back at school I had noticed that some teachers, like Burnet, went to extreme lengths to preserve the literal credibility of Bible verses. Reading Salle's manuscript I recalled how our divinity teacher had ascribed a number of natural phenomena from Exodus (ongoing darkness, a 'pillar of fire' by night, poisoned water) to the eruption of Santorini in the days of Moses, 16 centuries before Christ.

At the time I had loved explanations like that, they gave the epic story of the flight from Egypt a seal of authenticity. But still, when you stopped to think about it, you stumbled upon one conundrum after another. (What is manna, anyway? And how could it come raining down from Heaven?)

In Salle Kroonenberg's manuscript I read that geology's patriarchs had also come to the conclusion that an all-too-literal approach to God's Word led only to more paradoxes. To fit their new discoveries into the scheme of things, therefore, they were forced to stretch the limits of Biblical exegesis. The seven days of Creation were to be seen allegorically as seven eras, and the Deluge may not have destroyed the *whole* world (there simply wasn't enough water for that), but the world inhabited in Noah's day. The kneading and squeezing of scientific insights to fit the mould of the Old Testament became increasingly desperate, and persisted until people began to realise that the Earth must have experienced an ice age. Around 1840, a young Swiss glaciologist was finally able to convince the world's staunchest 'Diluvialists' that glacial ice provided a much better explanation for geographical phenomena than did the waters of a general deluge. Scratches on travelled boulders were traces of moving ice masses, and the stones used in the megaliths of the northern Netherlands had not been tossed there by waters rushing from God's heavenly floodgates, but had been carried by glaciers from Scandinavia. With the acceptance of an ice age, the Diluvialists' time had run out, and the Bible as geological manual was laid aside.

I told Salle that I had experienced something similar with the twentieth-century insights revealed to me bit by bit at school. In my case, of course, it had happened in fast-forward, but it boiled down to the same thing: the knowing, with which I had been all too pleased to have myself inoculated, had begun working as a vaccine against believing.

I stopped there. What I didn't tell him, but what I was thinking, was: and still I am not an atheist. 'God does not exist' was not a claim you'd ever hear me make. Although you could not logically demand that anyone prove the *non*-existence of a Supreme Being, the dogmatism of the atheist seemed suspect to me. How did it differ from being a believer?

Salle Kroonenberg shifted in his chair. 'Well,' he said, 'that's all completely foreign to me. I'm an atheist.'

That was how he had been raised. 'When I was about ten, a group of tough kids cornered me on the street once. "Are you a Catholic or a Protestant?" they asked. I was at my wits' end, I had no idea what to say. I didn't know those words. I'd never heard them before.'

There was only one line from the Bible with which he agreed wholeheartedly, and which he always had in readiness. 'Dust thou art, and unto dust shalt thou return.'

'So that's all there is to say about the fate of mankind?'

'Yes, actually. Nature is indifferent to human suffering, but almost no one dares come to terms with that.'

The corridors of the mining faculty were growing quiet. Salle gave me his Soviet-Russian book on volcanism, and a printed overview of hundreds of scientific papers with the word 'Ararat' in the title: all I had to do was mark what I was interested in and he would order it for me. The professor packed his checked suitcase and suggested a walk: past his house, where he had more books about Ararat, and then on to a good restaurant.

On our way out we passed a derrick that had been built in one of the stairwells, on a scale of 1:5, in a spot where one would normally expect to find a marble bust.

Out on the street, leaning as though into an invisible wind and taking huge steps, Salle began telling me about his Jewish father, who had worked as an ophthalmologist on the islands of Zeeland province, and his Dutch Protestant mother, who had also gone to medical school. 'They met at a meeting of the Humanist Federation. People didn't believe in God there, but in man.'

He took me the scenic route, through a medieval city gate and along little canals choked with water lilies. Religion had never played a role in the Kroonenberg household. Salle's grandfather was an army physician in the former Dutch East Indies, and had barely given a thought to his own Jewishness. He was white; otherwise his background wasn't particularly relevant. But that changed – through no fault of his own – when he returned to the Netherlands in the 1930s. While the Jews in Germany were being isolated and persecuted with increasing zeal, he was appointed director of the Dutch-Israelite Hospital in Amsterdam. His position there meant that he had to act 'more Jewishly' than he would have liked. His three sons finally had to be circumcised. 'My father told me he was suddenly no longer allowed to walk around on the Sabbath with a pencil in his breast pocket. You weren't supposed to work, so you weren't allowed to write either.'

During the first few years of the Occupation, Salle's grandfather had not realised – or refused to see – that his family was in danger. Even when Jews were already being transported out of Amsterdam, he made no attempt to go into hiding. His hospital was emptied, room by room, but Medical Superintendent Kroonenberg continued caring for his patients as long as he could. When everyone else was either gone or in hiding, on 8 August 1943 he and his family were put on a transport to Westerbork, and from there to Theresienstadt. 'My father and his younger brother were at home when they came for them, they climbed out of the cellar window and got away. But their youngest brother was just arriving home at that moment, they arrested him on his way up the stairs. He was sent to Bergen-Belsen, without his parents.'

We crossed a shopping street at a spot where a bleached-blonde pharmacy employee was lowering the steel shutters. A taxi sounded three short blasts of its horn, like after a football victory. Salle greeted the driver with a wave of his suitcase. 'He's a good fellow. A Surinamese Indian. I met his father back when I was working on my thesis along the Corantijn River.'

I took it, I said, that none of them ever came back. 'Neither of my great-grandmothers did, no. They were sent to Auschwitz. But amazingly enough, my uncle and my grandparents did.'

At Theresienstadt, Grandpa Kroonenberg had first been assigned work as a boilerman, and later as physician in the children's hospital. There was a typhoid barracks no German dared enter, where the patients were brought in by wheelbarrow like living corpses. 'Somehow, he and his wife survived until the Russians came.'

Salle slowed and looked at me triumphantly. 'That's why I speak Russian: my grandfather was so in awe of the Russians that he taught himself the language. After the war he took out a subscription to the magazine *Ogonyok*, the socialist *Firebrand*. He kindled my enthusiasm too.'

On weekdays Salle lived alone in Delft, weekends he spent with his wife in Wageningen. His pied-à-terre turned out to be a real bachelor flat, above a shop for baby clothing, prams and rockers. Standing in front of the shop window, waiting for him to find his keys, an image came back to me of his practical classes in stone identification. Once a year Salle would send his students out to the most chic sections of the local shopping street, amid the jewellers' and the fashion boutiques. You would see them then in groups of two or three, not staring in shop windows but standing in front of the marble pillars or kneeling on the granite paving stones. They would place their loupes against the stone of the façade, or scratch at it with the pieces of quartz they'd brought with them, to test its hardness on Mohs' scale.

Salle's bicycle was in the hallway. Upstairs was a landing, a kitchenette and a narrow room, made even narrower by the bookcases on both sides. He put a cold beer in my hand as I stood tilting my head back and forth to read the rows of titles: a tilt to the right for English

43

or Dutch books, to the left for German, French, Spanish and Russian publications. I'd noticed it before, but I mentioned it anyway, this seemingly insignificant fact, this mad demarcation line in printing practice that ran straight across Europe. That was one thing we had in common, our amazement at the apparently trivial. Salle could even be engrossed by a pencil stub, which brought to his mind images of graphite mines and cedarwood from Lebanon. We also discovered that we shared the same weakness for peculiar place names.

'Gzyel,' he said. 'For years that was the password for my computer. It's in Russia, they make a kind of delftware there.'

'Ouagadougou,' I said.

He: 'Krk.'

'Kommerzijl.'

Salle pursed his lips; mmm, that one was just passable. Generally speaking he thought Dutch names were merely clumsy.

'So you'd prefer Aracataca?'

'Yes, or Chiquinquirá, which skips like a stone across the water.'

'Ararat,' I said.

'Ararat will do,' he said. 'A toast to Ararat!'

The evening had grown muggy, and we drank our beers in thirsty gulps. The notion that I was the student and he the teacher had vanished. From the look of his bookcase, I realised we also shared more or less the same literary tastes. Salle had a separate shelf for W.F. Hermans, with several different editions of *Beyond Sleep* and the rare *Erosion*.

We broke the silence by swapping Hermans aphorisms. 'A hero is someone who has been careless with impunity,' I said.

'Man is a corpse poisoned with life,' he said. Salle felt an affinity with Hermans' nihilistic body of thought.

I might, I remarked, be able to take stock in such a bleak and chilling universe, were it not at loggerheads with the creative gifts of a person like W.F. Hermans.

Sitting on the windowsill, watching the Delft rush hour passing, I realised that Salle's cheerfulness stood in strange contrast to his sardonic way of looking at things. One lovely word or a powerful aphorism, it seemed, was all it took to arouse his enthusiasm, and that surprised me. I asked Salle how that worked, that poetic transport – where did it come from?

He thought about that for a moment, then started talking about love. Love, he said, served a purpose. It could express itself by sophisticated means, or boorishly, but it always served the preservation of the species. 'I've noticed, for example, that I look at brunettes more often than I do at blondes. Apparently there is some urge in me that causes me to look for a partner outside my own gene pool. I have no idea how it works, but there's no denying its functionality.'

I started to put in my own two bits' worth, but he wasn't finished yet. 'When is it that love blossoms between two people? Only when chance brings them together in time and space, under a lucky star. What if my father hadn't escaped through that cellar window in time? Or if some other woman had been attracted to him after the war?' The fact that he existed, that he was who he was and not someone else, was a one-in-a-million chance.

His train of thought was almost getting away from me. 'So if there *is* a God,' I said, 'then he operates by a roll of the dice? He's a compulsive gambler?'

'Take our cat,' Salle said. 'He's been living with us seventeen years. I've watched him carefully, his foibles, his feline behaviour, and I've often wondered: are Corrie and I really so very different from him?'

I was allergic to cats. 'You two are conscious of your own existence,' I said. 'The cat isn't.'

'Perhaps. It's true, humans are believed to possess consciousness, and a free will. But have you ever heard about that survey taken in Jacksonville, in the United States? In Jacksonville, it seems, a proportionately greater number of Jacks and Jackies are born than in comparable cities. Maybe the citizens of Jacksonville are simply proud of where they come from; that would be a logical explanation. But when they were asked about it, the vast majority of those parents said they'd named their child Jack or Jackie without even considering it. "Wow, now that you mention it . . ." That's what they said.'

'But you and I are individuals who act consciously. Don't try to tell me that your son just happens to be named Salomon.'

'All right, our tomcat doesn't recognise himself in the mirror. In that way, at least, we're different. But how uniquely human is that? They say dolphins recognise themselves in the mirror too.'

I wasn't convinced. Man could clone cats, or calculate the mass of the universe. Dolphins could not.

Salle admitted that I was right about that. But, he said, biology makes you realise how minimal the differences between man and animal really are. The genome of the mouse bore a strong resemblance to ours. The deeper science penetrated a given subject, the more easily things seemed to fit together. Without batting an eye, Salle remarked: 'I believe that one day we will finally understand the mystery of life.'

That seemed a long shot to me. Like the presumption of those theoretical physicists who believe that the secret codes of the cosmos can be cracked, that all we have to do is give them a little more time. In the end, the universe would surrender a logical explanation – expressible within a single mathematical formula. But what made people assume that a philosopher's stone like that existed?

For Salle, it was the way one discovery followed another, the pattern. Every once in a while a milestone was reached, a revolutionary breakthrough like Darwin's theory of evolution or the fathoming of the twisted rope-ladder structure of DNA. 'There's still a lot left to be explained, of course. The behaviour of stem cells, for example. You ask yourself: how can these cells develop into different, specialised cells? It's a deep mystery, a wonderful thing to see. But those who shout, "Look, this is the hand of the Creator!", well, they're slamming the door, they're cutting science off at the pass. If you ask me, within a few years biology will produce new insights and we'll understand how the stem cell works as well. That's the way things have always happened.'

In fact, he saw only one obstacle. Religion. By which he meant any doctrine of faith assertive enough to obstruct the freedom and independence of scientific research, the way the Biblical dogma of the universal Deluge had done with geology.

Salle Kroonenberg cited the pioneer Charles Lyell, the first scientist to realise that a phenomenon like erosion could wear out an entire Grand Canyon, and that wind and water had taken millions of years to do exactly that. Lyell had once estimated how much precious time – 'at least two and a half centuries' – had been wasted by his predecessors clinging to the idea that all fossils and travelled stones bore witness to the great deluge of Noah's day. And, Salle said, there were still pockets of religious resistance to the established insights of geology. Even today one had schools of pseudo-scientists involved in what was called 'diluvial geology' and the 'young Earth theory': attempts to prove that the Earth's history was identical to that described in Genesis. It seemed a hopeless struggle, but the participants would not give up. In the mathematical models of the young Earth creationists, the Grand Canyon had not been eroded particle by particle: the greatest gorge of all was nothing but a drainage channel for the waters of the Deluge.

'Wait,' Salle said. 'I have an excellent example of that just here.' He went over to his shelf of miscellanea and took down *The Flood: In the Light of the Bible, Geology and Archaeology*. The author, Professor Alfred Rehwinkel, was a theologian who had also made a study of geology. I weighed the book in my hand and saw that it had been published in 1951, as a textbook for Protestant schools.

I flipped from the title page to the foreword and read:

The shock received by the inexperienced young student is therefore overwhelming when he enters the classroom of such teachers and suddenly discovers to his great bewilderment that these men and women of acclaimed learning do not believe the views taught him in his early childhood days.

I began reading aloud:

'"First he begins to doubt the infallibility of the Bible in matters of geology, but he will not stop there. Other difficulties arise, and before long scepticism and unbelief have taken the place of his childhood faith."'

This book was obviously meant for me; the Dutch translation had been published five years before I entered a Protestant secondary school.

'Have you read this?' I asked.

'Are you kidding?' Salle said. This was an example of the kind of religious fanaticism that tried to thwart science. 'It's yours. Please, take it.'

I slid *The Flood* into my bag like a purloined treasure.

Thou shalt not

EVERYONE I KNEW had something to say about Mount Ararat. I had barely scratched the surface of the subject, and already found myself buried beneath a landslide of commentary. Someone turned up with the old *Red Knight* comic albums, more particularly that volume in which the Flemish comic-strip hero finds Noah's Ark. A friend who frequently climbed in the Himalayas gave me a strip of Diamox, a diuretic pill normally prescribed for glaucoma patients. 'In the event of altitude sickness: 1 x 250 mg (and descend immediately). Drink large quantities of fluids. Second pill if needed only after 6 hours. Max. 2 tablets (= 500 mg) every 24 hours.'

My publisher brought back a present for me from London. 'But please,' he said, 'I want you to promise me one thing . . .'

He handed me a pocket-sized guide to climbing Mount Ararat, which consisted of a folding map with routes and traveller's tips. The guidebook looked dated, with its drawings of Kurdish shepherds and minarets in a vast landscape, but to my surprise I saw that it was from 2004.

'And that is?'

'That halfway through the manuscript you won't suddenly start writing "he" with a capital H.'

I looked up from the guidebook. 'And if I do?'

He folded his arms and upped the ante: 'Then I won't publish it.'

As far as my wife was concerned, I could capitalise whatever I liked, as long as I didn't come down off the mountain a convert.

Horrible, she thought, to spend the rest of one's life with a stranger.

Light-hearted as the comments may have been, religious feeling in my immediate surroundings appeared to be locked away in a concrete bunker. To me, the 'risk' of becoming a convert to one religion or another seemed almost nil, for I had no such intention. But I did want to travel as open-mindedly as possible.

The degree of difficulty ascribed to climbing Ararat was greater than I would have expected, at least when you looked only at its steepness or the danger of avalanches. What kept most climbers at bay was not the three- or four-day climb itself, or the need for crampons and an ice axe. A far greater threat was the rattle of machine guns heard in the region from time to time. With true British understatement, the climber's guidebook noted that the mountain was located in 'a politically sensitive area'. That had always been the case and would not change soon, not as long as Ararat lay on the fault line between Christianity and Islam. Flying the banners of the cross on one side and the crescent moon on the other, countless armies had hacked each other to pieces here since time immemorial. Masis / Ağri Daği / Kuh-i-Nūh had found itself within the boundaries of the Russian, Turkish and Persian empires by turn, and strikingly enough always at their outermost edge, standing like a massive sentry. As soon as the clash of arms fell silent even briefly, travellers came from far away to Noah's mountain, including hermits who settled in the caves along its slopes in order to snuggle up as close as possible to 'the cradle of humanity'. They believed that where God had entered into his covenant with Noah and his descendants (i.e., all of us) was also the place from which the chosen ones would be taken up into heaven.

Both pilgrims and adventurers had made mention of Ararat's indomitability. 'In the heart of Greater Armenia lies a very high mountain, in the shape of a cube, where, it is said, Noah's Ark still lies,' Marco Polo had reported during his journey to China in 1271. 'That mountain is so huge and so long that more than two days are needed to get around it. At its top lies snow, so much that no one can climb it.'

That Ararat could not be conquered was an official article of the Armenian Church. The slopes above the snowline were guarded by angels with shining swords, and were inaccessible to mortals. The first person who challenged the dogma and claimed to have stood atop Mount Ararat had spent the rest of his life suffering the consequences of this myth. In September 1829, Dr Friedrich Parrot, a German in the service of the Czar, had come down from the snowy slopes in a state of euphoria, feeling 'like the patriarch Noah'. Parrot set off flares he had received from a Russian artillery captain, and thanked the Lord. He had, he swore, been to the summit, where he had planted a cross made from his own walking stick. But the cross was too small to be seen from the valley, and the German was not believed.

Parrot's report, *Reise zum Ararat*, the veracity of which was questioned in Europe as well, had been published in both German and English during his lifetime and could still be found in antiquarian bookshops. I ordered both versions.

The little climber's guide described the history of Ararat ascents since Parrot's day. During the nineteenth century there had been a total of 28 expeditions; thereafter, local, regional and global wars had followed in rapid succession. For most of the twentieth century Ararat had been off limits. Only during the period 1982–89, when the Kurdish guerrilla forces seemed to have been crushed in this part of the country, did the Turkish army open one route to climbers. That was the southern ascent, starting in the garrison town of Doğubayazit, pronounced *dough you ba ya suit*. With the exception of an oriental fairytale castle that had once belonged to a local pasha, Doğubayazit did not even faintly resemble a scene from *The Thousand and One Nights*. Nissen huts and demonstratively parked armoured vehicles characterised the town and the nearby border crossing to Iran.

As the border zone between NATO member Turkey and Soviet Armenia, the far north face of Ararat, with its views of the drab concrete architecture of Yerevan, had been restricted ground during the Cold War. The decline and disintegration of the Soviet empire had done nothing to change that. On the contrary, this section of the Iron Curtain, the 300 kilometres between Turkey and Armenia, had actually been more heavily secured, with infrared sensors and new rolls of razor wire.

At the time the guidebook was published, in early 2004, Ararat was open only to climbers with 'military permission'. 'We must emphasise, however, that only the southern route (by way of the village of Eli) has been opened. Climbers who stray may be fired upon without warning by army patrols.'

So how did one go about obtaining military permission?

The procedure was explained under the heading 'Regulations and Restrictions'. First of all, at least three and preferably four months before departure, foreign nationals had to submit a request to a Turkish embassy. If that was awarded, you then had to hire an official guide from the Turkish Federation for Alpinism, and to pay separately for his travel and lodgings.

'Note carefully: do not leave without the special Ararat visa in your passport. You will not be allowed on to the mountain.' Another comment had been added in apparent haste: the ceasefire between the Kurdish PKK separatist movement and the Turkish authorities had expired on 1 September 2003.

The back cover consisted of an advertisement, quite chipper and cheerful, for Executive Wilderness Programmes, a travel agency that claimed 20 years' experience of mountaineering expeditions in 'difficult' areas: 'WE RUN SCHEDULED TRIPS TO ARARAT.' And, not unimportantly: the mandatory climber's visa was included in the price (1,380 euros). I was tempted, but finally, because I preferred to make my own plans, I decided to apply for an Ararat visa independently.

Friedrich Parrot had lent his name to the Persian ironwood tree (*Parrotia persica*). The Parrotspitze, an Alpine summit on the Swiss–Italian border, had been named after him as well. The German scholar was seen as the founder of 'scientific alpinism' and was, in any case, one of the pioneers of mountain climbing, although he did not climb for the sake of climbing as alpinists do today. Parrot's penchant for high places was 'in the service of the natural sciences'. I read this in the epilogue to his 1831 account *Reise zum Ararat*, which had been republished with loving care in 1985 in East Germany.

Before setting his sights on Ararat, Parrot had already stood atop two previously unclimbed Pyrenean summits, the altitudes of which (3,355 and 3,404 metres) he had established with the help of a barometer. Even earlier, as a student participating in a cartographic expedition to the Caucasus, he had found his way up Mount Kazbek, which triangulation showed was above 5,000 metres. That was even higher than Mont Blanc, where legend had it that climbers encountered atmospheric conditions that allowed them to see the stars in broad daylight. The thinner the layers of atmosphere one entered, the theory went, the deeper and darker became the blue of the sky. To monitor those gradations the cyanometer was developed, a kind of paint fan displaying all possible hues of the firmament, up to and including the blue of night. These were the days – the early nineteenth century – when Mount Chimborazo in Ecuador was considered to be the world's highest mountain at 6,310 metres. Parrot's compatriot Alexander von Humboldt, who had climbed that peak to a height of 5,880 metres, believed he held the world record for high-altitude mountaineering. Personal pride, the pursuit of fame – in Parrot's day these also mattered, however earnestly the expeditions wrapped themselves in the cloak of scientific research.

Parrot explained his fascination for Ararat as a corollary of Christian devotion: 'What must not be the feelings of a Christian when he fixes his eyes on that sacred mountain . . . a witness of one of the most remarkable events in the history of the world, and of God's immediate dispensation for the preservation of the human race!'

It was precisely for that reason, Parrot knew, that such great honour lay in store for the first man to climb Ararat. Had he genuinely been prompted by religious motives, I wondered, or perhaps by more worldly ones? What had moved him, what was he looking for?

The epilogue of the East German edition contained a biographical sketch that offered a few possible clues. The son of a labourer from the grand duchy of Württemberg, Friedrich's father, Georg Parrot, had worked his way up to become rector of the German-language Imperial Academy at Dorpat (present-day Tartu in Estonia). The adjective 'Imperial' referred to the Russian czar, who had annexed the Baltic coast. The portrait of Georg's youngest son Friedrich, with his black curls and firm jaw, bore powerful witness to the young man's un-German good looks. After studying medicine and physics at Dorpat, and serving as a medic in the Czar's army in the war against Napoleon, Friedrich assumed his father's rectorial gown.

In 1828, when the Russian empire – at the expense of the Persians and Turks – succeeded in expanding its southern border beyond Mount Ararat, Parrot realised that his time had come. Now that the sacred mountain was finally within the 'domain of Christendom', his travelogue begins, the moment had arrived when 'a long-suppressed aspiration' could be gratified. Less than a year after the Treaty of Turkman-chai had been signed, the 38-year-old Parrot was on his way. His entourage included a mineralogist, an astronomer, two university students and a *feldjäger*, or armed guard, appointed by the Czar.

Nicholas I provided a stipend of 1,600 silver roubles for the purchase of scientific instruments. By the hand of his secretary, he noted: 'The enterprise enjoys my wholehearted support. Select a *feldjäger* of proven reputation to accompany the travellers and serve them until they return.'

Parrot, in his account of the journey, portrays himself as a zealot alight with curiosity. He proves to be a highly empathetic observer, a kind-hearted character who pauses to reflect on the Buddhism of the Kalmuck people along the Caspian Sea. ('They are without any regular performance of religious worship, even on the Sabbath,' he notes.) The urge to proselytise is foreign to him. When he considers taking on a fatherless Kalmuck boy as his servant, he warns the boy's mother and uncles that he will not be brought up in the Buddhist faith. As I read, I began developing an affection for the man's broad-mindedness.

Having crossed the Caucasus, with a wine-drenched stop in Georgia, Parrot and his crew – who have been on the road for three months by this time – finally catch sight of Ararat. The view fills him with an 'overwhelming sense of the mighty works of the Creator'. In the foreground they see the outlines of the Armenian monastery of Echmiadzin. And as the little convoy of horse-drawn carts reaches the floodplains of the Arax, the sky turns yellow and green and gusts of wind roll in. The local farmers make a run for it, but Parrot doesn't go looking for shelter, not even when lightning starts splitting the clouds at ever shorter intervals. This is the kind of spectacle for which he came, an experience he speaks of with the reverence of a pilgrim: 'Was I not at the foot of Ararat, the hallowed mountain of the Ark, where the soil . . . retains the most indubitable traces of those waters which were once commanded to subside from its cloud-capped summit, to leave a resting-place for all that survived of the human race? Was I not now before the walls of Echmiadzin . . . where Christianity, ever since the first century of its propagation, has maintained a habitation . . . ?'

Echmiadzin was (and still is) the Vatican of the ancient and autonomous Armenian Christian Church, founded in the year 301. Parrot and his companions are given quarters in the monastery, yet the reception is as chilly as the rough-hewn galleries and chapels. The *katolikos*, the Church's spiritual leader, turns out to be an old man of 93 who fails to make an appearance. The monks speak only broken Russian and, to Parrot's annoyance, neither Greek nor Latin. When they sing hymns the sound is 'devoid of melody, harmony or fervour'. The walled Echmiadzin, draped over its hill, may believe itself the Vatican's equal, but the demeanour of the *katolikos* is anything but papal. A few days later, when the prelate finally grants the travellers an audience, his only comment on their plans to climb Ararat takes the form of 'apathetic and chilling' sounds.

Parrot acts as though the aged man is feeble-minded. He refuses to hear his objections or protests, and mentions nothing of the doctrine claiming that Ararat is 'insurmountable'. Does Parrot really know nothing of the ecclesiastical ordinance, or is he simply ignoring it? At the last minute, with obvious reluctance, the *katolikos* lends him one of his interpreters: a 20-year-old deacon by the name of Abovian. But did he really have a choice? Could the Armenian patriarch have refused anything to an expedition that enjoyed the Czar's patronage?

Armenia, Parrot comments upon leaving the monastery, was in 'urgent need' of a genuine, ecclesiastical seminary.

A day's march further, that annoyance has lifted and he herds his oxen and horses across the rushing Arax. The clay flats make way for the coagulated, weathered basalt fans of Ararat.

Regarding the choice of a suitable base camp, Parrot hesitates between Doğubayazit ('a Muslim town on the southern slopes') and Arguri ('a Christian village on the north flank'). He finally chooses Arguri, built at the end of the mountain's one gorge and the only settlement close to a glacier. News of their arrival has preceded them, and during the last few kilometres they are accompanied by a pack of boisterous shepherds who trot along beside them. The reception at Arguri is warm, with wine and solemn greetings, but there is also a hint of suspicion, as though the crowd is subjecting the newcomers to an inspection. The announcement of their plan immediately meets with ridicule, for the sparkling dome of ice in the distance is simply impassable. The 175 or so families of Arguri are convinced that, after the great disembarkation of man and animal, God intentionally covered Ararat with a crown of ice. Anyone who dares to venture above the line of eternal snow will lose their footing and die.

The myth of the unconquerable mountain, Parrot must have realised when he arrived at Arguri, was much more than a well-intentioned safety tip. It was not a caution against rash behaviour. Whether a climber chose to risk his life was not the point. The point was that you were not allowed to climb Ararat. The eleventh commandment read: '*Super Masis nullus debet ascendere quia est mater mundi.*' ('No one may climb Masis, because she is the mother of the world.') The Armenian Christians were not the only ones who knew this rule; it had been expressed in identical terms by Willem van Ruysbroeck, a Franciscan from Flanders, as early as the thirteenth century. After all, the reasoning went, how could one hope to re-enter the womb from which one came?

This mystification intrigued me. Why was it that human curiosity had to be suspended as soon as religion entered the picture? Every faith, no matter how primitive, had an altar or a tabernacle or suchlike that no one was allowed to see or approach. There was always a circle within which it was forbidden to dance, or a tree from which you were not allowed to eat. Don't look back, or you will be turned into a pillar of salt! Something always had to remain hidden, it seemed, whatever the cost; that was a feature of every religion. The mysterious had to remain mysterious, in order that one might believe in it; that was the general gist. But I couldn't help wondering what was being hidden. What was it that had to remain concealed from human eyes? It aroused the lurking suspicion that the rigour with which priests cordoned off their holy places could be prompted by only one fear: that there was nothing there.

One spring day in 2005, I phoned the Turkish embassy in The Hague. They referred me to the consulate in Rotterdam.

'What is it that you want to film?'

I said that I didn't want to film anything. I wanted to climb. 'Mount Ararat.'

'Ah yes, Ağri Daği. Then you'll need a sporting visa. Only the embassy is authorised to issue that.'

'A sporting visa for Ağri Daği? Contact our consular services. In Rotterdam.'

I learned to pronounce Ağri Daği without the ğ's, with the i's as a barely audible ooh, so that almost nothing remained. *Ah rooh da* was enough. Literally: the Mountain of Pain.

At the embassy, after some persistence on my part, I finally made contact with the right person. She held the rank of third secretary, her name was Beliz. I was never to meet her in the flesh, but during the months that Beliz and I spoke to each other on an almost weekly basis, we established a bond. 'We are always pleased to hear your voice,' she would say in her most congenial tone.

During our first conversation Beliz asked me to submit a written request, accompanied by all the relevant information. 'On the basis of that, we can continue our correspondence.'

'Fine,' I said. 'But what do you consider relevant information?'

'The equipment you're planning to bring into the country, the names of the members of your expedition, the time of year and the duration . . .'

I interrupted her by asking whether I could also submit an individual application.

That was possible, so long as I didn't forget to send along my CV.

I asked whether I needed to mention, for example, my training as an agricultural engineer. Was that what she meant?

'Yes, but we will also need a list of your most recent publications, and a brief description of what you are planning to write about Ağri Daği.'

For a moment, I was left breathless. How did she know what I was planning to do? Or even the fact that I wrote?

'Just start off with the letter,' I heard Beliz say, and for the time being we left it at that.

In planning my ascent of Ararat, insurmountable obstacles were not something I had reckoned on. Snowstorms or lightning or altitude sickness could keep me from reaching the summit, but that was all. Those were within the realm of possibility, but I had never foreseen problems with obtaining a visa. This was 2005, the year of the – admittedly awkward – embrace between Turkey and the European Union, which meant that the political tide should be turning in my favour. As soon as Turkey actually entered the EU, Ararat would be the highest mountain in the Union. Textbooks all over Europe would be due for revision: Mont Blanc, at 4,810 metres, couldn't hold a candle to a bona fide 5,000 metre peak, and would be automatically relegated to the minor league. Should the Turkish embassy happen to ask, I had my answer ready: I wanted to explore 'what will soon be the highest peak in the EU'.

But now everything had changed. My application was not being evaluated in The Hague, but in Ankara. Beliz would send the papers along to 'the proper authorities', by which she meant the ministries of Internal Affairs and Defence.

Just to be sure, and in order to avoid any blunders, I called Ahmet Olgun, a journalist of Turkish origin at my old newspaper.

'Does the Ministry of Defence have a say in the matter?' Ahmet asked incredulously. 'Did they really say that?' He was less surprised about the embassy being well-informed about me. Make no mistake, he said, there are always a few newspaper-clippers in the diplomatic corps who do nothing but assemble dossiers. Ahmet strongly recommended that I be completely frank with them. Were I to proffer obviously misleading motives, that could be used against me. 'Look at it this way: mountain-climbers are welcome. The question is whether they're ready for mountain-climbing writers.'

I asked Ahmet what I should treat as the most sensitive issue.

He burst out laughing, then said with a politician's earnestness: 'First of all, there's the Armenian question. Secondly, you have the Armenian question. And thirdly: the Armenian question.' To understand just how sensitive this 'question' was, all I had to do was follow the news about the Turkish novelist Orhan Pamuk. The to-do surrounding him had begun a few weeks earlier after his comment – in a Swiss newspaper – that no one in Turkey dared to talk 'about the thirty thousand Kurds and the one million Armenians who have been killed'.

Official and not-so-official Turkey had come down on him like a ton of bricks. He'd been charged with three counts of libel and slander. One parliamentarian had said that he was 'not worthy of the air he breathed', and a provincial governor from central Turkey had ordered all of Pamuk's books to be removed from the libraries in his district.

But as long as I left the Armenians unmentioned, Ahmet saw no reason why my visit should pose any problem. Then he stopped suddenly. 'When you were a correspondent, you didn't write about Armenia, did you?'

I wanted to say no, but the truth was yes. Some of my stories about the Armenian cognac industry and other innocent matters had been in the paper. 'But that was years ago.'

That didn't make any difference, my former colleague said. If I had written about Armenia, the Turkish memory might be more tenacious and selective than I'd like. Maybe it would be better for me to sign up with a regular expedition, as one participant among many.

With all these 'ifs' in mind, I finally chose to take the narrow road in the middle: I wrote to Beliz to say that I wanted to climb Ararat in order to write a travel book, for a publishing house by the name of Atlas.

Our correspondence began. She sent me the application forms 'for the performance of archaeological excavations and film activities in Turkey', which I dutifully filled out to the best of my ability and returned to her in fivefold, along with five identical passport photos.

It was 10 April 2005. I had given them my mother's maiden name and her two middle names: my application was ready to go to Ankara.

While Friedrich Parrot is busy establishing his base camp at Arguri, he hears that the village's name is a combination of two words: *argh* (he planted) and *urri* (vines). The entire group, recently joined by two Russian border guards, is packed into the close quarters of the monastery of St Hagob (Jacob), a little less than an hour's walk uphill from the clay huts of Arguri. The hills of pumice piled against the slopes behind the monks' gardens rearrange themselves every few hours with a nerve-shaking clatter. The noise of these miniature avalanches sometimes drowns out the roar of meltwater rushing out of the gorge into the irrigation canals beside the monastery.

The guests are given fresh bread, baked against the walls of a clay oven. The flat, limp patties of dough, Parrot notes, serve as 'both spoon and napkin'.

After the welcome dinner, the monks, dressed in their ankle-length robes of blue serge, show Parrot the floor plan of their middlemost chapel, in the shape of a cross. At the point where the cross intersects there is a flat stone: the very stone Noah used as an altar for his sacrifice of thanksgiving. The 'sweet savour' rising up from this altar had pleased God and led him to make the promise of Genesis 8:21: 'Neither will I again smite any more every living thing, as I have done.'

Like their colleagues at Echmiadzin, the monks of Arguri swear to their guest that Ararat cannot be scaled. Was this starting to get on Parrot's nerves, I wondered, all these stubborn assertions about the certain failure of his mission?

To my surprise, I discovered that the English translation of his travelogue was peppered with waspish remarks made in hindsight. *Reise zum Ararat* (1831) was unbiased. *Journey to Ararat* (1846) was full of hard feelings.

The British publisher had felt it necessary to note that Parrot was 'constantly guided by the love of truth'. The reader would do well to realise that he now had before him nothing less than the one true account of the first successful ascent of Ararat. The author, who could no longer defend himself – Parrot died in 1841 – had done nothing to deserve the slanderous claims that he had never stood atop Noah's mountain. From the prologue to *Journey to Ararat* I deduced that Parrot's reputation had been under fire even before his journey to Armenia. The Berlin pharmacist and chemist Martin Heinrich Klaproth, whose discoveries included the element uranium, had dismissed his ascent of Mount Kazbek in 1811 as 'impossible'; another authoritative academic had branded the young student a windbag. Parrot, disillusioned, pointed out at the time that he had never claimed to have reached the *summit* of Kazbek, but that did little to clear his name.

Journey to Ararat, as it turned out, was a thoroughly enhanced version of the original manuscript. Following Dr Klaproth's lead, another scholar now came forward 'to cast the first stone', this time in the 1831 edition of the *Tiflis Chronicle*, volume 11. The crux of this detailed attack was that Ararat's icecap was too steep and too slippery for human feet, no matter what 'Professor Parrot' said.

The maligned explorer, who had been anticipating praise and

public acclaim, felt 'grieved', 'persecuted' and 'stabbed in the back'. Since the era of the duel to the death was drawing to a close, Parrot chose instead to defend his honour with a rational reply. He addressed himself to his expedition's patron, the Czar of Russia, with a request for signed affidavits from the helpers with whom he had conquered Ararat. The office of Prince Lieven, a government minister in St Petersburg, thereupon issued directive 5793 to the commander of the Trans-Caucasian provinces, who in turn charged a major general with tracking down and questioning those who had climbed Mount Ararat. The men in question were two Armenian farmers from Arguri and two Russian soldiers from the 41st Regiment of Chasseurs. The fifth man, Deacon Abovian of the monastery at Echmiadzin, was either not sought or not found; instead, the village headman of Arguri was questioned, even though he had not taken part in the climb. Parrot received five sworn affidavits, which were included word for word in the English edition of his book.

Upon reading the documents, I was overcome by a feeling of despondency. The three witnesses from Arguri, the farmers and the village chief, had sworn on the Bible that neither they nor Parrot had reached Ararat's summit. The two Russian soldiers were unsure about the exact date, but were able to confirm that they, in September of 1829 and in the company of Professor Parrot, had indeed stood on the summit.

That was three against three, if one was willing to accept Parrot's word. Or two against two if you put stock only by the direct eyewitnesses to Parrot's achievement. A draw? Not according to Parrot. He assumed without question that the truth tipped the balance in the Russians' favour. The Armenians, after all, were illiterate and ignorant, fettered by superstition.

In light of the controversy surrounding Parrot, I had the tendency to read his account of the actual climb with great suspicion. Was he playing along with the obscurantists, or had he actually exposed the myths for what they were?

Apparently, during the weeks that the group camped at Arguri, three attempts were made to reach the top. The first was only half-hearted, nothing more than an exploration of the snowline, which lay at 3,800 metres, as Parrot established with the help of a barometer. He had left at sunrise without porters, taking along with him only Karl Schliemann, one of the two students from Dorpat. Using their walking sticks, they crossed a snow-field with a slope that 'did not quite amount to thirty degrees', and at three in the afternoon, having established that the route was free of 'insuperable obstacles', they turned back. Then, while traversing the icy slope, near-disaster struck. 'While the footing is generally less sure in descending a mountain than in ascending it, at the same time it is extremely difficult to restrain one's self and to tread with the requisite caution,' Parrot lectured. 'The active spirit of my young friend . . . was yet unable to withstand this.' Schliemann took a wrong step and slipped. The professor flung out his arm and grabbed his student as he tobogganed past, but also fell; both men ended up hundreds of yards below their own footsteps in the snow. Parrot got the worst of it: he crashed against a pile of debris, breaking the tube of one of his barometers. His chronometer was shattered as well, and spattered with blood.

Back at St Hagob's monastery, despite the pain in his ribs, he insisted on saying nothing about the accident. Schliemann was also forbidden to mention it; the expedition's leader had no intention of encouraging the monks in their narrow-minded assumption that anything other than Newtonian gravity could be at play here. He did, however, thank the Lord for saving his life, and that of his student.

During the days needed to recover, Parrot conversed with the cowled monks. Over dinners of lentil soup, they told him about the early days of the Armenian Church, and St Hagob, the monk after whom their monastery was named. Hagob had hoped to put an end once and for all to discussions concerning the reliability of scripture by finding the wreck of Noah's ship. Carrying only his staff and a bag of dried apricots, he climbed the slopes of Ararat till darkness fell. He lay down to sleep in the shelter of a rock, but awoke the next morning only to find himself back at the foot of the mountain. This happened time and again, until an angel visited him in a dream and explained why his enterprise could never succeed: the eternal snow of Ararat was forbidden territory for mortals, but as a reward for his efforts, and to help satisfy human curiosity, the angel gave him a piece of Noah's Ark. When he awoke, Hagob found the relic beside his staff and his bag of apricots.

'And this story,' Parrot noted with a certain degree of scepticism, 'is sanctioned by the Armenian Church.' Back at the monastery of Echmiadzin they had shown him the relic: a piece of wood the size of a man's hand, reddish-brown, set in an icon of silver and gems. A silver cast had also been kept of St Hagob's fingertips, the first to touch the remnants of the Ark.

During his stay on Ararat, Parrot did not go looking for slivers of the Ark. It seemed probable to him that the wreck was preserved somewhere inside the glacier 'like a Siberian mammoth', but he was not seeking proof of God's existence in the form of a gopher-wood plank. Parrot's goal was to stand on top of Ararat. As soon as he was feeling stronger, he therefore made a second foray into 'the realm of eternal winter', promising his porters a silver rouble or a gold ducat should they accompany him all the way to the summit.

Due to more misfortune, this second foray took him no higher than just below the altitude of Mont Blanc. But in his third and final attempt, Parrot applied what he had learned from his mistakes. Spend the night as close to the snowline as possible. Do not eat mutton or other hard-to-digest foods before climbing. Onion soup with bread and a few sips of rum, that was the ticket. Start out as early as possible; beware sudden gusts of wind and crevasses.

On 27 September 1829 the weather was perfect. One Armenian farmer, suffering from altitude sickness, remained at the camp at 3,900 metres. Two other helpers stopped after the first rest period, but the remainder pushed on. By 10 a.m., Parrot and five of his companions had already passed the cross left during their previous attempt. It had been too big and too heavy;

the man who carried it on his back had almost collapsed beneath the burden. With no desire to re-enact the drama of Golgotha, Parrot had chosen a more portable model this time: two oaken slats, the longer of which could be used as a walking stick. The snow that had fallen a few days earlier was now compacted to ice, forcing the team to hack steps in the glacier. The air grew thinner, and after hours of toil the barometer showed that they had surpassed Mont Blanc. Although the sky was cloudless, there were no stars to be seen.

Just above the 5,000-metre line, the group arrived at a treacherous passage: a steep wall of ice. Having navigated that, the six men suddenly found themselves in a windstorm that took their breath away and chilled them to the bone. But the lashing of the wind could not deter them; the only thing left between them and the summit was a gently sloping field of ice.

'Before my eyes, now intoxicated with joy, lay the highest pinnacle . . . and at about a quarter past three . . . WE STOOD ON THE TOP OF ARARAT!!'

That is what it says in *Journey to Ararat*.

In *Reise zum Ararat*, the upper case was absent, and a single exclamation mark sufficed.

Despite his ecstasy at reaching the top, Friedrich Parrot remained focused, rational. His first act was to pull out his barometer to establish Ararat's true altitude: 5,155 metres. The planting of the cross he left to the deacon from Echmiadzin, who had made the ascent in his monk's habit. Parrot revelled in the view out over the range of the Caucasus, but was careful not to relax his powers of observation. Ararat, he noted, was a volcano without a visible crater. But that was not his most striking observation: during the climb he had examined the arrangement of loose boulders along the way, which seemed to him to have been sorted by size *by receding waters*. Even here, at such great heights, huge volumes of water must once have flowed. Parrot was aware of the doubts among geologists concerning the global nature of the Deluge, but says: 'the physical proof of the correctness of the historical narrative of the Flood cannot easily be flung aside'.

Whatever the sceptics or unbelievers may say, here lay 'a great truth, derived from pure sources'.

The climbers remained on the summit for 45 minutes. Before starting their descent, the deacon filled a flask with Ararat ice, and Parrot poured a libation of wine for the patriarch Noah.

In the final years of his life, Friedrich Parrot grew emaciated and bitter. To anyone who would listen, he said: 'Put an Armenian on the summit of Ararat and he will still cling to the idea that it is unconquerable.' Even more hurtful was that 'the educated Europeans' set no stock by his achievement. Despite his persuasiveness, Parrot was not equal to the myth, which proved stronger and more stubborn than he. That in itself was food for thought; it said something about the human need for mysteries and the accompanying urge not to solve them, but to keep them firmly in place. It almost seemed as though belief and the will to know were mutually exclusive.

Notwithstanding his waning health, Parrot brooded until the very end over plans to return to Ararat and show to a delegation of doubting Thomases the route he had taken. But that resolution was thwarted at a single stroke: in the summer of 1840 – one year before he died – Parrot's trail up Ararat was obliterated for all time. The mountain had begun to move. On 2 July, half an hour before sunset, people in the area heard a subterranean rumbling. The ensuing tremors went on for several minutes, soon followed by a deep thundering that began at the top of the gorge and gradually rose to a deafening roar. From a distance, shepherds saw a column of reddish-grey dust or smoke rising, which then came rushing down as though a torch-bearing giant were running down the mountainside. Seen from Echmiadzin on the plains of the Arax, it looked as though Ararat was 'boiling' within; eyewitnesses said they had seen 'steam' rising from chasms along its sides.

The monks of St Hagob's and the inhabitants of Arguri, alarmed by the approaching cataclysm, had only a few moments to look upon the avalanche of gulping, roiling mud before it dragged them along and then buried them.

$\sqrt{-1}$

Aʟʟ ᴏꜰ ᴛʜᴇ letters my former mathematics teacher sent me had something paternal about them. The first had appeared suddenly in 1995, 12 years after I had taken my finals. His opening was like a chess move. 'On occasion they send me things, a dissertation, a thesis, but when one of my former students writes a book, I buy it.'

Dr W. Knol – known to us as 'Calculus Knol' because he seemed so at one with the subject he taught – had lost none of his severity. He had perused my debut with a proofreader's eye, 'slowly and attentively, as I ordinarily do only when reading the Bible or mathematical treatises'. The more precise my formulations, the greater his appreciation. And when he encountered sloppiness it resulted in a rap on the knuckles. 'There is a tautology on page 38. A square is by definition a surface. You learned enough mathematics from me to know that what it *should* say is: "Vukovar had four city squares, with a joint surface *area* of 60,000 square metres."'

Calculus Knol observed that I had made history my profession. He wrote: 'History is a difficult subject, more difficult than mathematics, although the latter has greater depth.' As though wishing to deliver proof of that claim on the spot, he had enclosed an old exam of mine which he had dug out of his files. Recognition wafted up from the mimeographed sheet with his handwritten exercises. But a closer look produced only estrangement. I had, it seemed, solved without error problems like 'Draw in a complex plane the collection of points corresponding to $|z - 1 + 3i| = |2z + 1 - 3i|$.

Apparently there had been someone who went by my name and who understood formulas like that. On the morning of 11 February 1983, that person had turned in six pages of calculations and was rewarded with an 8.8 out of 10.

It's never too late to take your degree.
With kind regards and all respect,
W. Knol

Calculus Knol was viewed as the terror of the school. Only those certain they were beyond range of his hearing dared to mimic his heavy northern accent. 'What'd be y'r problem, boy? Dunno ha' to draw a margin?' King-sized margins were needed to accommodate his comments in red ink. Anyone who forgot to add an extra margin line during an exam automatically sacrificed a full grade – a hideous caprice to those teetering on the verge of passing or failing.

While still at primary school I had once come home to find my sister, who was four years ahead of me, lying on the sofa, sobbing and holding a cushion over her head. My father had tutored her at the kitchen table; along with her friend Trudy she had crammed to memorise the 'red rules' from the maths textbook. But during the exam both she and Trudy had drawn a blank.

'Forgot to do yr home'rk again, ah suppose?' Calculus Knol had commented as he handed her her umpteenth unsatisfactory mark.

My sister had refused to eat but my parents made her sit at the table anyway. My father cleared his throat and launched into the Lord's Prayer. When he got to the part about 'deliver us from evil', I glanced up at my sister in solidarity. She had her eyes open, and she was not praying along.

One Sunday afternoon in Amsterdam, walking the narrow streets of Prinseneiland, I told my sister about my correspondence with our former maths teacher. It was 'open-studio day'; we were just entering a silkscreen printer's.

'Did you call him "Calculus Knol"? We always said "Knol

Rigmarole" or "Square-Root Knol" . . .' My sister, as it turned out, had an entire arsenal of nicknames for him. That I was actually exchanging letters with the man felt to her, even after all those years, like a form of treason.

Moving from door to door, from attic room to basement studio, only half aware of the passing ranks of tin soldiers and decorated shop-window dummies, we reminisced about other things as well. Mostly about home, where we had spent more time together than we had at school. Despite our age difference, we had equally clear memories of the one occasion we had been allowed to watch TV in our pyjamas in the middle of the night. Our mother, keen to watch as well, had woken us. We tiptoed down the stairs to the living room, where Dad was already adjusting the rabbit-ear aerials to find the best reception. Later, in his folder of memorable clippings, I had come across the article that went with that event: a front page from the *Algemeen Dagblad*, 22 July 1969, bearing the headline MAN ON THE MOON. I was four and a half at the time. We must have heard the excited voices of newsreaders, historic words, but all I see today in my mind's eye is how we sat close together on the rug, in front of a flickering screen.

'Did you know that Mother had a weakness for astronauts?'

I had no idea; little brothers don't pick up on things like that.

'She saw them as real heroes, but that was partly because she thought the Russian cosmonauts were so pitiful.' It was as though my sister was supplying subtitles to the grainy archive footage of my childhood.

'Pitiful?'

'Yeah, because they always said they had gone into space and hadn't seen God anywhere. She would always say: "I feel so sorry for them, they have to say that, otherwise they'll send them to the labour camps."'

That explained a lot. My mother's Cold War allegiances had never been any secret to me, but now that my sister mentioned it, her strong aversion to the Soviets had everything to do with their godlessness.

It reminded me of the time I had read about a space quiz in *Kijk* magazine; first prize was a telescope powerful enough to see the rings of Saturn. I dreamed of that thing on its tripod at our attic window, but the problem was that I didn't know who had been the first man in space. Was it John Glenn? Or was it actually Yuri Gagarin?

'John Glenn,' my mother said.

My sister and I arrived at a little square where two performance artists were engaged in launching a 'dead horse' into the air with a giant catapult. My sister, an artist as well, was comforted by the thought that these two, like her, were producing completely unsaleable art. Next to the office where she practised as a dietician, she had a studio where she made perishable sculptures from butter (a dining-room table and four chairs) or sugar (sprinkled in the form of a knotted rug, or caramelised into a tangle of vines).

We ordered iced tea at a pavement café. I told her I was busy rewinding the home movie of my memory, looking for the moment when I had started to doubt the Bible as being God's Word, and the existence of God himself. It seemed to me that my faith had been chipped away at gradually, more or less without me noticing.

We had never spoken about faith before, but she knew exactly what I meant.

'For me, the first real shock was during history lessons,' she said. 'We were talking about Marxism, and about the role of religion as Marx saw it.' The teacher had explained his famous statement about religion being the opiate of the masses, but also said that Marx was convinced that man had created God, and not the other way around. 'I was astonished by that. That you could also view faith as a human invention.'

I had never been exposed to Karl Marx's ideas about God; I had dropped history as soon as I got the chance. Just as my sister had dropped maths.

Back at school I would not have admitted it, but I had always been fond of Calculus Knol. To start with, I preferred the exact sciences, not the vague liberal arts. Having been forewarned, I had started – as soon as Knol became my mathematics teacher – drawing extra margins of my own accord. He had bushy eyebrows like Brezhnev's that merged at the bridge of his nose. When students received unsatisfactory marks from him, they were told: 'If you don't understand it, at least admire it.' But if you displayed insight into algebra or geometry, he took care of you; he would bring a chess problem of the type 'white to checkmate in three moves' especially for you, or pass along a titbit of information about the beheaded King Louis XVI, whose death sentence in 1793 may have been due to a miscalculation: according to Knol, a fatal error had been made while counting the votes in the French Assemblée.

At school, rumour had it that his first name was Wouter, or Wout, but in fact it was Wolter. I had discovered that in the school library, where his dissertation could be found on the science and mathematics shelf. There wasn't a single lending date stamped on the inside cover. I borrowed it, out of compassion and curiosity. The text was in English, but that wasn't the difficulty. There was, in fact, almost no text; the pages were full of long series of numbers, punctuated by logical if/then symbols, after which the numbers took over again. Wolter Knol had received his doctorate for this.

From all three pre-college classes of 25 students each, only seven signed up voluntarily for Maths II, 'mathematics for weirdoes'. I was one of them, though I did my best not to be viewed as a creep. Good marks put a drain on your popularity, a principle driven home hard from the very first day of secondary school. The exception to the rule, however, was Harro 'the alchemist', a skinny boy who, despite his consistent top marks, commanded respect by conjuring up recipes for smoke bombs and underwater explosions in the pond opposite the school. By becoming an accomplice in his stunts, I had hitched my wagon to Harro's success, and so I shared in his prestige as well. By the time we arrived in classroom 3b for our first chemistry lessons, our reputations preceded us. Both of us were able to lay claim to an enviable seat in the back row, which helped greatly in the pecking order. Sitting at the back never gave a greater sense of power than it did in chemistry, which was taught in a tiered room with built-in taps, sinks and Bunsen burners at each level.

It was during these chemistry lessons that Mr Beltman confronted me in unorthodox fashion with the Book of Genesis. The wrath of Beltman, a teacher extremely serious about his subject, was focused from the very first lesson on Harro and me. Each time he described the consequences of the incautious handling of chemicals, he gave the two of us a meaningful look. He would speak of hydrochloric acid splashed in your eyes, unslaked lime on your skin, and about the statistical probability of death by mercury poisoning. In this classroom, special safety regulations applied, Beltman said, which did not mix well with puerile behaviour. Anyone who thought they could get away with practical jokes was sorely mistaken.

Before opening the cupboard containing hazardous materials, Beltman first put on a pair of square perspex spectacles that accentuated his pointy chin. He donned a stained lab coat, showed us a steaming vat of sulphuric acid, then pointed out to us a chain with a handle on it, hanging beside the blackboard. Pulling the chain turned on a shower: a cascade of water would come pouring from the ceiling, potentially saving the life of anyone who had caught fire or spilled a bottle of peroxide on themselves.

Beltman took off his protective glasses. 'Misuse will be punished.' He opened the door to show us where the water would go: out into the hall, past the lab assistant's cubicle and all the way down to the physics lab. 'I'm the only one who knows how to turn off the shower, but let me assure you: if anyone plays around with it, I will not turn it off until the hallway is under water all the way down to biology.' The culprit, so much was clear, would have to mop it up all by himself.

Every misdemeanour had its appropriate Beltman sanction, and the first ones to undergo such punishment, even before the autumn holidays had arrived, were us.

'Frank W., Harro K.,' he scribbled on one of the blackboard's side panels (we did not yet know that it was Beltman's wont to publicise his punishments for all to see). 'Come in after school. Copy Genesis chapters 1 to 10.'

What had we done to deserve this? Harro and I were unaware of having broken any rules. That morning, during devotionals, Beltman had suddenly become angry with us for no good reason. Devotionals were a daily ritual: every morning at 8.15, the first 10 minutes of school were spent in Bible reading and prayer. There was no getting around it. The only way to act suavely was to treat your school Bible as carelessly as possible. Anyone with a neat Bible was an immediate outcast. Harro's was covered in inkspots, mine no longer had a spine, its pages held together by the remains of glue and tattered linen. That morning, after ordering me to read aloud, Beltman's gaze had fallen on our much-abused Bibles; in four or five long strides he was standing beside us, at the top and back of the classroom.

Genesis 1 to 10 doesn't look like much. Eight pages, comprising the stories of Adam and Eve (the Fall from Grace), Cain and Abel (fratricide) and Noah (the Deluge).

'You two can skip the begots,' Beltman said that afternoon, by way of concession. He went on filling flasks of chemicals in the otherwise deserted lab.

Reading and copying are activities of a completely different order. Never before had I absorbed a Bible text so assiduously, and in a way that made the stories I thought I knew by heart more mysterious, more obscure. I had not realised, for example, that God had created Man twice, the first time in Genesis 1, and then all over again in Genesis 2 (this time by 'breathing life into his nostrils'). Another, at least equally strange dissonance was tucked away in the first verses of the Flood story: suddenly there was talk of 'the sons of God'. Plural, in other words, even though everyone knew that God had sent his only Son to save us. But here, in black and white, it said that Jesus had had older brothers who had been on earth as well and who had not behaved like saints: 'The sons of God saw the daughters of men that they were fair, and they took them wives of all which they chose.' I read to my amazement that in 'those days' there had been 'giants' walking the earth, as well as 'mighty men which were of old', offspring of the sons of God and the daughters of men. The Lord was angered by this lawlessness, and regretted having created them.

Then came the Deluge, and the extermination of all living things.

It was and always has been a monstrously exciting story, even if you know how it ends. What I liked was Noah's blind faith in building that Ark, with only instructions to go on, while everyone else mocked him. And he went on imperturbably. Another of my favourite passages related the arrival of the animals, lined up so tamely two by two, male and female. As soon as the animals, Noah's family and finally Noah himself (eight people in all) had entered the ship, the 'windows of heaven were opened' and it began to pour.

'And the Lord shut him in.' That was no normal remark: you could almost feel the tremor as the door slammed shut.

'And the waters increased, and bare up the Ark, and it was lifted up above the earth.' That, in my mind, was a literal lifting-up, like a rocket rising from the launch pad in slow motion as the scaffolding collapses on all sides. The Ark, too, had floated through empty space, not weightlessly beyond the atmosphere, but adrift on a film of water. 'And every living substance was destroyed which was upon the face of the ground, both man, and cattle, and the creeping things, and the fowl of the heaven; and they were destroyed from the earth. All in whose nostrils was the breath of life, of all that was in the dry land, died.' Only 150 days later would God decide to close the floodgates of heaven, so the water could subside and the Ark could land safely – atop Ararat.

The school my sister and I attended, the Christian Community School for Greater Assen, had a reputation for being Biblically and doctrinally sound. The teachers, however, made no bones about teaching evolution or the origins of the universe. Darwin was dominant in biology, and in physics the Big Bang was presented as the actual 'in the beginning'. Such theories, though, were described as 'explanatory models' which were not definitive per se or the final word.

The only religious conflict that I can recall being fought out tooth and nail related to one's moral position on the arms race: whether one, as a Christian, should oppose it. This was in the early 1980s, when the Americans hoped to station nuclear cruise missiles in the Netherlands as a counterbalance to the Soviet SS-20s. The church elders and our teachers were divided into two camps, both of them basing their views on the New Testament. The opponents of the cruise missiles quoted the Sermon on the Mount ('Ye have heard that it hath been said, An eye for an eye, and a tooth for a tooth: but I say unto you, That ye resist not evil: but whosoever shall smite thee on thy right cheek, turn to him the other also'), while the advocates availed themselves of Paul's letter to the Romans ('For he is the minister of God to thee for good . . . for he beareth not the sword in vain'). I remember how furious it made me that this latter group awarded greater importance to the words of an apostle than to those of Jesus. 'The congregation of hypocrites' was what I wrote, in my notebook of 100 per cent recycled paper, about those church members I knew to be in favour of Ronald Reagan's 'Star Wars' programme.

Concerning my aversion to the Americans and exactly what one should think about the cruise missile, I looked to my sister. From behind her bedroom door I could hear the songs of Bob Dylan and John Lennon. Each year on Boxing Day, she and her girlfriends marched past the airbase at Havelterberg in the peace demonstration. American nuclear warheads were stored there, no more than 40 kilometres as the crow flies from our house. I had a recurring dream in which the bunkers at Havelterberg exploded in a burst of light. Above the flats on Speenkruidstraat there rose a mushroom cloud that blotted out the sun, and everyone watching in the street was incinerated by the wave of fire, leaving behind only a sooty smudge on the pavement.

One day, in a kitchen cupboard, my sister came across a rusty tin without a brand name, tucked away behind a pile of pans.

'Oh, those are Cuba biscuits,' said my mother, whom we had called over immediately.

It was a funny-looking tin. The label read 'CD Emmen'.

'CD stands for Civil Defence,' my father said. Curious himself now, he went to the garage to look for a hammer and chisel.

While waiting, we examined the strip of iodine pills we'd found beside the tin. According to the directions, they were to be taken in the event of radioactive fallout. In the same cupboard we also discovered a folder entitled 'Tips to protect you and your family', about what to do in case of nuclear attack.

'An atomic explosion is marked by an extremely bright flash of light.' After the flash, you and your entire family were to seek shelter 'beneath a table, bed, workbench, etc.' and stay tuned to the radio.

The folder had been published in 1961; one year later, at the height of the Cuban missile crisis, my parents had picked up the tin of biscuits and the pills from the neighbourhood coordinator of the local civil defence unit.

Dad clamped the tin in the bench vice and had it open in two whacks of the hammer. The biscuits that came rolling out tasted like cardboard, but were still unspoiled after 20 years.

You could make fun of those emergency rations and those pills for the prevention of thyroid cancer, and we did. But at the same time it awakened me to the possibility that we could die any moment, that I, at least, might never live to see 18. We were enduring the chilliest years of the Cold War, when fear of the bomb perched on one's shoulder, like a punk rocker's pet rat: on rare occasions, you almost forgot it was there.

The only one who understood our fears was Dr ('just call me Niek') Govaerts, our physics teacher. As a nuclear physicist opposed to nuclear power, he was on our side. Govaerts also shared his pupils' views about the insanity of the neutron bomb. He wore a wispy beard that suited his boyish build. 'Half of all physicists sooner or later end up working for the arms industry,' he said when we asked him why, with a PhD, he had chosen to teach in a secondary school (like Calculus Knol, in fact, though you would never have asked *him* a thing like that).

Niek Govaerts showed us films that most pupils never saw, like the ones of the surface nuclear tests in the Nevada desert in which shrieking caged pigs were irradiated and roasted in a single flash. He wanted us to be able to talk sensibly (to him, that meant rationally) about the dangers of radiation, without being swayed by polemics. Radioactivity was a natural phenomenon. Hold a Geiger counter above a few blocks of basalt and it will react wildly. As long as you knew what you were doing and didn't expose yourself to excessively high doses for too long, there was no danger.

For Niek Govaerts, the important thing was that we approached Nature with as few misgivings as possible, so that we could look her straight in the eye. 'Is there life on Mars?' Govaerts would write on the blackboard as that week's theme, then go on to discuss the discoveries made by the Viking I and Viking II probes that had taken soil samples from the red planet with their robotic arms and analysed them on board. Microbes were all one might expect to find on Mars, but what if there really was intelligent life in space? Wouldn't that turn all our preconceptions upside down? Would we still be able to see man as the pinnacle of creation? Those were the kinds of things we talked about.

I remember when Govaerts started a lesson with a story about a French genius of the seventeenth century, Blaise Pascal. This great man, hitherto unknown to us, was not only a theologian but also a mathematician, and had, Govaerts told us, done a lot of thinking about the infinite nature of the universe. When looked at next to the unfathomable vastness of the cosmos, Pascal felt, man was nothing but a measly creature, even when you took his imaginative powers into account. That imagination could extend to great lengths, but never far enough to unveil the deepest secrets of creation. There would always remain the unknowable; by way of example, Pascal had cited the physical make-up of the stars. Mankind could never know about that, because no one could ever go to a star and bring back a sample. I thought his reasoning extremely sound, and I suppose I nodded.

But this whole story proved only the prelude to a practical lesson in which our teacher handed out photographic contact sheets of starlight refracted through a prism. Within that colour spectrum there were thicker and thinner black stripes. Each wavelength devoid of light corresponded to a specific element in that star's make-up. With a set of instructions to hand, we were able in two 50-minute sessions to unravel what Pascal had considered part of the divine mystery: we determined the composition of the stars on the basis of their bar codes. This was the triumph of science; I thought it was fantastic, and I suppose I sniffed in pride.

Looking back, it must have been those same sciences that made me doubt most. Biology, physics and chemistry divested the world of a great deal of its mystery. The knowledge I took in gave me self-confidence and something to cling to, and caused the conviction with which I prayed to dwindle even further. Where was God? Our little group of four or five like-minded souls talked about that in the school café. One of us had heard an American professor on TV explain that black holes might actually be portals to another dimension. We knew that a black hole emitted no information and no energy, that it reflected and radiated nothing. So why couldn't they be portals to heaven?

My notebook from those days also contained a few comments under the solemn heading 'Remarks on the Story of Creation'. In one of them I entertained the possibility that God's creation had also included the 'plough of logic' – with which Adam and Eve could till the soil in the Garden. 'But the plough of logic hit upon something hard and broke, dooming all their descendants to lives of fear and uncertainty. What should have become the Kingdom of Reason ended up being the realm of religion.'

I'm quite sure that at that point, however, I had not rejected God or religion. The only person in our class who dared to say out loud that God did not exist was Jacoliene Dop. Jacoliene wanted to be cremated, not buried, because she already knew what it was like to be dead.

'So what's it like?' I asked.

'Exactly the same as before you were born.'

Her remark stunned me, and left me feeling cold and uneasy. On the other hand, I was quite capable of being rude to the little group of born-again girls who walked the halls flouncing their ponytails and clutching canvas bags with a rainbow emblem and the slogan 'THERE IS HOPE'. They sealed themselves off from all doubt or discussion; as soon as things got serious they would say: 'God is love.'

'Yeah,' Harro once replied, 'and love is blind.'

Exactly what I thought about death and what followed it remained unclear until my sister, who had gone to Groningen to study health science and nutrition, gave me a book containing the letters of Vincent van Gogh. The passage I read aloud in a corner of the café went like this:

Is life as a whole visible to us, or are we familiar with only one of its hemispheres before we die? . . . For myself, I declare that I know nothing about it at all, yet seeing the stars always causes me to dream, in much the same way that the black dots on a map showing towns and villages cause me to dream. Why, I ask myself, should the shining dots on the firmament be less accessible than the black dots on a map of France?

The way we take a train to get to Tarascon or Rouaan, we take death to get to a star . . . In short, it does not seem impossible to me that cholera, kidney stones, consumption and cancer are heavenly means of transport, in the same way that steamboats, omnibuses and trains are earthly ones.

Dying peacefully of old age means one goes there on foot.

'Nonsense,' my friends ruled. But I insisted that van Gogh's idea could be just as true as any other, because something like *poetic* truth did exist.

That I continued to believe in God, at least during my secondary school years, was down to mathematics. Maths was not like biology, physics and chemistry. It was purer. A realm unto itself. Applied mathematics (he who mastered the cannonball's parabola could strike the enemy) didn't interest me. I was enchanted by the abstract side of maths. Accordingly, I fell under the spell of the number π. There was even a period when I combed the school library for everything I could find about π. In nature, π was everywhere (in a flower's calyx, in the shape of the moon). It was simply the circumference of a circle divided by its diameter. It existed, yet (or rather: and at the same time) it was unknowable, it surpassed our powers of comprehension. Two centuries before Christ, Archimedes had tried to calculate π: he arrived at a value of 3.14. The display on a pocket calculator listed eight decimal places: 3.14159265. But there were already computers that could calculate π to millions of decimal places. Even then, you weren't there yet. You would never get there.

Mathematics revealed a logical universe, and at the same time introduced you to the unknowable (and not to the seeming unknowableness of stellar make-up). It was a magnificent thing indeed to see how Calculus Knol proved the correctness of Pythagoras's theorem ($a^2 + b^2 = c^2$) in less than no time. If you were handy in the logical juggling of numbers, you could use it to explore unknown territory. That was what we learned in Mathematics II. What had been mathematically impossible during Maths I became possible in Maths II. Finding the square root of negative numbers, for example, was out of the question. Until we, the seven pupils of Maths II, were initiated by Calculus Knol into the world of the 'imaginary numbers', which depended wholly on the assertion that the square root of -1 was equal to i. The imaginary number i simply could not exist, but the gist of the idea was: all right, it's not possible, but just imagine it *were*. When you imagined that, it turned out, you could use i to calculate without limits – and the most wondrous thing of all was that the results of those calculations could be applied in turn to the real world.

To me, this bordered on the divine. Mathematics, it seemed,

allowed you to create nonexistent worlds that still had an impact on reality. Was that not *the* proof that there was more to reality than what we could quantify?

For weeks, Calculus Knol's most recent letter had been lying on my desk, unanswered. It contained, as usual, a reprimand – this one concerning my previous book – that called urgently for a confession of guilt: 'Page 8 made me frown. Next to cranial index you write: breadth divided by length times 100. That should be: 100 times breadth divided by length. Converting formulas into words demands great precision. What was I teaching you all those years?'

In my reply I promised to describe the cranial index with greater accuracy in subsequent editions. After this and a few other formalities, I moved on to some questions I'd been meaning to ask him for a while: 'In the book I'm working on at the moment I find myself in the shadowy area between believing and knowing, based in part on the bafflement I experienced twenty-five years ago as a secondary school pupil. The knowledge and insights passed along to me then served as a double-edged sword: the world around me became easier to understand, while at the same time the mystery only deepened.'

What I hoped to hear from my former maths teacher was this: how were matters of belief and knowledge related in his mind? And did the two ever cause a short circuit there?

The relationship between science and religion, I posited, might be comparable to that between mathematics and language; the one being precise and traceable, the other elusive and full of loopholes. To me, these were two distinctly different filters through which one could view reality.

His reply came two months later. He had sent me a four-page epistle, complete with a number of addenda tucked into clear plastic document wallets.

Dear Frank,
   Your letter, dated 28-7-2005, contains a few themes to

which I, despite my ignorance in the fields in question, would like to add a few comments of my own.

Calculus Knol set out to refute the parallel I had drawn between the science–religion dichotomy and the relationship of mathematics to language. 'The conflict between religion and science cannot be compared to that [the precision of mathematics versus the imprecision of language]; a conflict with religion supersedes all else.'

Well, I thought, you've got me there.

But this wasn't a dogmatic letter. In fact, the tone was different from his earlier ones. 'Even as a young boy, I was struck by the fact (which can be illustrated in the form of a diagram) that the stories of Christ's resurrection as told in the four gospels contradict one another.' It took me a moment to get used to the idea that an authority like Calculus Knol had ever been a boy. 'I also remember that later, at the Christian secondary school in Leeuwarden, our divinity teacher (a pastor) made us memorise five proofs of God's existence. As though one proof alone wouldn't have been sufficient for us, as budding scientists. That's how it started out.'

As a secondary school pupil, Knol had apparently struggled with the same kinds of questions. I had never been forced to regurgitate proofs of God's existence, but I could easily imagine the scepticism that must have provoked. Five proofs!

Once he became a teacher himself, however, I understood his letter to say, the religious doubts were relegated to the sidelines. 'The views and opinions of individual teachers may have been discussed at home or in smaller circles, but not in the teachers' common room. The only heated discussion I can remember had to do with the cruise missiles.'

I knew what Niek Govaerts' view had been at the time, but Calculus Knol was still skirting the issue.

When he applied for the job at our school, the headmaster had given him a set of 'guidelines concerning our approach to controversial issues'. A copy of that two-page directive was included as one of the addenda.

'Science is no longer the handmaiden of theology,' I read in this document from 1961. I discovered that we, the pupils, were to be informed of modern insights 'concerning the age of the earth and the development of living creatures'. Christian education could no longer afford to ignore 'the flood of popular publications serving to disseminate the findings of science on this score'. Marxist exegetics, however, were strictly taboo: 'A very clear point must be made of the reprehensible, anti-Christian character of nineteenth-century materialist evolutionism.' The teacher was, 'of course', free to express the belief that 'Genesis 1 constitutes a straightforward and chronological account of God's creative activities six thousand years ago.' But only on one condition: he must at the same time point out that this opinion was in conflict with current scientific insights!

Strangely enough, the document's shilly-shallying comforted me. I had not been the only one to be tossed back and forth between belief and knowledge: the teachers who had formed me were apparently of two minds as well.

Calculus Knol did not elaborate on the concrete examples I had given from geology and biology. He stuck to mathematics, and closed his letter with a few thoughts about the relationship between mathematics and faith, followed by a remarkable credo:

Mathematics, the science of the meticulous, of extreme accuracy.

Mathematics, which its practitioners believe is an autonomous creation of the human mind.

The problem being: what is the human mind?

Does it work 'independently' . . . of the brain's profusion of signals?

And what is belief? Belief in one of my teacher's five proofs of God's existence? *Thinking* that one of them must be right?

Is belief a projection? Of what, from where, to what end and in what way, the mathematician urgently desires to know.

83

The Source, or so I expect, will show us some day.
Sincerely yours,

W. Knol

PS Don't let Noah's Ark drive you to distraction. The fog of the past is bound to be very thick.

The north face

THE NUMBER 26 minibuses to the holy seat of the Armenian Apostolic Church leave from near the Yerevan cognac distillery. Across the former Soviet-Russian empire, these shared taxis are still known as *marshrutki*, a name imbued with the rhythm of Cossacks marching off to parts unknown.

The next bus in line was not yet half full, which gave me time to walk down the wakening avenue and buy something to supplement my hotel breakfast. When I returned 15 minutes later, only one other passenger had shown up: a Japanese man.

Even on a Sunday, route 26 to the monastery of Echmiadzin did not seem heavily travelled. The driver punched the accelerator and took an exit just past the distillery. Ararat was hidden from sight. That was unusual for this time of year; although spring was well underway, the Arax valley lay under a blanket of cloud through which the sun only occasionally burned pale spots of light.

Outside the bowl of the city we passed through a strung-out corridor of casinos. GLORIA. FORTUNE. CHICAGO. Pole-dancers, palm beaches and Formula One cars rolled by on their painted façades.

'First time to Armenia?' The question, coming from a fellow passenger with a briefcase on his lap, was addressed to me and the Japanese man beside me.

The Japanese man nodded.

Parked on the pavement in front of the casinos were gangster vehicles with the hulking posture of armoured cars. 'I was here in 1999,' I told the man, 'but I don't remember seeing anything like this.' I was paying attention to very different things now, I noticed; this time I was seeing Armenia as a country in the shadow of Ararat.

'Back then we did not yet have this mini Las Vegas. As you can see: Armenia is prospering.'

The special green ink used to print dollar bills, the Japanese man and I were told, had been invented by an Armenian, a fact that seemed to mould itself to such surroundings. Neon hedgerows advertising SAUNA, MASSAGE and PRIVATE DANCE CABINS lined the road to the monastery of Echmiadzin. I was reminded of Friedrich Parrot, who had braved thunder and lightning on this same road back in 1829; it was here that the vista for which he had been longing had opened up: Echmiadzin, with Ararat in the background.

The landscape to our left and right should have been lush, green and verdant, with apricot orchards and babbling irrigation canals. Instead I saw the dismal Soviet-style tower blocks, and bus shelters in the shape of a hollow fish. Then, without warning, the *marshrutka* stopped next to the monastery wall of Echmiadzin. The Japanese man and I walked past stalls selling incense, devotional pictures and vials of 'Armenian soil' and 'Armenian water'. After sizing each other up a little, we admitted that we had both come for the same thing: the fragment of wood from Noah's Ark.

Yun Yamashita had a black fringe that danced on his forehead and tended to slip down under the top of his glasses. He worked for Panasonic in Peking, a Japanese expat in China, but had taken time off for a more-or-less direct trip to Echmiadzin.

We made an unusual duo: two grown-up men from opposite sides of the globe, travelling thousands of kilometres to see a piece of wood. A Japanese and a Dutchman, neither of us particularly inclined to believe in fables, but both drawn simultaneously to a relic from a primal story: sufficient evidence it seemed of the Flood story's universal appeal. Knowing that the treasury of Echmiadzin is usually closed to outsiders, we agreed to join forces in our attempt to goggle at that petrified piece of flotsam.

Was Yun a believer, or simply curious? At first I couldn't read him. His attention seemed focused on a clumsy concrete sculpture commemorating a visit by the Pope in 2001. I was more interested in the seminary where Parrot had spent the night almost two centuries earlier, the one attended by Deacon Abovian, the young monk who accompanied him to the summit of Ararat and later became nineteenth-century Armenia's most famous writer. The rafters of the grey stone building were wrought with busy-looking woodwork. Somewhere I had read that, during the First World War, which had taken such a disastrous course for the Armenians, the seminary at Echmiadzin was packed with refugees. The school was closed down, and after the violence had subsided, the new Soviet authorities had been in no hurry to reopen it.

In the eyes of most Armenians, the Russians had always been their friends and liberators, or at the very least their guardians. There was, of course, a world of difference between pre-1917 Russians (fellow Christians in the fight against the Muslims) and the (atheistic) Reds who came later. But as a people at the very edge of the European-Christian landmass, grinding against the tectonic plate of Islam, the Armenians went on regarding the Russians as a source of support, regardless of whether they served the Czar or the secretary-general of the Communist Party.

Amongst my baggage was a book written by a female American-Armenian journalist who had visited the Soviet Socialist Republic of Armenia in 1930. Like a human plumb, she had given her journey the form of a longitudinal beeline from Leningrad on the Gulf of Finland to Leninakan along the Turkish–Armenian border.

'Can one be moral without religion?' the journalist had asked herself. She had shared a train compartment with a group of girls from the Komsomol, the Communist Youth Federation, who stared out of the window in awe at a hydroelectric dam that had cost 'eleven million roubles'. The girls were absolutely uninterested in the ancient, moss-covered monasteries 'and other things of the past'.

From the balcony of her hotel in Leninakan, Armenia's second-largest city, hung a red banner with white letters:

RELIGION IS THE ENEMY OF THE FIVE-YEAR PLAN.
DOWN WITH RELIGIOUS HOLIDAYS!
ENTER THE UNION OF FIGHTING ATHEISTS.

Such was the spirit of the times. In accordance with the
Communist cosmology of scientific atheism, houses of prayer were
converted into planetariums. Painters climbed into the domes to
turn the All-Seeing Eye into a shining sun. On Sundays, students
wearing red armbands would tell visitors that the Earth was a ball
which rotated on its axis once a day, that it was illuminated by the
sun and revolved around it once a year: nothing could be less mysterious.

'The fury of Soviet anti-religious activism has not borne down as
heavily on the Armenian Church as it has on the Russian Orthodox,'
the readers of the *Christian Science Monitor* were told. 'No priest
is shot at dawn or sent to Siberia *because he is a priest*, but only
because, it is alleged, he is often a kulak or a counter-revolutionist.'
At Echmiadzin the journalist was told that the *katolikos* had died
not long before, after having lived in seclusion for years. He had
locked himself in his study to avoiding communicating with the
Bolsheviks, whom he saw as the angels of the Antichrist. Stalin had
'collectivised' the vineyards and the flour mill at Echmiadzin, and
the monks were forced to live off charity. On the other hand, the
Commissar for Education and Culture had acknowledged the value
of the monastery's antique manuscripts (including the apocryphal
'Gospel of Lazarus' from AD 887) and ordered them to be rebound
in leather covers bearing the hammer and sickle. The relics in the
Mayr Tachar, the Mother Cathedral, including the spearhead with
which a Roman soldier had pierced Christ's side, and the piece of
wood from the Ark, had escaped the comrades' iconoclastic frenzy
as well.

Did I know that some Armenian monks prayed daily in the direction of Ararat?

'Masis is their spiritual true north,' Dr Armen Petrozian had told
me shortly before I left. Petrozian, in his sleeveless photographer's
vest with sew-on pockets, was a wiry little man. Seventy-two years

of age, grey but for his eyebrows, a seismologist by profession. As the author of a 'historical catalogue of earthquakes in Armenia', he was able to tell me that Armenia's ancient church-builders had taken into account the possibility of severe tremors. The belfries they designed were solid and relatively blunt, their domes situated above a cruciform nave. A circle atop a square; at the time, Petrozian explained, that had been an architectural revolution. By determining which of those churches had survived and which had collapsed, he had been able to deduce the characteristics of two legendary earthquakes in the tenth and seventeenth centuries.

Petrozian's catalogue, which appeared in 1997, was the last thing he had published. In the autumn of 1999 he had fled Armenia along with his wife and their two conscription-aged sons. They had packed their bags and traded in their apartment in Yerevan (with its view of Ararat) for a prefab unit in a refugee centre in a Dutch polder four metres below sea level.

'Hendrik-Ido-Ambacht,' he said. 'I can't get my tongue around it . . .'

That was where they lived now, in a state of abysmal boredom amid all the other abysmally bored Kurds, Somalis and Iraqis. How was he to know that, as a refugee in Holland, you weren't allowed to work until your 'status' had been established? Armen's wife was under 65 and so had received a summons to attend mandatory Dutch-language courses, leaving him 'home' alone. That was the world gone topsy-turvy. 'A man isn't supposed to stay at home. The house is the woman's domain. I know things are different here, but with us in the Caucasus, that's the norm.'

Among the belongings he had brought with him was an out-of-date calendar with pictures of Ararat, photographed 12 times, at each month of the year, from the Armenian side.

'We came here for our sons,' Petrozian said. 'They should be studying, not fighting.'

Armenian refugees: an apparently timeless phenomenon. I remembered coming across them in Assen as well. Families, children with dark, close-cropped hair, whom we helped out with charity collections. When the going got tough they were given asylum in the church. The strange thing, though, was that they weren't actually from Armenia, they were from Turkey. People called them 'Christian Turks' or 'Turkish Christians', but if you said that to them they became angry.

'We're not Turks.'

And that was the mildest reaction one could expect; it was precisely in those days, in the 1970s and 80s, that some of them carried out attacks on the offices of Turkish Airlines in Amsterdam, on the Turkish consulate in Rotterdam, on the young son of the Turkish ambassador in The Hague. A group calling itself the 'Avengers of the Armenian Genocide' claimed responsibility for these acts of terrorism. At the time I'd had no idea what was being avenged, but I did notice some sympathy for their cause. The special church services held in support of the Armenians, the little votive candles we lit for them as schoolchildren; the sense of solidarity was so strong at times that you could almost touch it.

To me, the fact that Armenian refugees were more welcome than their non-Christian fellow sufferers seemed only logical, something to which I never gave much thought. Only now, talking to Petrozian, did I realise that that sympathy could be traced back to the Crusades: the Armenians in Turkey had provided the medieval European Crusaders with support, both moral and material, during their marches on Jerusalem. In the villages, they had lined the roads in welcome, tossed food to the passing armies. Some of them had also joined the ranks.

Petrozian taught me my first word of Armenian: *baron*. It was an echo from the days of the Crusades, bastardised through the centuries until it simply came to mean 'sir'.

The second was *yergrasharh*, which had nothing to do with holy wars, but all the more with the seismologist's daily reality. It was Armenian for 'earthquake'.

'*Yer-gra-sharh*,' I tried: three syllables that slid and ground against each other like a rumbling underfoot.

In Armenia, Petrozian had been the country's leading seismologist, the man who in the Soviet era had tested the earthquake-resistance of plans for the country's only nuclear power station. If there was one thing he had believed in all his life, it was progress. The secularisation campaign which went hand-in-hand with the Soviet-wide drive for literacy had ultimately borne fruit. 'My father and mother were only children when Lenin came to power. They received a secular upbringing, and I never knew any different.' The four cooling towers looking out over the Arax, those were the temples of twentieth-century socialism, the cosmonauts and proletarians hewn in granite in Yerevan's metro stations its icons.

For Armen Petrozian, even Ararat had no Christian connotations. He had been raised with the official Soviet doctrine that dismissed the story of Noah's Ark as 'a fable that has long obstructed the path of science'.

Glancing at his expired calendar, I asked him how he *did* see Ararat then. As a focus for national pride?

'Yes, but I have to admit that my first thought in the Soviet days was always: what a fantastic NATO lookout point . . .' Was I aware that during the Cold War the mountain's north face had been completely covered in electronic surveillance and espionage equipment?

Petrozian was proud of having contributed to the construction of Armenia's only nuclear plant, which also happened to lie in full view of the enemy. After thorough seismic investigation it had been decided to locate the two Chernobyl-type reactors on a spur of Mount Ara*gats* (4,090 metres), a volcano and the highest mountain fully within Armenia's borders. In the late 1960s, Dr Petrozian's team had estimated that the plant should be able to withstand shocks of up to 7.0 on the Medvedev-Sponheuer-Karnik seismic intensity scale.

According to the literal specifications of the MSK scale, 7.0 spelled 'Panic. Many buildings damaged. Chimneys collapse. Waves in ponds. Church bells sound.'

On the morning of 7 December 1988, Armenia was rocked by a quake that registered 6.9 on the MSK scale, but which paid no heed to the specifications: within 30 kilometres of the epicentre, not a house was left standing.

I asked Petrozian about that day and that exact moment, 11.41 a.m. Where was he at the time?

'I was at the wheel of my car,' he said, his hands resting on the edge of the table. 'And the amazing thing is, I didn't notice a thing.' He'd seen office workers running out into the street in shirtsleeves, and when he arrived at his institute he found his colleagues standing in the car park. 'I wound down my window and asked them what was going on.'

'"Armen," they said, "that's what we should be asking *you!*" One hour later I was on TV, explaining that Armenia had just been struck by one of the most massive earthquakes in our history.'

Barely 100 kilometres away, at Leninakan on the Turkish border, all the Soviet tower blocks built after 1960 had been destroyed with their inhabitants in them. Entire working neighbourhoods imploded with the slow collapse of obsolete factory complexes demolished with dynamite. Twenty thousand bodies were buried beneath the rubble at Leninakan alone.

The nuclear plant outside Yerevan was put out of action by the shock, but remained intact: 6.9 was still less than 7.0.

Soviet Armenia descended into chaos that year; there was a shortage of cooling equipment, coffins, gravediggers. Meanwhile, the winds of glasnost and perestroika were shaking the Soviet Union to the core. The Berlin Wall fell without a sound and wars flared up in the Caucasus, including the Armenian–Azeri conflict over the enclave of Karabakh, an Armenian time bomb awarded by Stalin to neighbouring Azerbaijan. The two fraternal socialist peoples went for each other's throats as deadly rivals. Under the motto 'Death to the Muslims', Armenian soldiers with crosses tattooed on their forearms flushed the Azeris out of Karabakh in a war that claimed 30,000 lives.

By the early 1990s, the geological and geopolitical upheavals had once again produced waves of Armenian refugees, but Petrozian was not one of them. With his specialism, the time was ripe to make a career as researcher at the newly established Seismic Protection Service, which even had a budget for palaeo-seismology: the study of earthquakes in the past.

I asked him about the *yergrasharh* of 1840, the one that had buried the hamlet of Arguri on Ararat beneath a river of mud.

'That was a bad one,' the seismologist said. 'According to our estimates it measured 7.4 on the MSK scale.'

I showed him prints of the articles I'd ordered through Salle Kroonenberg. They were written by an Armenian geologist with a Russian first name: Arkadi Karachanian.

'Oh, Arkadi!' Petrozian cried. 'I know him very well. He worked for me.'

This Arkadi, I told him, claimed that the 1840 earthquake had been accompanied by a volcanic eruption in the Arguri gorge, and that scientists were mistaken about Ararat being an extinct and harmless volcano.

'Masis is as dead as a doornail,' Petrozian interrupted.

'But according to this article, that is precisely the misconception.' The publication was recent, from 2002, and its author saw unnerving parallels between Ararat and Mount St Helens in the United States; the volcano that had erupted in 1980, releasing the energy equivalent of 27,000 Hiroshima atom bombs.

'You mean he thinks that Ararat may blow its top tomorrow?'

Without really meaning to, I began defending Arkadi, who had provided carefully annotated evidence that Ararat had erupted on 2 July 1840 and had buried Arguri not only beneath a landslide, but also beneath a flow of volcanic mud, a 'lahar'. I pointed to the words 'eruption', 'volcanic origin' and 'sulphur fumes', but Petrozian had turned his head away and was looking outside.

In the pasture, framed neatly by the window of his prefab, a cow stood chewing the cud.

'If you visit Arkadi in Yerevan, be sure to give him my regards and tell him that he is spouting a lot of nonsense.'

I gathered my papers, said goodbye to Petrozian and left without hearing exactly why, in 1999, a full five years after the war against the Azeris, he had left Armenia.

The Mother Church of Echmiadzin had a serene air to it. The Armenian Apostolic Church's most important cathedral was understated, not weighed down by pomp. The decorations consisted largely of frescoes in the hues of autumn leaves, showing familiar scenes from the Bible: the baptism of Jesus in the River Jordan, the Last Supper, Jesus' feet disappearing into a cloud at the Ascension.

The church had no pews or chairs and smelled of melted wax. Something was in the offing; monks came and went, some wearing pointed cowls with trains that hung down to their waists. The first handful of visitors on this Sunday morning shuffled about, coughing nervously.

Yun and I did what everyone else was doing: we bought a bundle of candles and planted them in a tray of sand in one of the aisles. Meanwhile, we kept our eyes fixed on the door to the right of the altar, which we knew led to the sacristy and the adjoining reliquary.

We saw monks in black going in there, and coming out a little later dressed in red and blue vestments.

I went up and spoke to one of them, a red one.

'Hovannes,' he told me his name was. He was a blushing young fellow with a large, round face and a less than full beard. He spoke English with an American accent.

In a whisper, Hovannes told me he was a novice; one more year at the seminary and he would become a deacon. 'The ones over there in blue are deacons already, and today they're being ordained as *apegha*.'

An *apegha*, as it turned out, was a celibate priest, and the four men in blue were about to take their vows of chastity. When Yun and I expressed interest, Hovannes gave us a little tour.

Echmiadzin, we were told, meant 'Light of the Only Begotten Son'. That light had come down to earth at this spot in AD 301, the same year that St Gregorius had converted King Trdat III of Armenia to Christianity.

The novice took Yun and me by the elbow and herded us down a flight of steps to the crypt beneath the church. Switching on a fluorescent light, he showed us a low wall with a few clay cooking pots and a pile of shards: the remains of a heathen fire temple. When the Mother Cathedral arose above these remains, Hovannes said, the prehistoric gods had been chased out by the Only True One of the Bible. At his urging we laid our hands on blocks of granite placed there 17 centuries ago; this was, in Hovannes' words, 'the foundation of Christ's Church on earth'.

The Armenians, he went on to explain, were descendants of Noah's son Yapheth. After the debacle with the construction of the Tower of Babel, Yapheth's clan had settled on the plains of the Arax. The way Hovannes told it, it seemed only logical that Christianity had first established itself as the state religion here, amid a decor so imbued with the Old Testament. Starting in the fourth century AD, he said, Echmiadzin had flourished for a time as the capital of a Greater Armenia that stretched out on all sides of Ararat. The most momentous achievement of that period was no devastating battle this time, but the creation in AD 405 of an alphabet exclusively for the Armenian language. One of Echmiadzin's bishops, Mesrob Mashtots, had worked on that alphabet, which had finally crystallised in the form of four rows of nine letters each, 36 in all. I said the letters reminded me of goblets and candlesticks, but Hovannes dismissed that association as meaningless. The first letter, the Ս, was also the first letter in the word 'God', while the last, the Ֆ, was the initial letter of the name 'Christ'.

'God the Father and His Son are the guardians of the beginning and end of our alphabet,' he said proudly.

I had read about this interwovenness of faith and language, about the Word and the word. The first thing the Armenian community that arrived in Amsterdam in the seventeenth century had done was to build a printing press and, in 1688, to print a Bible in Armenian. To them, the Bible in their own language was every bit as much a staple of life as bread itself. Even today, almost all Armenians of the diaspora – and there are many more of them than the three million souls living in Armenia proper – regard the Apostolic Church and the Armenian alphabet as the vessels of their Armenian identity.

Hovannes, who had returned from exile only a few years earlier, confirmed this. In Los Angeles, where he had lived until the age of 19, he had never become part of the proverbial melting-pot, thanks to his faith and the language spoken by his parents.

And what about us? Hovannes wanted to know what had brought us to Echmiadzin. 'Or have the two of you perhaps come here to be baptised?'

'I've already been baptised,' I heard myself say.

'Me too,' Yun said. 'I'm a Baptist.'

Hovannes' lips curled in the pained semblance of a smile as he led us back up the stairs.

Many more people had arrived by now; a women's choir in green and white headscarves had assembled in a side chapel. My evasive 'I've already been baptised' had left me feeling cowardly. Oh really? And did that actually mean anything to me?

Hovannes excused himself; he had duties to attend to. I reached out to shake his hand, but Yun intervened. Pointing to the door on the right at the back of the church, he asked whether we could still visit the reliquary.

'Perhaps after the ordainment,' Hovannes said. 'It's being used as a dressing room at the moment.'

We would have to wait an hour or two, but I didn't mind. How long had it been since I last attended a church service? Fifteen years? Twenty? The women's singing spun a silken net, airy and harmonious. After that we were borne up on the cantor's baritone chant, and the monks made their entrance. Hovannes, swinging the censer and blushing, was easy to pick out. In a singsong voice, an older priest called the four deacons forward. Not understanding what was being said made it perhaps even more enchanting. And standing, I noticed, was also more pleasant than squirming in a pew. Shifting my weight from one foot to the other, I asked myself what I was here for. It was the same thing Hovannes had asked me: what was it that had brought me to Echmiadzin?

Not the piece of wood from the Ark: that was at best an excuse. My circuitous approach to Ararat, I knew, was more than a search for facts. In one of my notebooks I had written about my desire to embark on a kind of experiment, as 'Job in reverse'. In the Bible, the devout and wealthy Job had been the subject of a wager between God and Satan. The devil would be allowed to heap misfortune upon him – poverty, the most hideous of skin diseases (which finally left him scratching at his boils with shards of pottery) – simply to see whether he would finally curse God's name. And what was my plan? To put to the test my own resolve as a non-believer. I had wanted to seek out places and situations like this, to see whether faith would touch me or not. Standing here, my elbow resting in one hand, the other hand clenched in a fist against my lips, I could only laugh at my own naivety. I hadn't embarked on an experiment at all; what I had done was to seek out precisely the kind of place I knew so well. No church service could shake me to the core, of course not. It was ridiculous to think that I was 'clean': the leavening had done its work, I was permeated with Christianity.

It reminded me of an evening I had spent with my publisher; we were sitting in a restaurant in Amsterdam called Heavenly Mud, the wine flowed, and talk turned to God. All of a sudden he, the atheist, relinquished a millimetre of his godless universe. 'The few occasions that I've had the urge to thank something greater than myself have always been at moments of extreme happiness.'

I, or the wine in me, had agreed. 'I know what you mean. That's what I call the "eternity feeling".' I went on to describe the conditions under which the eternity feeling descended on me: alone, far from home, and preferably moving at a constant speed through an unfamiliar landscape. Long ago as a hitchhiker in the high cab of a lorry moving through the French countryside, later in a helicopter above the smoking crater of the Ivan the Terrible volcano on the Kuril Islands. At such moments I was plunged into a state of total bliss; for a little while everything was *good*.

'That's why I love to travel,' my publisher said. 'It makes you more susceptible.'

I was travelling now. Standing beneath the dome of the Mother Cathedral, the scent of incense in my nostrils, I thought I felt a tingling in my non-extinct religious senses.

But that was it. It didn't go on, it had no staying power or even the shadow of a chance. On the contrary: as soon as the men in blue fell to their knees, I felt repulsed. All four let the priest run his hand over their head. Why did devotion always have to involve submission? Or, indeed, humiliation? With an almost animal servitude they shuffled around the altar on their knees, their faces contorted in pain.

I looked at Yun to see his reaction, but he was filming the service impassively, his camera held at arm's length.

When it was all over, Hovannes led us into the sacristy. Stepping over a row of shoes, we made for the display case containing the church's treasures. At shoulder height lay a diamond-shaped piece of wrought iron: the tip of the lance that had pierced Christ's side on the cross ('. . . but one of the soldiers with a spear pierced his side, and forthwith came there out blood and water' – John 19:34). Yun and I were already glancing around to find the splinter of Noah's Ark, but I saw that Hovannes was still loitering in front of the spearhead. He stepped back and bowed his head briefly. Then he showed us the case containing the silver cast of the hand of St Hagob, the monk who had tried in vain to find the Ark. The piece of gopherwood, however, which the angel had given him in his dream, was missing. The perspex stand was still there, as was the small cardboard sign explaining what it meant. But the relic itself, as it turned out, was 'on loan'.

'On loan?' Yun said.

Hovannes shrugged apologetically. 'Yes, to the Hermitage.'

Throughout the rest of my visit to Armenia, Ararat remained hidden from sight. That felt very peculiar; at home I had become accustomed to peering at her three times a day through the 'Ararat webcam' of an Armenian telecoms firm. On a clear day, through that static eye mounted on top of an apartment building in Yerevan, you could watch the summit turn from blue to pink at sunrise. During the course of the day, the smog would rise and cause the icecap of Greater Ararat to hover above the earth, like a floating object in a painting by Magritte.

On a related website, which went by the name www.ourararat.com, ordinary Armenians gave vent to their passion for the mountain:

Dear everyone, I'm proud to be an Armenian and on behalf of all Armenians in Iran I can promise you that we will never give up. One day we will have our Ararat back.
Lala, Teheran

To my brothers and sisters in Armenia. Don't give up. One day soon the Turkish–Armenian border will be opened and all Armenians will be able to embrace Ararat. Ararat was, is and will always remain ours.

I salute the souls of the victims of the Armenian genocide.
Hagob, Vancouver

As for me: Ararat = Armenia. I'm mad about Mount Ararat. I see Him every day (to me, Ararat is a He) and every day I would like to hug him, but I can't . . . I hate Turkey! Ararat is mine, and no one can keep us apart!
Seda, Yerevan

For Armenians, Ararat was more than Noah's mountain. To the associations that usually accompanied it (the cradle of civilisation / the clean slate / God's covenant with mankind), a more urgent aspect had been added: for almost a century, the Armenians had seen Ararat first and foremost as the symbol of the promised land.

For the past 90 years, the route Friedrich Parrot took from Echmiadzin to Mount Ararat had ended abruptly at the border. The railway and the road to the Turkish town of Kars were barricaded, blocked by tank traps and razor wire; the guardhouse was today still occupied by Russian border guards. During the Soviet era, the border crossing at Leninakan had been one of the few openings in the Iron Curtain through which the privileged class could travel – aboard the Doğu Express from Yerevan to Istanbul – but since the early 1990s even this Turkish–Armenian Checkpoint Charlie had been closed tight as a noose. Watchtowers loomed over the cornfields, the rolling mist making them look like they were sailing by; at the roadside, fields of poppies swayed in the wind.

The two-headed volcano rising from the plains was so close, but also so unreachable, that an Armenian might justifiably wonder whether this was a mirage, or a sky-high cinema screen hung there by the Turks.

According to Armenian newspaper columnists, there was only one proper way to cross the Turkish border: armed, with the purpose of reclaiming Ararat. They glamorised Armenia's isolation, calling it the 'the cross we must bear', and bemoaned the painful situation in which Armenians were forced to look each and every day at their own mountain fallen into the hands of their mortal enemy. Their longing for Ararat, I came to realise, had become a ritual that kept alive the memory of the fatal deportation of the Armenian people from eastern Turkey ('western Armenia!') in the early twentieth century. To speak the word 'Ararat' in Armenia was to speak the word 'genocide'.

At first I had had no desire to acquaint myself further with the unfathomable horrors and the accompanying claims for and denials of a poorly documented tragedy, but there was no escaping it. The 'Armenian question' pounded away in the background with every step I took in the direction of Ararat. Even my chances of receiving a climber's visa, the application for which was still being reviewed by 'Ankara', seemed to depend on it. Precisely because of the Turkish–European rapprochement, which was being bitterly squabbled over in both camps, this century-old crime had returned to the fore.

A German newspaper had recently devoted a full page to a 100-year-old speech entitled 'An Appeal to Europe's Conscience'. After I had wrestled my way through it, there was no going back. The text was an impassioned address delivered in Berlin in 1903. The speaker, a Danish philosopher and literary critic, was commenting on the persecution of the Armenians within the doddering Ottoman Empire. The Sultan's troops, he told his listeners, had killed 300,000 Armenians between 1890 and 1900.

'But if one says: three hundred thousand lives have been sacrificed . . . that makes only a slight impression. It does not call upon the imagination.'

If one wished to make an indelible impression, the speaker said, one had to speak of individual, personal suffering, which is precisely what he went on to do.

'A woman fell to her knees and begged the soldiers to spare her life – which amounted, in fact, to two lives.

'"Is it a boy or a girl?" the soldiers shouted. And they wagered seven silver *medjidies* that it would be a boy.

'"Let's take a look!" And they tore open her belly.'

What followed was a catalogue of eyes put out, ears cut off, clerics nailed to crosses and mothers with young children locked up in churches and then burned alive. It was hard for me to read: since I had become a father myself, I could barely stand descriptions of suffering children.

'I know it and have felt it throughout: you have listened to me reluctantly. You have had to force yourself not to cry out: "Enough is enough." I have also seen that a great many ladies have left the hall . . . Yet still I ask you to consider: all this and more has been experienced by the Armenians a hundred thousand times over; this has happened in our day and age, only four or five days' journey from here – and we have allowed it to happen, and done nothing to stop it.'

In retrospect, this call to action seemed even more galling, having come only a few years before 'the first genocide of the twentieth century'.

In 1908, three young officers – Enver, Talat and Cemal – had deposed the Sultan, to the initial joy of the Armenian minority. A year after the outbreak of the First World War, however, things went wrong: Turkey, which had entered an alliance with Germany, was attacked from the east by Czarist Russia. Many Christian Armenians, oppressed as they were by the Islamic landowners, saw the Orthodox Christian Russians as liberators, and some even supported them. In the eyes of the new Turkish triumvirate, the Armenians therefore constituted a fifth column. On 25 April 1915, after charging them with collaborating with the enemy, the military leaders had some 800 prominent Armenians hanged in squares around Istanbul. Talat Pasha, the Minister of Internal Affairs, simultaneously ordered the deportation of all Armenians. In that summer of 1915, during forced marches to dumping-and-dying grounds in the deserts of Syria and Iraq, and under 'escort' by gangs of Kurdish robbers and underpaid soldiers, hundreds of thousands of Armenians (or was it more than a million?) died of starvation, dehydration and despair.

In 1920, the newly established League of Nations planned to intervene, but before it could act, the Soviet Union annexed the territory of present-day Armenia, with the sole exception of Mount Ararat.

'*Tsavet danem*' were the words with which Armenians still greeted each other on a daily basis. It meant: let me bear your pain. Only after I had left Echmiadzin did I realise that, for Armenians like Hovannes, the spearhead that had pierced the side of the Lamb of God must be a more important relic than the fragment of wood from the Ark.

Arkadi Karachanian offered me the choice between Armenian coffee (with dregs) and American coffee (without). He removed the mess of papers from the table and opened his wireless laptop, while his assistants pretended to work on at their desks. His casual attire, a polo shirt and jeans, and the fox terrier he had brought to work with him meant that he could only be the managing director. GEORISK, his assessment-consultancy firm, was housed in three or four stately rooms in a Stalinist colossus that looked out on the houses of the Armenian parliament. Arkadi told me that he led a team of 10 top geologists and seismologists, all of whom had formerly worked for the prestigious, but now defunct, Academy of Sciences and Seismic Protection Service.

'In fact, my first job was also with the Service.'

'Under Dr Petrozian,' I ventured.

'I wouldn't exactly say *under* him,' Arkadi said warily. 'He was my senior, but not my superior.'

I passed on the greetings from his former colleague Petrozian, but not his comment about Karachanian 'spouting a lot of nonsense' about Ararat. It was, after all, for that very nonsense that I had come.

Whether out of courtesy or real interest, Arkadi asked how the Petrozian family was doing. 'The last publication of his we saw was a historical catalogue of earthquakes. To be honest, I've never understood why he left the country.'

I told him what I knew: that Petrozian and his wife had had two conscription-aged sons.

'Armen's wife is Azerbi,' one of the assistants interjected. 'The boys are half Armenian, half Azerbi. That placed them in an impossible predicament.'

'I didn't know that,' Arkadi said. Conversation flagged. Arkadi's terrier, lying half curled around the table leg all this time, shifted and sighed.

The director got up to pour us two cups of Armenian coffee. When he sat down again, he resumed by turning his laptop to face me. The screen was lit up by a photo of a snowy volcano. The mountain had the same contours as Ararat, and was equally pointed, but one of its faces had been blown away, allowing you to look horizontally into the crater.

'Mount St Helens.'

Arkadi clicked to a photograph of Greater Ararat with the same, but closer, view into the Arguri gorge.

'A striking resemblance, don't you think?'

I had come here to find out more about Ararat as a geological phenomenon, and I was getting what I'd come for. These outward appearances, as I was about to find out, were only the beginning; in one respect, volcanoes were like fashion models: their looks offered no clue as to what was going on inside. And so Arkadi and his assistants had also analysed satellite images and consulted historical documents about the torrent of mud that had wiped Arguri off the map; old reports from Friedrich Parrot and other natural scientists, as well as eyewitness reports from the annals of the Armenian Apostolic Church.

Arkadi brought over a pile of documents and began reading aloud the account of an Armenian farmer from Arguri: '"I was out working on the land with my wife and children, a few versts removed from Arguri. We were just getting ready to go home when there was a horrible thunderclap. The earth shook so hard that we were thrown to the ground. We panicked, and then the cyclone came."

'Look,' Arkadi said. 'When someone describes a cyclone like that, that's interesting information for us.'

Arkadi had assembled all the information that might possibly indicate a volcanic eruption. Shortly after the first tremor, a column of smoke was seen above the gorge at Arguri. Shepherds had witnessed red and blue lights flashing inside the column. They had smelled rotten eggs and heard 'the thunder of cannons'; they had seen stones being jettisoned into the air. ('Ballistic ejecta' in volcanologists' jargon: in this case, chunks weighing up to 500 kilos that had landed as far as five kilometres away.) The column had risen as high as the summit of Ararat, and by that evening it had formed a cloud that rained down on to the plains. The puddles it left were a poisonous blue and stank like pools of sulphur; the monks had reported smelling it as far away as Echmiadzin.

While Arkadi was bringing in more evidence, I suddenly realised how severely this story clashed with the image of Ararat as the site of God's covenant with man. In the rainbow above Noah's burnt offering, the believer saw the promise that the Creator would never again punish mankind as cruelly as he had with the Flood. One could either believe that or not. Science, however, showed the exact opposite. The spot where Noah's altar was supposed to have stood, and a group of devout monks along with it, had been obliterated by a violent and indifferent force of nature. Where was the theologian who could explain that?

Assimilating all this background information, Arkadi and his team had arrived at the following reconstruction. In the late afternoon of 2 July 1840, the earth had quaked with an intensity that probably would have registered 7.4 on the MSK scale (this, so far, was in complete agreement with Petrozian's catalogue). That quake had produced an avalanche of mud and the eruption of Ararat. The mass of mud had swept down as far as the Russian army barracks beside the Arax, while higher up in the gorge a volcanic lahar had flowed out on top of the mud. That lahar could still be seen in the satellite photos, and had an estimated volume of 300 million cubic metres.

Ararat's eruption was of the Bandai variety, named after the Japanese volcano that had erupted in 1888.

With these findings, Arkadi had made even the Smithsonian Institution relent: to the most recent editions of its authoritative *Volcanoes of the World*, under Ararat (number 0103-04) had been added: 'Latest known eruption: 1840 (Karakhanian et al. 2002)'.

In my innocence, I asked: 'So there's no question about that any longer?'

'No,' Arkadi said. 'Although a few of our older colleagues claim that what we see as a lahar is, in fact, a moraine.'

I knew he was referring to Petrozian, among others, but that – for whatever reason – he didn't want to mention his name.

Arkadi clicked to another satellite photo with a nineteenth-century map superimposed on it. 'This finger of land is what it's all about,' he said. He tapped the butt of his pencil against a light grey stripe, which the scale showed to be about four kilometres long, on the floor of the Arguri gorge. The stripe lay in line with the 'Abich' glacier, and stopped a few hundred metres past the flattened monastery of St Hagob. Arkadi's opponents claimed that he was way off target, and had formulated a very different hypothesis: the only thing that had taken place on that day in 1840 was an earthquake which had destroyed Arguri and the monastery. The grey finger of land further up the gorge had not been vomited out of a crater, but was loose stone that had once lain under the Abich glacier and was now exposed by the retreating ice. Glacial moraine, in other words. Their theory ran that the Abich glacier had retreated four kilometres in a century and a half; the tongue of land was therefore an alarming indicator of the speed at which the earth was heating up, and the sea level rising.

'That of course provides them with something newsworthy,' Arkadi commented. He could imagine, he said, that in coastal regions 'like yours, in the Netherlands', the suggestion of a rising sea level constituted an urgent issue.

I nodded, but at the same time I could see the irony of this academic haggling, which served only to bolster Ararat's reputation as a mountain of mystery. Certainties were a rare commodity, and that apparently applied to the Earth sciences as well.

If I understood correctly, I told him, the debris at the bottom of the Arguri gorge was either a warning of Ararat's dangers as an active volcano, or an indicator of the threat of flooding in low-lying coastal regions around the world, a universal deluge in the offing.

'You could put it that way, yes.'

'So what now?' I asked.

'Now the *Journal of Volcanology and Geothermal Research* has asked both parties to prove their hypotheses.'

That, at the moment, was the way things stood.

There was only one problem: I simply could not believe that a doctor of geology was unable to tell a moraine from a lahar. But then I realised that Arkadi had never been able to visit it himself. He was an Ararat expert without ever having set foot on Ararat! And what's more, the same thing went for his opponents. There was no way they would ever be granted a Turkish research visa.

Was that it, was that the nub of it?

Arkadi spread his hands in a 'that's-just-the-way-it-is' gesture.

'But if you're planning to go anyway,' he said, 'I'd be very pleased to see any pictures you might take in the Arguri gorge.'

Homo diluvii testis

The Hague, 10 June 2005

The forms you have filled out for permission to climb Ağri
Daği have been conveyed to our relevant authorities in due
time. Our authorities informed the Embassy that the period
to climb Ağri Daği is usually 5–10 days and requested us to
convey to you that you should state a more reasonable period
of time (in the forms you have conveyed to us the period
mentioned was 3–3.5 months). Therefore it would be much
appreciated if you could convey to the Embassy the period in
which you wish to climb Ağri Daği as soon as possible.
  Best regards,
  Beliz Celasin, Third Secretary

I PULLED OUT the folder containing our correspondence and
found the copy of my visa application. Under question 16 ('proposed
dates of travel') I had indeed filled in 'from 1 July to 15 September
2005'. That was the entire mountaineering season; I had been meaning
to show how compliant I was, but that pliancy turned out to be the
root of the problem. Beliz had asked me before not to call back every
week; her embassy, after all, was only an intermediary. 'The procedure takes two or three months,' she'd said, sounding annoyed for the
first time. 'If permission is granted, we instruct the consulate to issue
a visa. We're not allowed to do any more than that.'

  'And if my application is turned down, will you hear about that
as well?'

'Why should it be turned down?' Her voice rang with indignation, or suspicion.

And now this news.

In order to think it over, I went for a run. Since starting a stringent training programme, I had learned to think to the rhythm of my own breathing. It was amazing how body and mind worked together during my runs in Vondelpark: the greater the effort, the greater the dexterity with which the brain seemed to solve problems.

There was never a lack of things to think about. In poisonous green letters on a container on the way to the park, someone had scrawled: STOP READING HOLY BOOKS. I had just started doing that. Two streets further, on a dead-end wall opposite the children's circus club, someone had spray-painted FUCK ALLAH. To the rhythm of my running, I thought about where those slogans came from. That grew easier as my body began producing more endorphins: a substance that kneaded one's thoughts and transformed them into visions of grandeur (world records, roaring crowds!) and, when the dosage was increased, dissolved them into a mild nothingness. Cycling home afterwards, the dregs of an insight or decision would come floating to the surface.

I was busy calculating now as I ran: 10 June, plus another two months of processing time for the Byzantine red-tape operation, took me to mid-August at the very earliest. What if I scheduled the 10 days allotted me as late in the year as possible? The advantage of climbing so late in the season was the receding snowline, which would then be at around 4,000 metres; the disadvantage was the lack of leeway. Sometimes the weather changed as early as the second or third week in September, and then the season was over.

Before stepping into the shower at home, I sent Beliz an email: 'Thank you for your message. I would very much like to climb Ağri Daği in the period 1–10 September 2005.'

On a day when my daughter stayed home from the crèche, I took her to the Teylers Museum in Haarlem.

'Come on, let's go to the shell museum.' Earlier that week we had taken the train one stop further, and gone to the beach to look for seashells. 'They have special stones there too. They're called "fossils".'

Vera, almost three and a half, let the words sink in, then asked: 'What is that, fossils?'

With Vera perched on my shoulders, we took the route from the station along the River Spaarne, with a view of the old panopticon. Three times already I had shouted: 'Don't put your hands in front of my eyes!'; shrieking with laughter, she would then slide them back under my chin, like the strap of a helmet.

I had come to see one fossil in particular, an exhibit that had been in the Teylers collection for more than two centuries. It was known all over the world as '*homo diluvii testis*', the man who witnessed the Deluge, uncovered in 1725.

A fossil is an imprint, I heard myself saying, of a plant or an animal in stone. 'Rather like your footprint in the sand.'

It was an explanation that begged more questions, but for the moment all was quiet up above. Strictly speaking, the 'Diluvian Man' was not even an imprint; it was a petrified skeleton. Its discoverer, Johann Jakob Scheuchzer, was a doctor from Zurich. Had Vera asked *him* 'What is that, fossils?', he would have replied: 'Evidence of God's omnipotence.' Or, more pertinently: 'Remains of the Deluge, etched in rock.' For how else could one explain the shells, ammonites and lobsters found in the cliffs of the Jungfrau or the Matterhorn?

Scheuchzer, the son of a dentist, grew up in a late-seventeenth-century Protestant environment in which dancing and the theatre were regarded as the devil's work. He attended university in the less orthodox Nuremberg, where he became acquainted with the controversial ideas of Spinoza, the philosopher who claimed that, rather than a consciously active arbiter of good and evil, God was an entity at one with His creation, who manifested Himself only in nature – for He *was* nature – no more and no less than that. Scheuchzer, averse to such modernism, believed that all knowledge of nature contributed to the knowledge and acceptance of the God of the Bible, and that such an acceptance was the chief end of all science. With that in mind he went to the

Dutch city of Utrecht in 1694 to teach medicine, but was so tormented by homesickness that he soon returned to the Alps.

Faithful to his calling as a natural scientist in God's service, Scheuchzer dedicated the rest of his life to the systematic explanation of all the physical events mentioned in the Bible – with Noah's flood as the jewel in the crown. In Scheuchzer's day, it seemed that only one link was missing in the chain of evidence that proved the Deluge had indeed happened according to the letter of the Genesis account: a human skeleton in stone. Never had the fossil of a drowned human been found in any cave or rock wall. The theological explanation for this omission was that God had deemed these sinners unworthy of survival, even in fossil form, but Scheuchzer was unconvinced. There had to be layers of earth teeming with the mud-bound figures of the drowned. He undertook one expedition after another, and finally – in a shale quarry by Lake Constance – found his *homo diluvii testis*. It consisted of a fragile set of bones which he presented authoritatively – and successfully – as indisputable proof of the flood.

In his magnum opus, *Physica sacra*, Scheuchzer provided the following description: 'It is certain that this shale contains one half – or almost one half – of the skeleton of a man, that the bones and the flesh as well, including those parts softer than flesh, have fused with this stone. In a word: this is one of the rarest remains of that accursed race buried beneath the waters.'

Vera and I entered the oldest museum in the Netherlands and crossed the tile floor from Fossil Room One to Fossil Room Two. I lifted her up to show her a giant ammonite. The display cases were filled with beautiful shells and crystals, but her eye was caught by a fossilised marsh tortoise. My daughter was captivated by turtles; at the zoo they were her favourite animals and she tried to imitate the way they moved: crawling along on her elbows with her head close to the ground.

'Is that turtle already dead?'

The footprint explanation had not been enough. Yes, I said, but I was willing to bet that he had lived to be a hundred. A hundred, Vera knew, was the age reached by grandmas and grandpas.

The next question, I could feel it coming, was about heaven: did animals go there too?

Not long before, we had reluctantly introduced the concept of heaven, after she had told us excitedly about how one of her friend's grandpas had gone there.

There was also room enough for the animals there, I decided.

Then, out of the blue, Vera announced that she knew what it was like in heaven. 'There you can't live any more.'

'Really? What's that like, not being able to live any more?'

'You can't move any more. Look, like this . . .' She stood with her feet wide apart, shaking her torso back and forth, her arms jiggling like rubber. 'Living is moving.'

In a corner of Fossil Room Two I found Scheuchzers' 'Man who Witnessed the Deluge'. Exhibit number 8432 was a marine-green stone with yellowish bones: a spinal column, merging with a skull with enormous eye sockets, and helplessly dangling arms.

Site of discovery: Oeningen.
Purchase: acquired with no little difficulty for 14 Louis d'or
by Professor Van Marum in 1802.
Scheuchzer's original caption: 'The dismal skeleton of an
ancient sinner, drowned thusly in the Deluge.'

Meanwhile Vera had wandered off to the Instruments Rooms, but she came back and wanted to know what I was looking at.

'A salamander.' I lifted her on to my hip. 'Look, you can see the two front legs; he used those to crawl across the ground.'

For almost 90 years, until 1811 to be precise, the 'Diluvian Man' was categorised as 'human'. It was only after Scheuchzer's death that cautious doubts were raised. Didn't the skeleton look strangely like a catfish, or a giant lizard? In the end, the man who witnessed the Flood was publicly unmasked by the anatomist Georges Cuvier. During a lecture in Paris, this French genius – a Protestant every bit as devout as Scheuchzer – had proven that the hairy creatures removed from the Siberian tundra were not 'elephants' washed away by the Flood, but part of a separate, extinct species – the woolly mammoth. During a visit to the Teylers Museum in Haarlem, he matched that achievement by further chipping away at the fossil of the Diluvian Man. He had brought with him a drawing of a salamander's skeleton, and he predicted to those present the exact spot at which the front legs would appear.

They were just where he had said they would be, and ever since, one can see in the empty eye sockets the religious blindness of scholars such as Johann Jakob Scheuchzer, a man of science whose faith in God made him mistake a salamander for a human being.

Beneath the glass bell in the museum restaurant were slices of fruit tart with a thin layer of marzipan icing. Vera chose the raspberry. We sat down at a table close to the window, and after three sips of her apple juice a new question came bubbling up. 'Papa, do you know what happiness is?'

I spooned the foam from my cappuccino. 'This moment, now,' I felt like saying, but instead I said: 'Well, what?'

Her thoughts obviously elsewhere, she pulled the straw from her glass and sent drops of juice flying everywhere. 'Happiness is . . . when you're at the crèche, and you want to have the pink cup, and then you get it!'

It was a foregone conclusion: my wife would not come to Ararat. We had chuckled at the title of a book I'd ordered from a second-hand bookshop: *Mit Weib und Kind zum Ararat*; in our case (man with a mission, wife and child as baggage) that would have led only to mutual irritation. No, I would make the journey to Armenia and Turkey alone, but she wanted to be directly involved in everything else related to it.

'I'm going to read your manuscript,' she said. 'So I want to know what you're writing about.'

I had no trouble accepting that, but was all the more surprised at her insistence on going mudwalking with me across the Wadden shallows.

My plan to slosh off to one of the northern islands at low tide was intended as a form of training. '*Wadlopen*', as it is called in Dutch, was sometimes referred to as 'horizontal mountain-climbing': the sludge on the seabed sucked on the soles of your shoes just as gravity did on a climber's legs. Whether wading through a channel or ploughing your way across a snowfield, the effort was more or less the same.

'But you don't come running with me, do you?'

She didn't like water, or gale-force wind, or stinking sludge. Still, she was adamant.

'Okay,' I said, 'but . . .'

She didn't let me formulate the rest of my 'but'. 'I promise you won't hear a word from me about how cold it is, or how tired I am, or anything.'

'All right, then we'll walk to Rottumeroog,' I said as tactfully as I could. 'That's thirteen kilometres from the coast. The group leaves from the dyke at seven fifteen a.m.' Assuming she would back down, I showed her the description of the hike on my computer screen.

'. . . Leaving the reclaimed land, we then enter the real shallows. What follows is a two-kilometre stretch of deep sludge, which we will wade through along the Ra. The Ra is a channel marked by poles . . . The water in the channel may vary in depth from knee-high in easterly wind to chest height in westerly wind . . .'

'What do you want to hear? That it sounds scary? I think it's really scary.'

'No, what I want to hear is why you want to come.'

What she wanted, she explained, was to keep a close eye on things and understand what was going on inside me, so I wouldn't go drifting off on some solo spiritual tour without her having seen it coming.

That, in addition to the training element, there was another motive behind my desire to walk across the Wadden shallows had not escaped her notice. 'You're going for the symbolism,' my wife said, and I couldn't deny it. 'You want to defy the water. For your story.'

She knew me, and she knew that I couldn't contemplate a hike across the bottom of the Waddenzee without also seeing the

113

children of Israel's crossing of the Sea of Reeds. The anecdote tangled up with this was one she'd had to listen to often enough. It was a memory associated with my school divinity teacher.

Of all our teachers, Pastor van Woerkom had the appearance (silver hair, leathery hands) that best suited his subject. Everyone at school knew that, as a missionary, he had been chased out of Indonesia, the largest Muslim country in the world. With his characteristic stoop, he would draw a map of the Old Testament world on the blackboard before each lesson, with Palestine/Israel in the centre, to the east the Mesopotamia of the Tigris and Euphrates, and to the west the Sinai Desert, Egypt and the Nile.

One of his pet topics was the fact that the Bible, unlike the Koran, was not a dictation exercise. With a dictation, the important thing was to cross your t's and dot your i's, to mind the full stops and commas; there was no room for interpretation. The Bible, however, was an essay, a book of lessons on how to live that didn't have to be learned by rote. On the contrary. Just imagine, for example, that we were to take at face value Jesus' statement that 'it is easier for a camel to pass through the eye of a needle than for a rich man to enter the Kingdom of Heaven'. Who, in that case, would ever enter heaven at all? On the blackboard, our teacher would then draw a sketch of the gates of a walled city such as Jericho or Jerusalem, with a tiny door in them. That postern gate, he told us, was called 'the eye of the needle': a camel could get through it, but only by shuffling along on its knees.

That was how the Bible was: the stories were true, but you had to know the background in order to understand them. One day he drew the route the children of Israel had taken out of Egypt. Their exodus was barely underway when there, on the horizon, they saw the clouds of dust thrown up by Pharaoh's chariots. How did the Israelites get away? Pastor van Woerkom said that Moses had not led his people through the Red Sea, as people believed. That was a mistranslation. The correct translation was 'Sea of Reeds', as our school Bible said, and that was important. Where reeds grew, after all, the water was shallow. In English Bibles, 'Red Sea' had these days been replaced with 'Reed Sea'. Only one letter's difference, but one which had major consequences for our understanding of this escape across the seabed. There had been no 'walls of water' (as in the awesome drawings in my children's Bible) that fell on the pursuers when Moses raised his staff. No, we should understand that crossing quite differently. 'Compare it to hiking across the Wadden shallows.' Our teacher was proud of his own comparison, and elaborated on the image of Moses as the first guide through the channels. Anyone who set out as the tide was coming in was sure to be swallowed by the rising waters. Witness the fate of Pharaoh's army.

'Listen to this. In Germany, back before the war, they were already crossing the shallows by horse and cart.' My wife was reading to me from a book about the pioneers of mudwalking: '"Along the marked twelve-kilometre route between Nordseeheilbad Cuxhaven and the isle of Neuwerk, enthusiasts enjoy not only mudwalking, but also mudriding . . ."'

Het Gemeentehuis Hotel, where we were staying, was close to the sea dyke. I checked our equipment one last time: cheap gym shoes, tracksuit bottoms, sweaters and waterproofs, hats and sunglasses, flasks for sweet tea, muesli and chocolate bars, bin bags with a set of dry clothes for the boat trip back.

'The pastor of the island of Ameland was a mudwalker too,' I heard her say from the bed beside the bay window. And a little later: 'Did you know that on spring tides there's seven metres' difference between high water and low water?'

As I arranged our backpacks, my wife flipped through my little collection of mudwalking clippings and brochures. I had marked some passages with exclamation marks, like the greeting extended by the guardian of Rottumeroog in 1939 when he saw three students approaching his island: 'Well, if it isn't the children of Israel coming in from the Red Sea.' I had underlined the verb 'to overflood', along with the description of this technique for covering longer distances across the mudflats: when the water begins to rise, mudwalkers inflate a rubber raft, anchor it between four sounding rods and wait – like modern-day Noahs – for the next low tide. There were other marks in the margin beside comments from a mudwalking pioneer, comparing his crossings to Mallory and Irvine's Everest expeditions. Their disappearance in 1924 at around 8,000 metres had been no vain sacrifice, because: 'Only those live in vain who allow the desire for uplifting exploration and higher adventure to perish in their souls. They shall never penetrate the fortress of nature and spirit.'

One bundle of clippings, however, I had left at home on purpose. They were articles with headlines like: 'Mudwalkers overtaken by tide', 'Gale-force winds and rising water fatal' and 'Trapped after sudden shift in weather'. They were accounts of the failed June 1980 attempt to guide a dozen Third World students across the shallows. Their story interested me because of the Floodlike experience.

The participants had only just arrived in Holland from Africa, Asia and the Middle East, for a course in applied geography. One of the first lessons dealt with the origins of the Wadden shallows, in preparation for a day of mudwalking. The group had heard how this shallow sea had formed only recently, when the level of the world's oceans had risen after the last ice age and the North Sea filled like a bathtub. About 7,000 years ago, the water had created a row of dune islands and sandbars. These gradually formed a barrier around which the sea flowed at high tide, and behind which a shallow saltwater landscape arose: the Waddenzee.

Most travellers took a ferry to the islands, but during the summer you could also cross on foot: a well-planned journey through the gravitational fields of sun and moon, which caused the water to run into and out of this sea with metronomic regularity.

The plan – by way of team-building – was to have the students walk across the shallows to the far side. 'You won't have to swim anywhere along the way,' they were reassured. It wasn't difficult or dangerous; even the Queen's husband had done it.

Standing on a pier outside the dyke, in the driving rain, the chief guide had repeated that there would be 'no need to swim'. Ameland, however, the hike's destination, was hidden from sight. The white-tops slapped in rapid succession at the water stretching out before them, as far as the eye could see.

Afterwards, the assistant guide, a trained water polo player, said there was no question of them having misread the tide charts. 'We started how you're supposed to, as the tide was going out, so the sandbars would be above the surface on our way across. But that day it never happened. We just sort of splashed through the water.' He remembered seeing a couple of men from the Department of Waterways, who stopped work on the ferry dock to watch the group leave.

After wading through the first channel, Comrade Tang from the People's Republic of China was exhausted. He was so light that the guides took turns carrying him piggyback. No sandbars had yet risen above the water's surface, but the group pressed on. After a few hours, the hikers – their jaws stiff from the cold – reached the most difficult section, a channel where the water was usually no more than waist-deep. The guide prodded about with his two-metre-long sounding rod, but it never touched bottom. The wind, blowing from the north-west at a sturdy Force 7 now, was driving the North Sea water back against the tide. A few of the students, sensing danger, beat a hasty retreat; the others stood shivering miserably, their teeth chattering. The guides pointed to the dunes opposite them; that was where salvation lay, not on the dyke that had already disappeared in the distance behind them. They shouted to those who had turned and fled that they were heading for a watery grave, but they didn't see it that way. None of them could swim.

'We kept the group together, but it was hard,' the water polo champion said later. With Mr Tang on his back, he was the first to dive into the channel. After 20 powerful strokes he reached the far shore. 'I swam back and forth a few times. First I dragged Hilda, from Zimbabwe, to the other side. Then I got hold of Rolf, a Dutch student who I saw going down. I didn't look around after that, but when I went for the last boy, he said: "I lost Mustafa! I let go of Mustafa!"'

Mustafa was a 28-year-old Iraqi, from a desert town where water

117

was so scarce that it had to be channelled to the date palms through small plastic tubes.

The guides had no marine telephone, no flares. Once they were across the channel, panic gripped them too. The water polo player developed cramp and had to put down the Chinaman. At that same moment, Hilda from Zimbabwe collapsed. Her lips blue with cold, she murmured something that sounded like a prayer. 'You people go on,' she said a few times. 'Leave me here.' Her passivity frightened the water polo player. He had no sooner begun speaking words of encouragement ('Come on! Just a little while longer! We'll make it!') when it dawned on him that Mustafa was not the only one they were going to lose. The group was trapped in the middle of the sea and could not continue. The water rose to their thighs, then to their waists.

'Look! A ship!' someone shouted. The hikers craned their necks like cormorants, but with the curvature of the Earth they could see only a small triangular object, rocking back and forth. A buoy, the assistant guide thought, a bloody fucking buoy bobbing on the horizon. But to his amazement the object actually came closer. 'It was a sloop from the Department of Waterways, the men who had stopped and watched us leave.'

One by one they were lifted on board and carried down into the cabin. Only Comrade Tang remained lying on deck. He was taken to the pilothouse, but after about 10 minutes stopped responding to heart massage and mouth-to-mouth resuscitation.

Holland would not be Holland had no investigative committees been set up afterwards, with announcements that a new system of permits and regulations was on its way. Among the pages I had printed off were the government's 'final departure times', based on the tide charts.

'Did you know that you're not allowed to leave for Rottumeroog any later than one hour and fifty minutes before low tide?'

I was brushing my teeth. 'Yeah,' I said, 'and one hour later you reach the point of no return.'

My wife gave me a piercing look; she was not going to turn back, I had to get that into my head.

*   *   *

Breakfast at six the next morning was eaten in silence. The hotel dining room was full; all the guests were wearing trainers. Elderly couples, overgrown German boy scouts, families with children (no younger than 12), and the two of us.

Even in the bus, after the five guides had joined us – bearded characters carrying red-and-white-striped sounding rods – no one spoke a word.

Once we were standing in the lee of the sea dyke, the head guide introduced himself as Jannes. A giant of a man, he showed us his entire arsenal of navigational and emergency equipment, from phosphor flares to a satellite positioning system. We were going to follow the line of the neap tide, he explained. That was the strip of seabed that usually remained driest in the course of a tidal cycle; the place where, later in the day, two tides, coming around the western and eastern ends of Rottumeroog, would meet.

Surrounded by herders carrying staffs, we headed into the sea; the sheep on the dyke grazed on imperviously.

The visibility was unusually good: you could see the dunes of a number of the coastal islands light up in the morning sun, you could see a container ship at dock in Emden and the lighthouse on the German island of Borkum.

Crossing the initial stretch of dry salt marsh, I thought about childhood dreams in which I had been able to walk on water. If your faith was strong enough, as I'd understood it, you could really do that – as Jesus had done across the Sea of Galilee. Down at the pond along Vredeveldseweg I had put my faith to the test once, but it was wanting.

'The group from Pieterburen's out on the mud, too,' were the first words spoken. A few bends in the dyke further along we could see a cluster of dots heading out on to the glistening shallows.

'They'll get there at the same time we do,' Jannes said. 'We'll be on the same boat back this afternoon.'

Clouds drifted across the August sky, and every time their shadow crossed you could feel the wind pick up and the temperature drop. A storm front was on its way from the Shetlands, but would reach the shallows only at evening.

We literally ploughed along. With every step you took in the mud along the dams you sank up to your calves, and the churning brought up not only cockles and worms and green laver, but also the sickly smell of rot. The five guides with their bright sounding rods, I noticed, walked barelegged, while we, their herd of 30, all wore long trousers. Trousers were warmer, but heavier too.

Forty-five minutes later we reached the Ra. There would have been no way to see where the depths began or ended, had it not been for the buoys marking the sides of the channel. When everyone had gathered at the edge, two of the guides leapt forward and sank to their waists. For a few seconds they struggled for balance, then clambered on to the far shore. The stubborn silence remained unbroken. My wife and I joined hands and stepped into the invisible hole. Our feet, or at least mine, slipped out from under us, I fell backwards and felt solid bottom only after my clothes were soaked with ice-cold water. I kept my eyes on one of the guides on the far shore. Suddenly I saw an expression of shock on his face. When I looked over, my wife's face was twisted in animal fear. She had swallowed seawater and was screaming at the top of her lungs, but without making a sound.

During our first break, on a sandbank now clear of water, Jannes asked: 'Is there anyone who wants to go back?'

'And cross that channel again?' I heard my wife say. 'No way!'

We had a 45-minute hike behind us, and another two and a half to three hours to go. No one turned back. From here it would largely be an endurance race, across the occasional stretch of soft ground where the mussels sieved their plankton from the mud. The group spread out in single file into a long ribbon. We were among the last to start, and soon found ourselves bringing up the rear. We had agreed to put a brave face on things: my wife would not complain, and I would stick to her pace without comment. Before long we were walking beside the second in command, the backup man.

I began firing questions at him. How did one become a guide? Did mudwalkers ever turn and run for it? Had he ever encountered strange situations during a crossing? That sort of thing.

He enjoyed talking about his experiences on the mudflats, I noticed that, but apparently there was a code that said one did not talk about accidents or near-accidents. None of it went beyond pure theory.

'You don't want to be out on the flats during an electrical storm. It makes you look at each other and wonder: which of us is the tallest . . . ?'

But had he ever actually been caught in an electrical storm on the flats?

'Well . . .'

I tried another tack: had he ever run into trouble halfway?

'No. Only that one time, in 1981 . . .'

I knew about 1980, about the Third World students, but 1981?

'I mean that time with the schoolchildren.' The head guide had mistaken the lighthouse on Borkum for the ornithologist's hut on Rottum. By the time they were back on course it was too late. But all 150 hikers were rescued, picked up by a hospital-church ship that just happened to be moving up the Eems.

'A hospital-church ship?' I echoed.

'One of the ships that goes out on to the North Sea with the herring fleet. I didn't know about them before, either. On Sundays they hold church services at sea, broadcast on the maritime frequency.'

Blind luck in the guise of providence, I thought. 'So I suppose the schoolchildren fell to their knees in that floating chapel?'

The guide shrugged and glanced at his diving watch.

I looked up from the sandy ripples beneath my feet. Everywhere you turned there was the same emptiness; I was standing at the centre of the hugest circle of horizon you could imagine. The story about the floating house of prayer reminded me of my childhood pastor, who liked to speak of the church as Noah's Ark: all those who entered were saved; those who remained outside would perish. We did well to realise that every church was a lifeboat waiting on dry land.

I had abandoned that ship years before, and now I was walking across a temporarily dry seabed, having put my faith in meteorology and Jannes' navigation equipment. Was that sinful pride, I asked myself, or simply common sense?

When I turned around I saw that my wife was trudging along like a robot. Her shoulders were stooped, and she seemed oblivious to everything around her. When I urged her to eat something, her only reaction was to push her sunglasses up on to the bridge of her nose.

The guide looked worried too, and went over to her. 'Listen,' he said, 'you need to eat something right now.'

Absently, with an air of indifference, she took a few bites of chocolate. A few sips of tea went down just as apathetically. When we suggested a five-minute rest, she began walking faster.

This was ridiculous; I was the one who'd been in training, not her. I caught up with her and laid a hand on her shoulder, but she twisted away from me.

'This is the last energy I've got,' she said. 'If I wait too long, it will be gone.'

'Then it would be better to take a rest.'

She picked up her desperate pace, as though trying to shake me off.

I looked to the guide for help. 'Don't say anything more, just stay with her,' was his advice. 'If it's only her blood-sugar level, she'll be okay in a few minutes.'

We ploughed off after her at a march. I expected to see her collapse at any moment. We would have to lift her from the mud, the guide would have to carry her the rest of the way. Like Comrade Tang.

After 15 minutes or so the colour returned to her cheeks. She slowed down, and suddenly I could get through to her again.

'Sorry,' she said, 'my world just sort of drew in on itself.'

I asked her if that was because of the story about the schoolchildren.

'What schoolchildren?' She hadn't heard a thing, her senses had completely shut down for a while. In her mind we had been walking through a tunnel.

*   *   *

After 30 minutes we reached a sandbar close to Rottumeroog. We were not allowed to go on to the island itself, which was reserved exclusively for nesting birds. There was no jetty or harbour. The long sandbar curved away from the island in the direction of the sea gate dividing the Wadden shallows from the North Sea, and we curved along with it. Our destination was the half-moon-shaped extremity of this sandy barrier; there we would be picked up by a flatboat from Noordpolderzijl, which had been waiting for us in the channel for some time. Slinging our packs on to the ground, we took off our trainers and snuggled up against the ridge of sand. There we lay like a colony of lazing seals, overlooking the rolling breakers of the North Sea.

The waves fanned out over the beach, but didn't wash back. Instead they covered each other in turn, again and again; the waterline was approaching quickly. Just when we had surrendered to well-earned indolence, we had to get up again. Unless they were moved to safety, our shoes and backpacks would disappear into the waves. The group huddled together instinctively on the steadily shrinking island, but before long the first waves were lapping over its highest point. Holding our things, we watched as the water churned around our ankles, then crept up our shins to our knees.

'Within the next few hours, four billion cubic metres of water will flow into the Wadden shallows,' one of the guides commented.

The idea was that the water would rise sufficiently for the boat now resting on the flats to float and come to us. The dunes of Rottumeroog lay 1,500 metres away; to swim there would now be impossible. No one had told us that we would have to wait to be rescued from drowning. The skipper was trying to get close to the sandbar. Motor growling, the flatboat ploughed a few metres closer each time, its stern stubbornly sweeping left and right.

Finally the ship gained enough clearance and came bobbing and weaving in our direction. The skipper's wife came out of the cabin, her braids blowing in the wind. She climbed on to the foredeck and, all the way up at the bow, hooked an aluminium ladder over the railing.

Tablet XI

THE PORTRAIT OF Ağri Daği was in every tourist guide to Turkey. And it seemed all the photographers had stood at the same spot, for every Turkish depiction of Ararat looked identical. Set beside the standard Armenian snapshot taken from the north, it looked as though Ararat had only a front and a back. Side views were nowhere to be found; it was either heads or tails.

In late July, when no reply had yet come to my request for a visa, I took the bull by the horns: I flew to Istanbul on a dirt-cheap weekend ticket. I wanted to find out how the Turks saw Ararat – what significance or symbolism did they attach to their highest peak?

After checking into my hotel I walked down Istiklal Caddesi (Independence Street), past clothing shops and bakeries that could as easily have been in Vienna or Brussels. Amid Turkish girls in vest tops I stood before the window of Robinson Crusoe, a bookshop with a wide assortment of English titles. I was looking for a chil-dren's book from the series *Goodnight Stories from the Quran*, which I found inside in the rotating rack opposite the till. These were picture books with titles like *Allah's Best Friend* and *The First Man*. On the cover of *The Tale of a Fish* I recognised a spouting whale that was clearly recovering from having vomited up the prophet Jonah. I took *The Ark of Nūh* – the volume I was looking for – down from the rack and began leafing through it. Here too: the animals, two by two. Elephants, giraffes, monkeys, snakes, hippos. But just as Jonah was missing from the drawing of the whale, so too was there no Noah on the deck of the Ark. He and his sons were nowhere to be seen; to judge from the pictures, the Ark had not been built by human hand.

The Ark of Nŭh reminded me of one of Vera's pop-up books, which consisted of two hard covers that conjured up a replica of the Ark when opened. In the envelope that went with it there were foldable animal pairs and eight human figures: Noah and his three sons, plus their wives. Islamic tradition did not allow the depiction of humans. Otherwise everything seemed the same.

I bought *The Ark of Nŭh* for Vera, and for myself as well, curious as I was to see whether she would miss Noah.

If you viewed Ararat as a mountain with only two faces, then Noah went with the north face, Nŭh with the south.

But did that make any difference? The Ark of the Old Testament (and the Torah) must have been just as solid as that from the Quran. The Islamic story of the Flood was simply a bit shorter and a bit more fragmentary than the Genesis account. Allah, too, had instructed righteous Nŭh to build a ship for his family and the animals: 'And thou shalt come into the Ark, thou, and thy sons, and thy wife, and thy sons' wives with thee . . . and of every living thing of all flesh, two of every sort shalt thou bring into the Ark.'

Concerning the fate of the rest of creation, the Quran was brief: 'Their lot is to drown.' A new dramatic element, however, was the refusal of one of Nŭh's sons – unlike any of Noah's children – to enter the Ark. Surah 11 put it this way:

> As it sailed with them
> In waves like hills,
> Nŭh called his son, who was isolated:
> 'O, my son,
> come ride with us;
> do not be with the disbelievers' . . .
> The waves separated them
> And he was among those who drowned.

125

Reading and comparing, I also had the impression that the Quran was more sparing with details.

> It was proclaimed:
> 'O earth, swallow your water,'
> and 'O sky, cease.'
> The water then subsided;
> The judgement was fulfilled.
> The Ark finally rested on the hills of al-Ǧūdī.

Neither holy book was completely clear about where the Ark had finally run aground. Al-Ǧūdī was Arabic for 'the heights', and could therefore refer to any mountainous area, including Ararat. Genesis, of course, spoke of 'the mountains of Ararat'; the word Ararat, however, was derived from Urartu, the Assyrian name for Armenia, which in ancient times reached all the way to the south-eastern area of what is now Turkey.

Quran scholars pointed to eastern Turkey as the most likely spot for the prophet Nŭh's Ark to have run aground. Muslims in Iraq, Iran and Saudi Arabia all knew of local mountains once called al-Ǧūdī. But Sunnis and Shi'ites alike recognised eastern Turkey as having the best credentials, with Ararat in the north and the mountain called Cudi (the Turkish spelling for the Arabic Ǧūdī, pronounced *czew-dee*) to the south.

The Turkish authorities, and more particularly the military, would have been much happier with less sensitive locations. Like Ararat, brush-covered Cudi lay at a strategic hotspot: at the place where Turkey, Syria and Iraq meet. Its rocky summit provided a fantastic view of the course of the Tigris, which left Turkey there on its way to the ruins of Nineveh, about 100 kilometres downstream. Cudi's unique qualification was not its height (2,114 metres), but the old custom of those living around it, both Muslim and Christian, to jointly commemorate the Deluge each year on the summit of the mountain.

Centuries ago, a shrine called Sabinat Nebi Nŭh – the Ship of the Prophet Nŭh – was built on Cudi. The only trace that remains of that place of worship is a photograph taken in May 1909 by the British archaeologist Gertrude Bell. What the photo shows is something that looks like a stone shelter of the kind built by shepherds: a few low stone walls roofed with branches and beams. In a meadow where tulips blossomed, the archaeologist was told, 'on a given day in the summer', Assyrian Christians from the villages on Cudi's flanks met with Turkish and Kurdish Muslims to make their offerings in honour of Noah/Nŭh.

Celebrations of the feast of the prophet Nŭh are still quite common in Turkey, Iran and Iraq, as well as among Turks and Kurds in western Europe. Once a year, to commemorate the blessings given by Allah to Nŭh and his descendants, they make *aşure*, a saccharine-sweet dessert with 12 ingredients – including walnuts, pomegranate, honey, almonds and apricots – to hand out to neighbours.

Amid the tulips on Cudi, however, the annual feast and the sharing of the *aşure* enjoyed special significance, but the tradition came to an abrupt end in 1915. Like the Christian Armenians, the Assyrians (belonging to the Assyrian-Nestorian Church) fell prey that summer to pogroms and deadly deportation marches. The survivors withdrew to a handful of villages from which, in 1993, they were finally evicted for 'security reasons': the army blew up their homes to prevent them being used by Kurdish separatists. But with the eviction of the Assyrian Christians, who later settled collectively in the Belgian town of Mechelen, Cudi was still not entirely 'clean'. The soldiers who had taken possession of this vantage point regularly encountered pilgrims and religiously motivated archaeologists from all over the world, all looking for the remains of the Ark. Since the same problem was encountered at Ararat, Turkey came up with a solution that entailed temporarily putting aside its secular principles: the authorities picked out a third, more convenient location as the 'official' resting place of the Ark built by Noah/Nŭh.

The catalyst was the discovery of a boat-shaped outcrop on a hillside not far from Ağri Daği, which was also promptly given the name 'Cudi'. This location, close to Ararat, could be championed as being in conflict neither with the Bible nor with the Quran. And those with a willing eye were able to see in the landscape's morphology the shape of a ship. A Turkish air force colonel had first noticed the formation in 1959 while analysing aerial photos. The discovery, in other words, had been made by a Turk, and all these factors taken together prompted the Turkish authorities to designate the boulder-clay aggregate as 'the fossil impression of the Ark'. A museum was built beside it, and a sign in English erected reading NOAH'S ARK VISITORS' CENTRE.

The subtext was: this is the shadow of the Ark, search no further.

During the Istanbul morning rush hour I took a ferry across the Bosporus. Like most of my fellow passengers, I stood staring at the boat's wake. The ferry left a V of foam between the two shores. A Ukrainian freighter from the port of Sebastopol cut right along behind us, causing confusion among the gulls: which of the two trails of water were they to follow? The quay soon shrank in the distance, and by the halfway point the view of European Istanbul had broadened into the famous skyline of hills punctured with the pointed staves of minarets.

I was on my way to Istanbul's Asian shore, feeling like one commuter among many. Each day tens of thousands of Istanbullus cross the Bosporus aboard these huffing, puffing boats, and somewhere Orhan Pamuk had written that when the wind was right, the smoke from their funnels remained hanging over the water 'like Arabic script'. Standing at the railing I bought a bottle of salty yogurt from a waiter who circled the deck with his tray held above his head. Whenever his supply was exhausted, he went back to the buffet for a full tray. Atatürk looked on from his framed portrait on the wainscot. His stern gaze and raptor's nose had gradually taken on a kind of casual familiarity; you saw his portrait everywhere: in museums, restaurants, anywhere you could think of. I was struck by how only one image was used for the Father of All Turks, just as for Ağri Daği, and that there was an official reason for that: both were cherished icons of Turkishness.

The only place I had come across different depictions of Atatürk was at my hotel, but that should have come as no surprise; the Pera Palas Oteli housed a miniature Atatürk museum. These days the hotel itself, built in the late nineteenth century as the terminus for the Orient Express, stood for French grandeur, with a supplementary room rate for nostalgia. The carpets in the corridors were worn to a sheen, but I was fond of places where you feel the aftershocks of history. It was in room 101, during the years immediately following the First World War, that 'the Perfectionist' Mustafa Kemal, who later assumed the name Atatürk, worked out the blueprint for modern secular Turkey.

Room 101 was not available to guests, but had been converted into a shrine. You were only allowed in to look.

'At this spot germinated the seed of the Turkish Republic,' the sign by the door announced.

In the room were forks, knives, spoons, a chipped cup, a toothbrush and a tin of tooth powder, a pair of army binoculars and a pair of reading glasses: '36 personal possessions' of Mustafa Kemal as a young general.

What intrigued me, however, was this: at the same time that Lenin was settling accounts with 'God's representative on earth', the Czar, and busy converting the faithful all across the Soviet empire to scientific atheism, Atatürk was launching his own anti-religious campaign. And like the Soviet Union, Turkey was secularised with an iron fist. In 1922 Atatürk had toppled 'God's Shadow on Earth', the Sultan, from his throne, and while Lenin was putting down Christianity, Atatürk forced Islam to its knees. In 1923 he abolished the caliphate, the religious authority that had served as the empire's guiding light for five centuries. He wanted to replace religion with 'knowledge and science'. 'We shall pound that into the head of every individual!' He took umbrage at the fez and the veil, regarding them as symbols of religious backwardness. The wearing of veils and headscarves was forbidden by law for Turkish civil servants. The fez was suppressed even more rigorously: to his subjects' astonishment, the hat was banned in 1925. Whenever the president came across a farmer still wearing the felt headgear, he would personally knock it off the man's head. Those who refused to abandon the fez faced the firing squad.

'I myself adhere to no religion,' Atatürk said shortly before his death in 1938, 'and sometimes I wish that all religions would sink to the bottom of the sea.'

Turkey, as it appeared in the year 2005, still bore his initials in every fold and wrinkle – just like the bedspread in room 101.

Turkey might have relegated Islam to the margins of society, but now it was steadily creeping back to the centre of power. Atatürk's legacy was under fire. As in Russia and Armenia, where the fall of Communism had rung in a religious revival, religion was on the upswing in Turkey as well. The president and the generals still swore to the strictly secular nature of the state, but these days the prime minister was a Muslim whose wife wore a headscarf and who, therefore, was not allowed to attend state banquets.

Equally unthinkable in Atatürk's vision of Turkey was the current popularity of Istanbul cleric Harun Yahya, a Quran scholar who lashed out in the name of Allah at 'the lies of science'. This Yahya, an interior designer whose real name was Adnan Otkar, led a collective with no fixed address that published books and DVDs in more than 40 languages. By means of pamphlets and documentaries that could be downloaded for free, Master Yahya's movement broadcast the message that Darwin was an unparalleled liar and impostor, and that only the Quran contained the literal – read 'divine' – truth. Yahya's book *The Evolution Deceit*, also popular among some Muslim students at European universities, enjoyed print runs of well over one million copies.

One of Yahya's addresses dealt with the Deluge, which in his view – and contrary to the tenets of geology – had taken place four or five thousand years ago. Nŭh's Ark had not left behind a 'fossil footprint', and certainly not at the spot dictated by the Turkish government; according to Yahya it had run aground on a hillside close to the mouth of the Tigris and the Euphrates. There, in southern Iraq, the devout Muslim could expect to find the most famous of all shipwrecks. To illustrate this statement, the book showed a modern-day painting of the stranded Ark – without Nŭh or his house-hold, of course.

It took some getting used to the notion that Noah was not exclusively the Biblical character I had known since childhood. In addition to the Quran, he also figured in the Jewish tradition, where the rabbis had embellished the Flood story with all kinds of special features. They even gave the name of Noah's wife: Na'ama. But the heroic figure of Noah/Nŭh was known beyond the three great monotheistic religions as well. The patriarch who had survived a flood sent by God (or the gods) appeared in many guises: in mythology, Noah/Nŭh was also known as Atrachasis, Xisuthros, Utnapishtim, Ziusudra and, among the Masai people of Kenya, Tumbainot.

One of those stories came from Ovid, a Roman poet and contemporary of Jesus Christ. He had included the Flood motif in one of the opening scenes of his *Metamorphoses*. When the council of the gods, chaired by Jupiter, decides to destroy mankind, Aeolus, god of the wind, unleashes the South Wind ('his terrible face covered by a pitch-black veil. His beard was thick with storm clouds, and streams of water rolled from his white hair') to hasten a devastating flood. Only two people, Deucalion and his wife Pyrrha, survived as the new ancestors of the human race. Since *Metamorphoses* was written centuries after the Old Testament, Ovid's Flood saga could only have been a variation on a common theme. The same went for the African myth about the devout, polygamous Tumbainot, who was not only allowed to take the animals on to the Ark two by two, but both of his wives as well.

In the nineteenth century, however, even older versions of the Flood legend were found, older than the Bible itself. When the existence of a precursor to the story of Noah's Ark was revealed in London in late 1872, it caused a theological concussion from which – in my view – the Bible's apologists had never recovered.

In the years preceding this discovery, an assistant at the British Museum had tirelessly been examining the cuneiform writing engraved on fragments of clay tablet. These fragile and often broken tablets – notebook-sized and frequently engraved on both sides – had been excavated in 1853 from among the ruins of the city-state of Nineveh. Ever since, they had been lying there, unscrambled, in the British Museum like a time bomb.

Ironically enough, this treasure was a prize of Biblical archaeology, a discipline that enjoyed the blessing of the Church. During the nineteenth century, at the very point when geologists had discounted the Old Testament as a source, digs in the Middle East began producing an increasing body of evidence that seemed to confirm the historicity of the Bible. The primarily British practitioners of Assyriology, the archaeology of the ancient civilisations along the Tigris and Euphrates, came up with one success after another: *objets d'art* such as high-reliefs and decorated vases showed scenes that corresponded with the accounts of battles found in Kings II; Nimrod, the mighty hunter, had really existed, as had the city of Ur, which Abraham once left at God's command.

This flow of discoveries contained a reassurance: natural scientists – Darwin chief among them – might have contested some Biblical truths, but there were also specialists who could substantiate the book's authenticity. Archaeology seemed to be a God-friendly science – until it brought to light the text of tablet XI of the Epic of Gilgamesh.

Most modern translations of this epic poem, which consists of 12 'books', are introduced with the thrilling account of how this cuneiform text was deciphered. The life story of the man who cracked the code alone contains enough material for a classic drama. His name was as plain as plain could be: George Smith, son of a working-class family, born in 1840 in the overcrowded London district of Chelsea. Forced to leave school at the age of 14 to help support his family, he went to work as an apprentice at the firm of Messrs. Bradbury and Evans, where he learned to make engravings for bank notes. He spent his free time in the nearby British Museum, where a new wing had recently been furnished with prized pieces from the excavations at Nineveh. The kings of the city-states along the Tigris and Euphrates had employed scribes to help preserve their chronicles by engraving them in cuneiform, using a blunt reed stylus on tablets of wet clay. This historical record contains countless dry facts, but also compelling literature, like the great epic story of the brutish King Gilgamesh of Uruk, who wanted to be immortal as the gods. The problem was that for as long as no one could read those 'chicken scratches', the stories remained unknown. Even when translators began to gain a grasp of the glyphs of lines and dots, the translation of Nineveh's clay tablets still seemed a hopeless task: there were, after all, including the shards, more than 20,000 of them.

George Smith, who had developed a passion for the anti-counterfeiting processes used for bank notes, attracted the attention of Sir Henry Creswicke Rawlinson, one of the two archaeologists who had uncovered the ruins of the palace at Nineveh. Sir Henry gave him a room where he could study cuneiform. There he spent hours on end, complaining on foggy days about the bad light. In order to go on working at home, the story has it, George Smith made papier-mâché moulds of the tablets. In view of his astounding achievements and devotion, the museum appointed him in 1867 as an assistant in its Assyriology department.

Five years later, one morning in 1872, George Smith fitted together two fragments of a clay tablet and a few lines of verse suddenly appeared. He read of a ship full of animals that, having survived a huge flood, 'ran aground on a mountaintop', and about a dove that was released on reconnaissance 'but returned because it could find no resting place'. This could only be Noah's dove, which had been released for the same reason and also came back when it could find no resting place. It could not be a coincidence; there were simply too many similarities between this 'Babylonian Flood story' and the Biblical one.

'I am the first man to read this after more than two thousand years of oblivion,' Smith is reported to have shouted. According to the otherwise singularly sober-minded commemorative volume from the British Museum, he then rushed about the room in a state of great excitement. 'And, to the astonishment of those present, began to undress himself.'

Before the year was out, the 32-year-old autodidact had presented his translation of the incomplete Gilgamesh epic to a gathering that included Prime Minister William Gladstone and a host of other dignitaries. The emphasis of his presentation, of course, was on the sensational lines found on the badly damaged tablet XI. From the context of the other tablets, or what was left of them, Smith concluded furthermore that the flood story he had discovered was an adaptation or retelling of even older texts. The epic poem he had deciphered dated from the seventh century BC, but referred to other written sources a millennium older. The true, original Flood story, Smith told his listeners, must have been first written down between 2000 and 1500 BC, somewhere along the lower reaches of the Tigris and Euphrates.

Smith's life took a new turn after his historic reading. The owners of the *Daily Telegraph* offered him the kingly sum of 1,000 guineas to lead an expedition of his own in search of the missing fragments of tablet XI. After a journey through Turkey, and having wasted many weeks waiting for the Sultan's permission to carry out archaeological excavations, he found what he was looking for amid the rubble of Nineveh. On the evening of only his fifth day of searching, he wired the *Daily Telegraph* announcing the discovery of a shard that belonged to the first column of tablet XI, and dealing with the instructions for building the Ark and filling it.

> O man of Shurrupak, son of Ubar-Tutu,
> tear down your house and build a ship;
> abandon wealth, seek after life . . .
> Bring up the seed of all kinds of living things into the ship!

Back in London, Smith was both hailed as a hero of science and vilified as a man who, with his own bare, working-class hands, had undermined the authority of the Church of England. As an archaeologist, it was said, he was 'slinging mud at the Bible', and that at a moment when – after the 1859 publication of *On the Origin of Species* – the Creation story was already under fire. Darwin had unfolded a new vision of the origins of life, in which there was no place for the Creator, or at most merely as Great Mover or Initiator. The lines of verse Smith had translated showed that God's Word was not original, but borrowed in part from pagan sources.

Far removed from the debates in London, George Smith went on digging and found a cuneiform chronology of the kings who had ruled over the Babylonian civilisation. He now had a timeline. Even more striking was the division imposed on the list: you had rulers before the Flood, and rulers after! This deluge, impressive enough to have driven a wedge into the 'List of Kings', must have taken place around 2900 BC.

Searching through the material he had collected, Smith found even more references to older texts from the Tigris–Euphrates delta, about 1,000 kilometres south of Nineveh. It was on those fertile, irrigable plains that the earliest human civilisations had arisen, with Babylon as the most celebrated city. Might it be possible, Smith reasoned, that – after a winter of extreme snowfall in what is now Turkey – the Tigris and Euphrates had once overflowed so violently as to inundate the entire lowland area along the Persian Gulf?

George Smith, the archaeologist who unmasked the Bible as the work of man, dreamed of discovering the origins of all the key passages of Genesis, but died early and alone – of dysentery, in the Syrian desert.

Albeit posthumously, Smith's prediction did come true: during the excavation of a temple complex between Baghdad and Basra around 1900, the oldest Deluge account (to date) came to light. On a clay tablet made in the seventeenth century BC, the Noah figure was called 'Ziusudra', a name which also appeared on Smith's list as the last king before the Flood.

Ziusudra had survived a flood lasting 'seven days and seven nights', sent by the god Enlil to drown mankind and thereby put an end to the bothersome noise they made. But Enki, the god of the waters, intervened by telling the story's hero to build a ship and to cover its planks with pitch (Genesis 6:14: '. . . Make thee an Ark of gopher wood . . . pitch it within and without with pitch'). When Ziusudra made a burnt offering after the flood (just as Noah did), the gods came flying to its scent and bore him up into their pantheon: Ziusudra, and his wife with him, were no longer mere mortals.

It was precisely in search of this secret of the gods, the secret of eternal life, that King Gilgamesh would later go. At the end of his wanderings he found the survivors of the flood. Gilgamesh ('eleven ells tall he was, nine-span wide his chest') listened carefully to this Noah figure's story and received from him the herb of eternal youth. On his way home, however, when Gilgamesh paused to bathe, the herb was stolen from him 'by a serpent'!

'Gilgamesh sat down and wept,' the final passage tells us. He realised that he and his kingdom would live on in people's memories only as long as his most solid construction: the legendary walls of Uruk, which indeed still stand.

'The supreme epic of the fear of mortality,' crowed the foreword to my Dutch-language Gilgamesh translation. The modern reader, it said, would be amazed by the beauty of this 'primal piece of writing, this first literature'.

I first read it when I was about 20 and had just started living on my own. I had stayed in contact with a girlfriend from secondary school who had gone on to study art history. Sometimes, when we met in a café, we would evangelically loan each other books: 'you *have* to read this'. I lent her Stephan Themerson's *The Mystery of the Sardine*; she in turn lent me the *Epic of Gilgamesh*.

My reaction was largely one of anger. Why had nobody told me about this, at school or at the very least in catechism classes? Important information had been withheld from me, to keep me from wandering away from the flock of the meek. I imagined forcibly rubbing the borrowed book – my fingers literally tingling with adrenalin – under the nose of my catechist. Catechism, after all, was the study of the Bible. In a brightly lit room at the Adventskerk we – 16- and 17-year-olds from Assen-Across-the-Tracks – had been made ready to publicly profess our faith. This meant that – under pastoral supervision – we could hold up all our doubts to the light of the

Book that contained every answer. The idea was that we would meet each Thursday evening for two whole years, before reaching the age of 18, to consider and discuss our faith freely and openly and to sing along with the sluggish organ:

I believe in God, the Father Almighty,
the Creator of heaven and earth,
and in Jesus Christ, His only Son, our Lord:
Who was conceived of the Holy Spirit,
born of the Virgin Mary,
suffered under Pontius Pilate,
was crucified, died, and was buried.
He descended into hell.
The third day He arose again from the dead.
He ascended into heaven
and sits at the right hand of God the Father Almighty,
whence He shall come to judge the living and the dead.
I believe in the Holy Spirit, the holy catholic church,
the communion of saints,
the forgiveness of sins,
the resurrection of the body
and life everlasting.

That I had given up before reaching that point did nothing to cool my anger. On what, after all, had we wasted our time during all those hours of catechism? On talking about weekly themes such as 'forgiveness', 'sin' and 'lust', based on mimeographed sheets in a ring-binder. On talking about a photograph of a young boy drooling over the picture of a pin-up girl with nipples, as I recall, the size of silver dollars.

Was it wrong, what that boy was doing?

But then why, if we were being drilled to consciously profess our faith, had the pastor neglected to tell us from the start that the Bible was one long act of plagiarism?

Instead, we were told that the 'roundings of a woman's body' were lovely because nature was lovely, for it had been created by God. The only injunction was that you were not to slaver over anything, and not covet what was not your own – that latter ban having actually been engraved on the stone tablets given to Moses.

After reading the Gilgamesh epic I felt like going back and calling the pastor to account. In fact, I had only one question for him: what authority did the Word of God possess if it was an adaptation of pagan texts?

In addition to anger, I also felt disappointment. Something had been taken from me. By gaining knowledge you could apparently lose something else, and in this case that 'something' seemed to be the enchantment the Bible had once exercised over me.

A year later, if I remember correctly, at my student lodgings I received a letter from the Reformed Church. They asked whether I wished to have my name transferred from the congregation in Assen to one in Wageningen. I seized the opportunity to resign my membership.

My destination on the Asian shore of the Bosporus was a mountaineering organisation called Dağ Keçisi – Mountain Goat. I had an appointment with Yildiz Aslan, a woman whose living was Mount Ararat. She was the mountain guide and managing director of Mountain Goat.

At the top of the stairs leading to her office, I greeted her with a carefully rehearsed 'Merhaba.'

'Hello,' she replied in a more mutual language.

Her gym shoes aside, Yildiz was dressed in mountaineering clothes: a pair of zip-off hiking trousers, a windbreaker and a terry-cloth headband that held back her curls. All of it a light blue – I could imagine her blending into a background of sky on a high, icy ridge.

In the email Yildiz had sent me, she said she would be organising an Ararat expedition in the period 2–9 September, which fell perfectly within the time limit of the visa I had requested. I could join her group if I liked, as long as I could show that stamp from the embassy. At summitpost.org, a website for mountaineers, I had read that a single visa for Ararat was often easier to obtain with the help of a Turkish go-between, preferably a guide from an official travel agency. Looking for a suitable candidate, I first checked with Anatolian Adventures ('we arrange your Ararat visa in SIX weeks') and stumbled upon Mountain Goat, which had been set up by a group of ecology students. I had asked Yildiz if she could help.

'Leave it to us,' had been her response.

Now she said: 'I know the governor of Iğdir province. And if that doesn't help, I can always try my contacts in the army.'

Her father was a retired colonel, and that made a difference. While Yildiz handily slid my passport under the scanner, she told me that she had grown up at a number of garrisons scattered around Anatolia. It was important for me to realise that the army defended the secular state ('the body of Kemalist thought') like a watchdog, and that officers charged with that special task formed a network that lasted a lifetime.

And by the way, she said, Ararat had been declared a national park, with an entrance fee of 50 euros. She showed me a government order apparently containing that information. I paid her on the spot.

Only then did I hear that the Ararat expedition she was planning included a group of experienced Lithuanian climbers, who would first climb the highest mountain in Iran. The entire crew would meet up with Yildiz at Hotel Isfahan, in the border town of Doğubayazit, on 1 September – five weeks from now.

'Would you like me to reserve a room for you?'

I said that might be a bit premature, but she laughed at the suggestion. The only possible difficulty, she said, was that she would be climbing with the Lithuanians via the north-west route, which involved scaling the full length of the Parrot Glacier. 'And a climb from the north is always a little harder than one from the south.'

'What do you mean, always?'

'At least in the northern hemisphere, anyway.' Yildiz sat down at her desk and checked her email. 'Snow always stays longer on the north face. We'll be heading out on to the ice, for example, at four thousand two hundred metres. On the southern route the ice starts at four thousand eight hundred.'

She could see that I was having doubts.

'Listen, you'll be using crampons, and we rope up.'

I was still sizing up this new hurdle when Yildiz announced another one. Because the north-western route had been opened this year to foreigners for the first time, she wasn't sure whether my current application for the southern route could be converted to a single visa for both north and south. 'The problem is that, administratively speaking, Ağri Daği is located in two different provinces.'

I wasn't sure I wanted to hear this.

Yildiz curled her legs up beside her on the chair and explained why Ararat had been 'closed' for decades. 'Do you have any idea what the real problem is?'

'The PKK,' I said. 'The conflict between the army and the Kurdish separatists. At least, that's what I've read.'

'That may have been true back in the mid-eighties.' In order to properly understand, however, I had to be prepared to 'look under the carpets'. What followed was a précis concerning Atatürk and 'the Kurdish question'. Atatürk had hoped simply to turn the Kurds into Turks, forbidding education in the Kurdish language and the publication of Kurdish newspapers. The goal was 'Turkification', a process enforced by the military with a great show of arms. At the garrisons where her father had served, Yildiz said, it was unthinkable to even speak of 'Kurds'. They were "Mountain Turks". Atatürk himself came up with that term. In Turkey you had Turks and Mountain Turks.'

I would see it with my own eyes as soon as I arrived in Doğubayazit: the Turkish army there kept a very high profile. 'Doğubayazit is one hundred per cent Kurdish.'

True enough, there had been no fighting around Ararat for years now, but it was still 'war'. Her index fingers traced quotation marks in the air. 'The spoils are tourists like yourself. The southern route goes via a Kurdish village. As Turkish guides, we're not safe there.'

A few of her colleagues from Istanbul, Yildiz told me, had actually tried to set up their own expedition in 1990.

'But that's what everyone's been doing lately, isn't it?' I interrupted.

She shook her head; apparently I hadn't understood. 'They take you to Doğubayazit, and there you get a Kurdish tent, Kurdish donkeys, Kurdish guides . . . Two rival families in Doğubayazit control Ararat. You might call them the subcontractors . . .'

But back to what she had started to tell me: about 15 years ago, two Turkish guides had tried to bypass that link in the chain, and their group was shot at and robbed; one member was even killed. 'And what did the army do? That's right, they closed down Ararat! For ten years! Their excuse, of course, was the PKK!'

A great deal had become clear to me during the last half-hour. Except for one thing: as a Turk, she herself was now organising an expedition without the assistance or interference of the Kurds, wasn't she?

'That's right, which is why we're taking a new route. You don't meet Kurds along the north-western route. We're going to start on the Korhan Plateau, and the only thing there is an army base.'

After my visit to Mountain Goat, I settled down at a pavement café overlooking the mouth of the Bosporus. On the far shore was Europe. You could see the bluish contours of the Hagia Sophia, once the greatest of all Christian churches. Since the Islamic conquest of 1453 it had been staked out at four corners with minarets, the 'bayonets of Islam'. Atatürk, however, had been prudent enough to restore the plastered-over frescoes of Jesus and the archangels, and to turn the Hagia Sophia into a museum.

I ordered a glass of the local brew, Efes – if only for the allusion to Ephesus, one of the world's first Christian settlements.

'I'm very sorry that I can't help you,' the waiter said.

I looked at him; this was highly unusual. Turkish hospitality (or mercantile spirit) had been perfected to such a degree that whatever was unavailable was always fetched from elsewhere, thereby making it available.

The waiter pointed to a sign reading NO ALCOHOL, and excused himself once more.

I decided to try at one of the kiosks down by the waterfront. Fishermen stood along the quay, hunched over like wading birds. Sitting with the lukewarm Efes sold to me from a street vendor's coolbox, I looked out across the water and saw the Bosporus, for the first time, as a breach. Crossing the water also meant crossing a border. I hadn't felt that way as I stood at the ferry's rail this morning, but now I saw the differences. In Asiatic Istanbul, the girls did not wear vest tops and alcohol did not flow freely. The atmosphere here was different.

On the European shore that morning I had wormed my way through a crowd of young people. In the square opposite the ferry docks, a stage had been erected. A DJ was whipping up a group of Istanbul teenagers to do their thing with blocks of coloured chalk. To get to the ticket office for the ferry, I had walked past and over huge Mona Lisas and Draculas.

That afternoon, near the dock on the Asian side, an entirely different subculture seemed to have gathered. The boys wore jeans, the girls wore full-length skirts and colourful headscarves. These young people also had microphones and sound systems; they were standing at long trestle tables covered in pictures of the torture that had taken place at the Abu Ghraib prison.

'We're organising a petition against Bush, Jr.'s crusade,' they said.

I added my name to their list. The war against Iraq, the Biblical Mesopotamia, was indeed a crusade.

Feeling that same hazy defiance, mixed with curiosity, I entered a nearby mosque. I could have done so closer to home, in Amsterdam, but I chose to do it here.

Worn stone steps led up to a patio with a fountain where men were washing their hands and feet. Here, beneath a tree full of rustling seedpods, one felt lifted above the almost mercantile hubbub of the square below. I put my shoes in the rack beside the others and walked in stockinged feet to a gallery with a view of the prayer floor. Below me, small groups of men were claiming their prayer rugs, I saw fathers and sons together, the mosque grew busier. A few minutes later the muezzin raised his voice in a wailing *'Allahu akbar'*, 'Allah is great', followed, as tradition has it, by the creed, 'There is no other god but Allah, and Mohammed is his prophet', distorted almost beyond comprehension by the loudspeakers.

All the kneeling, bowing and sitting up again took place as rhythmically as gymnastics exercises, an activity more communal than individual. It was fascinating to watch, but I did not feel moved by it. This collective submission was as repulsive to me as the individual kowtowing of the priests in the Armenian monastery at Echmiadzin.

It was not the first time I had been inside a mosque, but now that I had an eye for it I was struck by its sobriety. The simplicity and calm stood in stark contrast to the extravagance of the world's major cathedrals. Here there were no statues of saints, madonnas in mourning or replicas of Christmas mangers, only endlessly repeating patterns of blue-and-white tiles. I was standing in a space infused with geometry and algebra. For the decorators of this mosque, the Islamic prohibition on portraying mortals – who might otherwise themselves become the objects of devotion, instead of Him – must have been a blessing in disguise.

The houses of prayer I was accustomed to had also been plain and simple; it was no coincidence, after all, that the Reformation had begun with iconoclastic rioting. In the Protestant churches I knew, that had resulted in bare interiors with only a minimum of decoration. But the designers of this mosque had demonstrated that shying away from the too-literal use of images did not necessarily lead to whitewashed walls: in contrast to the empty walls of a Protestant church or Michelangelo's hand of the Creator in the Sistine Chapel, they had given us mathematics. Not only did it strike a familiar chord, but I realised that it involved a different conception of the divine. In a mosque, or at least in this one, you let your gaze wander over geometric figures that cut across walls and pillars before meeting their vanishing point at the dome's summit. The artists and artisans of Islam had applied principles like reflection and multiplication – and thereby summoned up a disquieting sense of the infinite.

The Genesis Rock

AUGUST WAS SULTRY and passed slowly. Not being one to wait passively, I went ahead and bought an Amsterdam–Ankara–Kars ticket for the thirtieth of the month, 48 hours before my visa came into effect. The only thing was that I *had* no visa. But what else could I do? Comments from friends like 'I thought you'd already left!' and 'So, did you get to the top?' became more painful with each passing day.

My friend, the one who had given me the Diamox tablets for altitude sickness, helped me assemble my equipment. In her attic, surrounded by old trunks full of 'mountain gear' (my referring to it as 'mountaineering equipment', she said, reminded her of St Bernards and kegs of brandy), she fitted me out as well as she could. From inside a nylon bundle the size of a tennis ball she plucked an orange bodywarmer, which she draped over my shoulders like a lifejacket. She handed me a pair of snow goggles that had been up Aconcagua, and strapped a miner's lamp around my forehead.

'A headtorch,' she corrected me. 'You're not going caving, are you?'

With a magic marker she checked off the items on her list for climbs above 5,000 metres. Next to those she couldn't lend me or that weren't my size, she wrote: 'Buy this!' Then she sent me to the best (and most expensive) mountaineering shop in Amsterdam.

I was inclined to put off my purchases for a few days, out of a

Calvinist sense that it was immoral to spend hundreds of euros on things you weren't completely sure you'd use. But having only one week left, I adopted the jaunty pose of the high roller who believes that luck can be finagled into happening.

The sales assistant at the mountaineering shop walked around with my list. Each time she would hold up two pairs of trousers or two windbreakers and say, shaking the hanger: 'This is the minimum you'll need above five kilometres. And this is what you'd really like to have with you.'

Sometimes I went for the most expensive (mittens that cost 140 euros), sometimes I went for the absolute minimum (a sleeping bag that would keep you warm down to 10 degrees below zero). When it came to shoes, I had little choice: I needed rigid soles, 'technical boots', and that automatically put me in the heaviest class: category D.

I bought two sets of thermal underwear, a pair of zip-off trousers, three pairs of socks and, very professional indeed, a 'camelback': a water bag worn between the shoulders, with a drinking tube to keep yourself hydrated.

Adversity has a way of making me only more fanatical, and so I began to prepare myself mentally for an illegal climb. I had read that some would-be Ark-seekers travelled to eastern Turkey on a standard tourist visa, then dodged the checkpoints and joined up with the Kurdish herdsmen at their summer camps in the saddle between Little and Great Ararat. After paying a daily fee in dollars, they could make that their base camp. Sometimes they were pulled down off the mountain by a Turkish army patrol and spent two or three nights in the cells. You were only released after signing a statement that you had not been tortured, a printed form Turkey used in its efforts to qualify for European Union membership.

Deportation, on rare occasions accompanied by the status of *persona non grata*, was the stiffest sanction; interrogations usually ended with only the confiscation of photo and film material.

This was what had happened to Jim Irwin, the most famous of

all 'Arkeologists'. In 1986, he and his wife Mary had been placed under house arrest for about eight hours in their suite at the Grand Hotel Erzurum. That Irwin was an American astronaut who had walked on the moon in 1971 was not considered relevant. He and the members of his expedition, including a Dutch television crew from the Evangelical Broadcasting Organisation, were accused of espionage. They had hired a Cessna and filmed Ararat from the air in search of remains of the Ark, but the Turkish authorities interpreted that as a flimsy attempt to cover up their real mission: mapping the military posts along the border with Soviet Armenia. Jim Irwin was a retired colonel in the US Air Force. So was *he* trying to claim that he'd been looking for the wreckage of a ship in a sensitive border area 5,000 metres above sea level? On the morning after the flight in the Cessna, the group awoke to find the Grand Hotel Erzurum surrounded by 20 soldiers. A police commissioner roused all of the participants in Irwin's High Flight '86 mission from their beds, while plainclothes policemen searched their rooms for rolls of film. Irwin followed their instructions without flinching, but Mary began praying loudly in the hotel foyer and tuned her radio to an American gospel station.

During one of Irwin's earlier Ararat expeditions, the authorities had made a fuss about a strange stone found in one of his suitcases. Irwin had given his word of honour that it was a replica of the 'Genesis Rock' from the moon's Spur Crater, a stone he had chiselled with his own hands. The original belonged to New York University. Cock-and-bull stories like that, a Turkish police detective pointed out, did little for Irwin's credibility. The man began drawing up a report of the theft of an 'archaeological artefact' from Ağri Daği and the (foiled) attempt to smuggle it out of the country.

This time too, in 1986, a barrage of calls to and from embassies and government ministries in Ankara ensued, and once again everything was quickly smoothed over. That evening Jim and Mary Irwin's group celebrated this particular happy ending with a battle song: *Stand up, stand up for Jesus, you soldiers of the cross.*

*   *   *

146

Ark explorers interested and irritated me. I brought their books home because I wanted to find out what made them tick. I had supposed they were looking for proof of God's existence, but that turned out not to be the case. Among them were no doubting Thomases who first needed to see things with their own eyes. Most Ark explorers were ministers of the Church, devoid of doubts, and at least equally devoid of humour. They undertook their Ararat expeditions in the conviction that *your* life depended on it. When the chance arose, they baptised their Kurdish helpers in the nearby headwaters of the Euphrates.

From their publications (books, DVDs and 'Flood screensavers' with or without Bible verses) there was no telling why, having already found God, they kept on looking regardless. No Ark-seeker ever considered that. There were those who predicted that God would reveal Noah's Ark to mankind as a prelude to the Day of Judgement. In that light, their search took on something of a mission: each cubic metre of Ararat rubble they turned over brought the Kingdom of Heaven one step closer. At the same time, their hustle and bustle with spades, earth drills and what-ever else they dragged up the mountainside served to remind heathens that they should 'walk in darkness' no longer, for time was running out.

Organised expeditions in search of the Ark attracted dozens of enthusiasts every year, and their numbers only seemed to grow. The tradition had been started in the early twentieth century by Russian Orthodox Cossacks. Before then there had been the occasional vague rumour of hermits and shepherd boys finding the wreck of the Ark, but none had ever led to large-scale expeditions. All that changed in the summer of 1916, however, when scouts from the 19th Petropavlovsky Regiment reported having stumbled upon the remains of the Ark on Ararat's northern flank. The Cossacks said they had seen a bowsprit sticking up out of a deep crater lake, but had been unable to get any closer. News of their discovery apparently reached Czar Nicholas II, who sent 150 royal engineers to take a look. Legend has it that they too saw the remains of the Ark in the crater lake, that they measured it and charted its location, but that the evidence they collected was lost in the chaos of the Russian Revolution.

It was not until after World War II, once Ararat lay within the borders of the NATO alliance, that Frenchmen and Americans picked up the thread. One of the pioneers of the postwar quest for the Ark was a French businessman by the name of Fernand Navarra. One day, in an antique shop in Bordeaux, he had seen a copperplate engraving of a kneeling Noah, with a mountain in the background called 'Ararat'. 'The name didn't mean much to me, but then I compared it with my own: Na-var-ra, A-ra-rat. The same number of syllables, and all three containing the same vowel!' For him, this was reason enough to believe that he had been called to find the Ark. And on the very last day of his search in 1952, he succeeded: at the conclusion of his hair-raising tale of adventure, *L'Expédition au Mont Ararat*, he and his companion saw in the ice of the glacier below them a dark shape at sunset. 'The form was unmistakably that of a ship's bow . . .' Their eyes blazed with conviction, he writes. 'Only a few decimetres of ice separated us from the exceptional discovery the world no longer believed possible: *We had found the Ark!*'

But the reader has to take Navarra's word for it, because the explorer was unable to get to the wreck. Photography let him down too; the reflection of the camera's flash off the ice blotted out everything.

The first photograph of the Ark, or what passed for it, was finally published in *Life* magazine in September 1960: it was the aerial photograph in which the Turkish army colonel had discerned the boat-shaped mound. Its publication brought a new procession of the curious to Turkey: once arrived, and not convinced by what they saw, they felt encouraged to initiate searches of their own. 'Arkeologists' they called themselves – most of them middle-aged men from Arizona, southern Switzerland or New Zealand – who swarmed out over Ararat each summer in search of petrified timbers.

Interestingly enough, the Ark-seekers never appeared to come from staunchly religious countries. No Saudi sheikh had ever invested money in an expedition to find the Ark of Nŭh. Without exception, they came from places where Church and state were separate, and where the belief in reason had gained much ground during the past century. From developed countries. The fast-growing number of representatives from Asian tigers such as South Korea and Taiwan was striking. The more prosperous and relatively apostate the country, the more Arkeologists it produced.

One of them, a Catholic Honolulu-based dealer in hotel washing machines, had recently been in the news. During a press conference in Washington in April 2004 he had unveiled satellite photos of Ararat made at his own expense during the previous, extremely warm summer. In those images, two black spots could be seen through the ice of Parrot Glacier, spots in which someone with enough imagination could see the stern and prow of a ship.

'We're going to photograph it and, God willing, you're all going to see it,' was his comment. Its discovery would be 'the greatest event since the resurrection of Jesus Christ'. The businessman, also known in Hawaii as an anti-abortion activist, announced his plans to locate this object. He had already spent 160,000 dollars on the satellite pictures, and on equipping a 30-strong research team of 'Jews, Christians and Muslims'. The season wore on, but the expedition never got off the ground. The visas were taking longer than expected and a meeting was arranged with the Turkish ambassador in Washington. The ambassador promised to do what he could, but in mid-August the requests of all the team members were rejected.

'Security reasons,' Ankara said, and the case was closed.

I had been surprised at first to discover that the Ark-seeking tradition was only a century old. Before then, apparently, no one had felt the urge to look; in those days there were still very few unbelievers. Friedrich Parrot in 1829 had considered it so obvious that the Ark was lying somewhere beneath the ice of Ararat that he hadn't even bothered to look for it. But now, in the year 2005, you had high-tech Ark-seekers who were out to evangelise, like the Hong Kong Baptists whose Creation TV broadcasting company was aimed exclusively at atheistic China.

One of Jim Irwin's companions, a pilot from Denver who had studied geology for a few years, wrote two books in which he revealed something of his deeper motivations. He expressed it this way: 'I was taught in college that according to theories of evolution, particularly the Darwinian Theory, natural selection and chance were responsible for my existence. In essence, life was an accident. I didn't buy it. "Chance" is not my God.' Then he brought to bear a line of argument first used by an eighteenth-century British theologian against the claims of the natural sciences: 'Suppose I had found a watch upon the ground, and it should be inquired how the watch happened to be in that place. When we come to inspect the watch, we perceive that its several parts are framed and put together for a purpose ... The inference, we think, is inevitable, that the watch must have had a maker ...'

Among Christians, this watchmaker analogy was a perennial favourite. Muslims, including master Harun Yahya, preferred the sand-castle metaphor: 'When we see a sand castle, we are sure that someone made it. And because nature is so much more beautiful and complex than a sand castle, the only possibility is that a "creator" was involved.' Both parables intertwined like the lines of a duet, and ended in the same refrain: 'It's harder to believe in evolution than in creation. We humans were made for a special reason, by an Intelligent Designer.'

Referring to an intelligent designer in this way is a modern and increasingly popular way to profess one's belief in God. The most intelligent adherents of 'intelligent design' leave it at that. The argument seems waterproof: you *want* to believe in that special, preferably benevolent purpose. I did, too. The image of Nature going about her indifferent business is harder to accept. Senselessness or aimlessness run counter to one's feelings, in apparent conflict with the human urge to survive. But what could that purpose be? In the course of all those centuries, in answer to the question 'Why have we been put on earth?', the Roman Catholic Church has come no further than a sophism: 'God made me to ... serve Him in this world and to be happy with Him forever in the next.' There was no deliberating it, that was the

150

whole point, and if you deliberated too hard or too long it could drive you mad. God is love. God is. Or otherwise you could echo Nietzsche: God is dead.

In my view, questioning the weak links in Darwinist evolutionary theory shows a healthy sense of scientific curiosity. Most propagators of intelligent design, however, are not interested in that. Like the Pope in the *Compendium Cathechismus* ('It is God himself who gives to us the light both of reason and of faith'), they seek to deny any conflict between faith and science. But, wisely enough, none of them attempt to explain how you could square Christ's resurrection with the tenets of medical science.

No matter how you looked at it, Creationism, in the guise of intelligent design as well, was a matter of faith and not of scientific theory. But authorities all over the world – from President George W. Bush to the Dutch Education Minister – continued to suggest that it might not be a bad idea to bring the intelligent designer back into biology lessons, as a worthy opponent to Darwin.

Everywhere you looked, religion was on the comeback. On more than one occasion, when I had talked about Ararat, friends said: 'You're not starting to flirt with religion too, are you?' – and they weren't joking.

Unbelievers were on the defensive. Studies appeared with titles like *The Twilight of Atheism* – dealing with the resuscitation, in America and Europe, of a religious consciousness until then deemed on the point of extinction. Not only in the former Eastern Bloc, but also in the West, a religious revival – seen most clearly in its fundamentalist Christian and Muslim manifestations – was underway. Much to his father's chagrin, Armen Petrozian's eldest son had let himself be baptised and now sincerely believed 'in that pure flimflam' of Noah's Ark having been found by the Russians in 1916. Children these days, it seemed, could hurt their parents by embracing faith. Barely a quarter of a century ago, atheism had been the forbidden fruit of which I, as a schoolboy, had not dared eat. Religion had taken its place. The unspoken nightmare in my closest, least religious surroundings was that one day your daughter would suddenly don a headscarf: then you would lose her, the way our parents 25 years ago could lose us to the squatters' or punk scene.

The Ark-seekers sensed that the tide had turned in their favour, and put themselves in the vanguard of the rising religious-conservative front. Uncompromising as they were, they hoped to quash the unholy trinity of 'Darwinists, humanists and Marxists' by producing a fragment of gopher-wood from Ararat. They read the Bible literally, and so for them the idea of intelligent design was too abstract and too noncommittal. With pseudo-science as their weapon, they fought tooth-and-nail against the most self-evident scientific conclusions. Their writings followed a pattern with which I had become acquainted in *The Flood: In the Light of the Bible, Geology and Archaeology* – the textbook for Protestant Christian schools I had borrowed from Salle Kroonenberg. The Ark-seekers' arguments were at the same time hilarious and pathetic.

The salt lakes of Utah? Unevaporated remnants of the Deluge.

Oil beneath the earth's surface? That was the mush of cadavers and vegetable material that had been washed up and had rotted away at the time of 'the great worldwide catastrophe spoken of in Genesis'.

From the very start, I had been plotting to find an Ark-seekers' camp and enter it. At night, around a camping stove and a pan of onion soup, I would sound them out. But what good would it do? These people, with their moustaches and ill-fitting trousers, acted like twenty-first-century epigones of the faith-blinded Scheuchzer, who mistook a salamander skeleton for a human being. I, however, had no desire to revisit those dark ages. If belief meant voluntarily flipping off the switch of reason, I would bow my head and pass.

Jim Irwin was the only one who couldn't be shaken off that easily. He was a deserter from the camp of science to that of faith. As a human standard-bearer for technological ingenuity, he had been shot to the moon in the tip of a rocket; back on Earth once more, he had submitted, as Ark-seeker, to a strict and archaic creed. The knowledge he had been injected with during his astronaut training had apparently not immunised him to faith. Jim Irwin had taken a unique path: by stretching human limits and relentlessly chasing after knowledge, he had arrived at God.

What had overcome him? If *he* had broken through the sound barrier of knowledge into the domain of faith, that could, in theory, happen to anyone. And so to me too. But what did it take to reach that point?

James Irwin, born in 1930 in Pittsburgh, was the eighth man on the moon. And the first to drive around on it, in a high-tech vehicle. In the moon dust he had buried silver plaques bearing the finger-prints of his wife Mary and their children. And he had saluted beside an unwaving, stiffly starched Stars and Stripes.

At the age of seven, in 1971, I must have seen him in black-and-white. Or at least seen the reflection off his visor. And I must have had petrol-station medals with his picture on them: coins with the portraits of all the Apollo astronauts that my father received each time he filled up at the pump.

Besides being a superhero for a period of seven days, Jim Irwin had also been someone before he went into space and after he came back. He was 41 when the rocket blasted off from Kennedy Space Center, and he had lived for 20 years after his splashdown off Hawaii. It was easy enough to imagine that a voyage to another celestial body, so horribly far from the rest of mankind, might leave one not entirely unaffected. Of the 12 moonwalkers, more than half had ended up with mental and emotional problems: one had hit the bottle, another had planned to commit suicide, two received long-term treatment for depression, and yet others joined religious sects.

Cosmonauts from the a-religious Soviet Union had encountered similar problems. Yuri Gagarin became addicted to alcohol and flew to his death – accidentally or otherwise – in a MiG fighter. After having reached as high and as far as a man could, what was left?

As a correspondent in Moscow I had posed that same question in 1997 to the first person to walk in space, Alexey Leonov. His moment of glory in March 1965, as he wormed his way through an airlock of the Voskhod 2 capsule and dangled in space on an umbilical cord, had lasted 12 minutes and 9 seconds. All that remained were a few grainy photographs and audio tapes, but then they were really remarkable. In a radio broadcast, the Kremlin had announced that Colonel Leonov had 'bravely opened the door to the cosmos', while Soviet TV appealed to its viewers' sentiments by bringing Leonov's four-year-old daughter Viktoria into the studio.

'Where's Papa now?'

'Papa is floating in open space,' she had replied, steady as a ventriloquist's puppet.

Only Soviet ground control in the off-limits suburb of Kaliningrad, east of Moscow, knew that her father was fighting for his life. Leonov had passed without incident through the two inflatable airlocks, but once in the vacuum of space his suit expanded more than anticipated, to the point where he looked like the Michelin man. His hands no longer reached the gloves and his suit had become too large and too stiff to crawl back through the inflatable airlock.

Alexey Leonov tried to elbow his way back in. That didn't work. Then he tried going feet-first. That didn't work either. Ground control could only watch helplessly as his pulse increased to 165 beats a minute.

For 30 years he had carried that story around with him as a state secret. Only when the Cold War was over, when the Red Army no longer existed and Leonov, Hero of the Soviet Union and the recipient of two Lenin Orders, had become an advertising executive for Omega watches, was he able to relate without fear how he finally came through: contrary to all safety instructions he had opened a valve in his suit, allowing it to deflate and enabling him to squeeze his way in.

Failure, at that point, was not an option. Within the American–Russian struggle for dominance in space, in which Yuri Gagarin and John Glenn had fought out the first round, Leonov had been deployed as the first spacewalker.

What I wanted to know was whether, in line with Communist

doctrine, he too had announced that God did not exist because he had not seen Him.

'Yes, that's only logical,' Leonov said. 'That was part of the whole thing.'

He didn't expand on the subject, so I asked him whether, looking back on it, he still thought that was so logical.

Leonov stood up to show me a calendar illustrated with reproductions of his paintings. He said that he always carried a sketchpad, in case he had to wait at an airport, for example. His pencil drawings showed cloud formations with seagulls or parachutists. And at home, in Star City, close to Moscow, he spent days on end at his easel. In his life, he told me, that tranquillity served as a necessary counterweight. And then it struck me what it was he painted: rockets and churches. Russian rockets and Russian Orthodox churches. In the calendar illustrations, the same golden-yellow glow of the church domes came back in the sunlight reflecting off the spacecraft.

I asked him whether, as a cosmonaut of scientific atheism, he had come to believe in God.

'Not in a man with a beard on a cloud somewhere,' he said. 'But there is something out there that we humans don't know about.'

Jim Irwin's volte-face had made more of a stir. A reasonably handsome, strong-featured man, he had hired a ghostwriter to describe his conversion. The things he told his readers about his marriage read like a dated film script. Born the son of a plumber, Irwin had worked his way up to test pilot. On his third date with Mary, a Seventh-Day Adventist who had once competed for the title of Miss California, he got her pregnant. 'So let's get married right away,' he proposed. But it wasn't that easy: her parents were opposed to a 'mixed marriage' with a Baptist. When they finally eloped, Jim told her that any daughters they might have would be free to go to church with her, as long as their sons became Baptists.

Mary also had her memoirs written, and if you laid the two autobiographies side by side you could stare in stereoscope into the endless vacuum of their marriage. In a fenced-in plot of single-family dwellings in the desert close to Edwards Air Force Base, the steadily expanding family personifies the profound anti-heroism of the Cold War. Mary pines away, while Jim risks his life in top-secret supersonic planes. He wants to fly, higher and faster; she feels like driving her car into a ravine. Or should it be a divorce? Either choice would have burst the bubble, and Jim would have been taken off the Apollo project. An astronaut selected for a moon mission had to have a charming wife behind him.

Jim and Mary's books both belonged to that 'confessional' genre into which my publisher hoped to prevent me from descending: they both included a complete about-face, after which He-with-the-capital-H appeared and everything turned out right. Mary's conversion took place on page 100 of *The Moon is Not Enough – an astronaut's wife finds peace with God and herself*. After yet another Sunday-afternoon quarrel, Mary slams the kitchen door behind her and sets off on a drive to nowhere in particular. When she stops at one point and gets out amid the empty bottles and scrap wood of a roadside dump, it occurs to her: 'God, my life is just like this garbage.' Jim's lift-off will be in three months; one rash move on her part is enough to ruin his career. But Mary is incapable of any move whatsoever; she feels empty and at a loss. And then something strange happens to her: 'In my mind, like on a big TV screen, I saw two wrestlers. I realised clearly that Satan was one of them, and Jesus the other. They were wrestling over my soul. I sat there for what seemed like a full fifteen minutes with my eyes turned inward, watching the scene. When the match was over, I saw Jesus with His arm raised in victory. I knew the battle for my soul was won.'

With Jim, it was all a bit more complicated. His ghostwriter wanted us to believe that he had repented on the moon. But no one at ground control in Houston had noticed anything of the sort, and when a journalist asked him later whether going to the moon had changed him, he had looked at his own hands and arms and stated that he felt like 'the same guy'.

Mary only noticed the change during the tickertape parade through generally so-sceptical New York. A banner hanging on Fifth Avenue read: YOU ARE SERVANTS TO ALL THE WORLD NOW, and that

156

had caused Jim to realise his accountability as one of the chosen few. To Mary's amazement, one sentence began recurring again and again in his speeches, to the effect that he, Jim Irwin, had gone to the moon on behalf of all mankind. His selection for this expedition (of four billion human beings at the time, only 12 would actually go) was so unique that he could not help but bear witness, although it was not exactly clear to what. During his public appearances he became more communicative, but at home he was still a tough nut to crack.

Mary addressed her prayers to God, fearing that her husband was beyond help. 'The pinnacle of Jim's hard-won, long-sought career had been reached,' she wrote of those days in 1971. 'And he was only 41 years old.' The route NASA had mapped out for him contained one unavoidable pitfall. At first he could bask in the limelight, for as long as it lasted, but as soon as he returned to his regular training the bottom would fall out of his life. Mary sensed this, and asked herself 'Could there be any challenge left for him in life?'

As a superstar whose photograph was on the covers of all the major magazines, Jim was annoyed by his wife's renewed religiosity, which prompted her to stop wearing make-up and eating meat. Mary was adept at playing the happy housewife, but he would have been glad to leave her at home during the obligatory European tour of places including Brussels (a reception with King Baudouin) and Rome (an audience with the Pope). A wife's presence, however, was a standard part of NASA protocol, and so Mrs Irwin attended the overseas banquets. In her role as wife-of-the-moonwalker, she was dumbfounded to hear how Jim kept fine-tuning the account of his experiences, putting less and less emphasis on his own achievements and capabilities. A normal person would have tended to play up his own bravery, but Jim had actually started filtering all bravura out of his story.

'On the moon I relied more on God than on Houston,' she heard him say during an interview. That statement set off a chain reaction, and back in the United States they found their postbag overflowing with invitations to speak at religious gatherings. Once the official tours were over and Jim was about to start his training programme as a standby astronaut, he chose to address a crowd of 50,000 Baptists at the Houston Astrodome.

'What a thrill it was to hear my husband speaking openly . . . concerning his faith in Christ,' Mary wrote. 'Especially when I remembered that he had never been able to communicate spirituality in previous years.'

With hindsight, Jim's autobiography traced the moment of his conversion back to his experience of God in outer space. Once outside the Earth's atmosphere, he had sensed 'God's presence'. It had felt odd to travel 380,000 kilometres through space without the sensation of movement, to see Earth move away from him through one porthole and the moon approach through the other. And once on the moon's surface, driving around in the Lunar Rover, Jim had watched Planet Earth rise, and was suddenly overwhelmed by the feeling of seeing 'the earth through God's eyes'.

The rest of the world, however, was watching the Apollo 15 activities in black-and-white, and what they saw was a resolute figure, averse to all dreaminess or introspection. For the camera, Irwin and his colleague Dave Scott carried out 'Galileo's experiment': simultaneously dropping a falcon's feather and a geologist's hammer to show that – in the absence of air resistance – both would strike the moon's surface at the same time. Carrying out this experiment was tantamount to celebrating a high mass for science. Intentionally or not, it amounted to the vindication of Galileo Galilei, who was charged with heresy and excommunicated by the Vatican in 1633 for claiming that the Earth revolved around the sun (his official rehabilitation took place only in 1996, by Pope John Paul II). But the astronauts' mission was a scientific not a religious one. With their discovery of a white moonstone at a crater's edge, they made an important contribution to knowledge about the age of our solar system. When analysed at a laboratory in New York, the stone proved to be 4.15 billion years old.

'With a margin of error of, give or take, 250 million years,' Jim consistently added, like a true academic.

The faith that manifested itself afterwards may have had a long incubation period, but its effect was total. A few months after returning to Earth, Irwin made a public confession of it at the Nassau Bay Baptist Church. Leaving NASA, he set up his own evangelisation office, the High Flight Foundation, which he tended to run from the saddle of an exercise bike in Colorado Springs. For the rest of his life, Jim Irwin, who had reached the limits of human exploration, found a firm foothold in the letter of the Bible. In my case, knowing more had led to believing less, but with Irwin the process had worked in reverse. In his reliance on a combination of mathematical calculations and technology (for that was what had brought him to the moon with such pinpoint accuracy), it seemed he had caught a glimpse of the future, and that in turn had caused him to scurry back to the days of the Diluvialists and Creationists.

He used the moonstone to which God had led him as his ace in the hole. He had a replica made of it, and always referred to it as the Genesis Rock. When visiting kings and presidents he would slide the white rock, as old as the oldest stone on earth, across the table like a chess piece. Without mentioning the scientific dating (!), he presented his find as proof that the Earth and the moon had been formed at the same time – just as described in Genesis 1.

By making selective use of the intellectual Meccano set his astronaut training had equipped him with, Jim Irwin did his best to underpin an antique view of the world. The astronaut who had climbed the slopes of Ararat again and again, six times in all, ignored the fact that his rock was more than four billion years old. When called to account for inconsistencies, he had a custom-tailored one-liner ready to go: 'I sincerely believe that God will allow me to find something on earth from the book of Genesis that is more important than the Genesis Rock.'

That never happened. Jim Irwin died of a heart attack in 1991, at the age of 61, his Ararat expeditions having failed to uncover Noah's Ark.

Halfway through the week before my departure, I phoned Yildiz in Istanbul. 'What do you think?' I asked her. 'Do I stand a chance?'

My ticket was for that coming Tuesday, which made Monday the last day I could actually collect a stamped visa at the Turkish consulate.

Yildiz didn't understand why I still had heard nothing, and asked whether she should cancel my hotel reservation.

'No,' I said, 'I'm coming no matter what.'

After that I dialled the number of the Turkish embassy in The Hague. This time I couldn't get Beliz on the line; she had taken refuge behind a switchboard operator.

'She is aware of it,' I was told in Dutch without a trace of an accent. 'Just a moment, she's saying something . . .'

Voices were buzzing in the background.

'Hello, mister?' Suddenly I was hearing a man's voice, it was the deputy secretary. His English was more formal than Beliz's. 'We are very sorry that we have been unable to inform you within a more reasonable period.' But, he assured me, serious attention was being given to my case, I just needed to have a little patience.

I tried to explain to him that there was no time left for that.

'I shall see what I can do for you,' the deputy secretary interrupted. 'Please contact me again tomorrow.'

On Friday morning, feeling I had nothing left to lose, I called the deputy secretary again.

'We are working on your application,' I heard him say. And also: 'We are sending a telex to Ankara. As soon as the ambassador has a moment today, I'll ask him to sign it.'

A telex! Did that medium still exist?

I left the house to buy the last few items on my list: water-purification tablets, anti-blister treatment, lip balm and 'comfort food' ('something you'd like to have most at the moment when you feel like giving up').

When I returned home late that afternoon, the light on my answering machine was blinking.

'Good afternoon, this is a message concerning your visa application. You can retrieve your sports visa for Ağri Daği on the following weekday at our consulate in Rotterdam. Please remember that consular affairs are dealt with only between nine in the morning and twelve noon. Thank you.'

The word

On my way, with more than a kilo laced to each foot, I was taken aside three times for being a suspicious character. At Amsterdam and at Ankara, and then again at the airport in Kars, in eastern Turkey. I handed over my spare change, my watch, my mobile phone, my belt. But the metal detectors kept flashing red, until the border guards ordered me to remove my boots and place them on the X-ray conveyor belt.

My climbing shoes slid on to the screen, and were stopped at the push of a button: 28 metal clasps, 14 on each one.

I finally entered Anatolia in stockinged feet. WELCOME, BIEN-VENU, WILLKOMMEN, BENVENUTO, WELKOM, I read on a placard bearing the European stars. Kars was 120 kilometres from Ararat. I slid my feet into the stiff shafts of my shoes, took delivery of my backpack and suitcase-on-wheels and shuffled, laces untied, to the taxi stand.

It felt strange to walk on asphalt half-mushy from the heat of the day, carrying a burden designed for polar conditions. I shot off a text message: LNDD AT K. SAFE&WELL.

After a serious struggle, I had embraced the Short Message Service as a pleasant medium: it broke language up into a guttural, hideous stammer of unvowelled words, but at the same time cut out a lot of superfluous static. A message composed primitively, with two thumbs, pared down its essence.

The decrepit Mercedes I climbed into smelled of taxicab air-freshener. Along the road from the airport into the town of Kars, leather-clad motorcycle policemen were directing traffic. Amid the rolling stubble fields an articulated lorry had jackknifed across the road. I saw chunky red stars on the asphalt, and someone busily scraping them on to the hard shoulder with a snow shovel. When the taxi crept past I saw that the trailer had been carrying watermelons; they must have rolled out from under the tarpaulin like bowling balls and splattered on the road.

My telephone hummed. GRT! V ASKS: CN U C SNW ALRDY?

The hilly landscape around me, covered in boulders and devoid of trees, had the dull sheen of mercury. NO. FR V: SNW IN TRKSH IS KAR. XX PAPA.

Since the summer Vera had been interested in words like *yes* and *sí* and *da*, in fact with the very existence of different languages.

'Ihre Frau?' the driver asked.

'Ja,' I said, arching my back and sliding the mobile into my pocket. 'Or actually, my two women.'

Rocking his head back and forth and raising an eyebrow, he expressed his wordless admiration. It broke the uneasiness that had arisen between us. Just before the bottleneck in the road my driver had announced that he didn't want to take me to the address I'd given. With a German vocabulary of no more than 100 words, he had tried to convince me to go to a hotel. Hote Karabağ, for example, was *sehr gut*.

But I wanted to catch a minibus at the *dolmuş* station.

Driving into town we passed a rubbish dump, a mason's yard specialising in gravestones, a car-repair workshop, a furniture showroom. But I was too distracted by the driver's insistence that I spend the night in Kars to take a good look at the surroundings.

I already had a hotel, I told him, in Doğubayazit. *Auch sehr gut*.

The man let go of the wheel and looked away from me in almost theatrical agony. He seemed unable to bear the thought that a visitor from far away might have no interest in his city, if that was indeed what was bothering him.

Finally, in emphatic silence, he drove his taxi across the railway tracks and on to the little square where most of the *dolmuş* operators had their offices. Adhesive letters stuck to the windows listed

162

the various destinations, along with their prices. My driver accompanied me into the office of the only operator offering DOĞUBAYAZIT, demonstratively ordered a ticket for me and then, just as demonstratively, turned to me with the announcement that the last *dolmuş* of the day had left around noon. '*Habe ich doch gesagt,*' he said, bending his knees slightly and holding his hands palms up in desperation. It sounded more like a barrister's appeal than a cry of triumph.

Then it dawned on me what he had been trying to say all along: that I would have to spend the night in Kars in any event, because there was no way for me to leave. I admitted my mistake: we patted each other on the shoulder.

My driver introduced himself as Celil, pronounced *Czheleel*. Before we drove on, he turned off the meter.

Kars was laid out in a chequerboard of streets, a Russian legacy from the nineteenth century, with lots of trees and even more traffic lights. The cab pulled up with two wheels on the kerb in front of a dealer in tractor tyres and troughs. Across the street was a concrete and glass building with a sign spanning its façade: HOTEL *** KARABAĞ. Celil bore my backpack like a child in his arms across the busy road. In the lobby with its worn parquet, easy chairs and umbrella stands, he handed me his business card. Pointing to the telephone number scribbled in ink, he patted the mobile phone in his shirt pocket – if I needed his services, all I had to do was call.

There could be no harm, I told myself, in stopping and nosing around after such a long flight. It gave your spirit time to catch up; wasn't that what the Mapuche Indians said? Sacrificing one of my 10 climbing days made me feel like a high-jumper who waives his first chance at the bar, be it out of self-confidence or overweening pride.

And since I was stuck in Kars anyway, I started seeing my unconventional entry as a welcome gift. The misunderstanding between Celil and me, the uncomprehending Westerner, could have come straight out of Orhan Pamuk, who delighted in letting his protagonists fall through the hidden layers of deepest Turkey. A disproportionate number of Pamuk's novels had been in the pile of books meant to prepare me for Anatolian reality; you could almost say that I had set my course by the compass of his fiction.

Having changed my climbing shoes for lighter footwear, I left my windowless hotel room to find Pamuk's Turkey. His latest novel, *Snow*, was actually grafted to Kars' street plan. The city (which in the course of the story is cut off from the world by a blizzard) not only served as a backdrop, but its dilapidation and lumpen provincialism made it a kind of character in its own right. Reading, I had the feeling that Pamuk was handing over a key to the hidden Turkey, which I could now try out on Kars.

Pamuk himself had warned against doing that when he had one of his characters say that it was futile to look outside the book for the country that lies beyond words. Still, I decided to explore the streets, to buy a Turkish edition of *Snow* (*Kar*) and talk to the bookseller about Orhan Pamuk the man.

The receptionist behind the red marble desk doubted whether Kars even had a bookshop, so I went out to see for myself. I passed coffeehouses, internet cafés and pool halls, kebab restaurants and a striking number of cheese shops, all selling the same insipid-looking cheese. Opposite a hospital emergency exit I was accosted by a group of street children brandishing a set of bathroom scales; for a handful of lira they would tell you how much you really weighed. Together, the pushbarrows in Kars' every nook and cranny formed a rolling bazaar lit by the neon glow of the regular shops.

I wandered in the footsteps of the poet Ka, the main character of *Snow*. At 42, Ka was two years older than me, a Turk who had become Westernised after emigrating to Frankfurt. As a 'superstitious atheist' and rank outsider in his expensive charcoal-grey overcoat, Ka comes to Kars to report on a wave of suicides among girls who refused to take off their headscarves. He has also come for his old flame Ipek, whom he has heard is divorced and living with her father and sister at the Snow Palace Hotel. Besides becoming snowed in, Ka also becomes embroiled in personal and politico-religious intrigues.

Some reviewers described *Snow* as a novel about 'the clash between Islam and top-down secularism'. In this prejudiced reader's mind, however, it all revolved around Ka's search for spirituality.

With bated breath I had read statements of his like: 'There's a lot of pride involved in my refusal to believe in God.'

Between a greengrocer's and a bank I found a stationer's, its window festooned with colourful mobile phone covers. The two girls behind the counter giggled when I mentioned the name Pamuk, but no, they didn't sell books.

In Kars, however briefly, Ka recovers his religious sense, encouraged by the inspiration he feels as 19 poems come to him and fall into place in the perfect form of a snowflake. Ka's budding readiness to believe in a God who 'pays careful attention to the world's hidden symmetry' amazed and fascinated me. But that this same God 'will make us all more civilised and refined' seemed to me a pipe dream, too naive to be credible.

Having combed every street in the city centre, I walked along the wall of an army barracks towards a busy carriageway. There, at the corner of a crossroads, I found a shop belonging to ÖZGÜN ÖDÜL; by the look of it, Özgün dealt in anything people might buy. At the back of the shop, beneath the toy animals hanging from the ceiling, a balding shopkeeper was sitting at a desk. To the words 'Pamuk' and 'Kar' he replied 'yes' and 'sure'. Jumping up, he fetched a copy with the poet Ka on its cover, pictured three times from the back, in his long coat.

As I paid, I asked: 'What did you think of the book?'

'Bad,' the shopkeeper said once he had handed me my change. 'I read part of it and stopped.'

'Why?'

Instead of answering, he pulled up a chair for me, and took out his mobile phone to place an order.

'Please, sit down.'

From one of the drawers he extracted a copy of the *Langenscheidt Universal Turkish Dictionary*, a concise work the size of my old school Bible. We were barely settled when a boy came into the shop, carrying a copper tray with glasses and a teapot.

The comment of Orhan Pamuk's that struck me most did not come from one of his books, but from an interview. To a German journalist he had said: 'The main character in *Snow* has a sincere desire for religious experiences, but his idea of God is very Western. He is after the individual experience, not the communal one of Islam.' Pamuk was talking about me: for me, belief was a private affair; what mattered was the contemplation involved, not the search for comfort with like-minded others.

Leafing back through *Snow*, I happened upon a number of references to the limitations of such a 'Western' conception of faith. On page 72, I read: 'As Ka had always known, in this part of the world faith in God was not something achieved by thinking sublime thoughts . . . Above all, it meant joining a mosque, becoming part of a community.' Seen from that perspective, I, like Ka, was unsuited to religions that emphasised the collective. Which most of them did. Processions, prayer meetings or immersion in the Ganges all owed their attraction to their mass character. Yet the stronger the 'fellow feeling' within a community of believers, the more it appalled me. The frills and commotion of Seville's Semana Santa, when the streets filled with masked and frenzied believers, made my hair stand on end. I, with my Protestant background, preferred being a loner. I liked to stand on the sidelines, and if there was any danger of being dragged along I would dig in my heels. Reason held the reins, except perhaps during flashes of infatuation or when listening to Shostakovich.

But was that stance something I had assumed of my own free will – as a conscious, autonomous individual – or was I a prisoner to my upbringing? If I understood Pamuk correctly, he was trying to get it into my thick skull that I, with my holy individualism, was merely a product of the Reformation or some other schism. And that suggestion made me uneasy.

Why did I distrust rituals? Did I really believe that they detracted from the heart of the matter? Or had Calvin whispered that in my ear?

'Faith starts at the point where you stop asking questions. And that is precisely *not* your forte,' my wife had pointed out to me.

She came from a Catholic family; her uncle had been a bishop, an aunt had served in a missionary convent. Beneath her parents' Christmas tree there was always an entire collection of porcelain shepherds, three kings of the Orient, the child in its manger, sheep and a camel – precisely the kind of nonsense we Protestants looked down on. At our home, the Word had been central, and the bond with God into which we entered during prayer.

Our differing backgrounds had a way of rearing up at the strangest moments. Noah's Ark *on top of Ararat*? My wife had never heard about that. The men of Emmaus, the Good Samaritan? If she knew about them at all, it was only in Rembrandt's etchings and paintings.

In the Catholic Church, the altar was the focal point; with us, the pulpit. That rearrangement could be traced back to Calvin and Luther, who had seen the infallible Word of God as having paramount importance. Unlike the Catholics, they had stopped seeing Nature as a manifestation of God's might, in which he revealed himself to mankind. He did that only through his Word. It had never occurred to me before that that rift had assisted scientific progress; the Protestant researcher could approach Nature without sacred awe, as a subject for study and dissection.

My own fascination with the Bible could probably be traced to the Reformation too, but that made it no less real. Esau, who sold his birthright for a bowl of lentils ('Feed me, I pray thee, with that same red pottage'), the burning bush that was not consumed by fire, water changed to wine at the feast of Cana – I had been brought up with all those stories, and I cherished them. In catechism class, new trails were blazed through the jungle of Bible texts with the help of the weekly Bible crossword: a puzzle devised by our pastor ('I am my master's faithful servant and can speak only one two-letter word, except for that one time . . .') to which we had to find the answer (Balaam's talking ass) at home.

Those who had done well in Bible reading and exegesis could revel in the first two verses of John's Gospel: 'In the beginning was the Word, and the Word was with God and the Word was God. The same was in the beginning with God.'

If I were to hear my own confession, it would be that I had

167

sought refuge in the word (without the capital) and no longer in the Word. I had traded in the one for the other. Back in biology, I had learned that life could be unravelled in strings of DNA, or, to be more precise, in the arrangement of the base sequence A, C, G and T. It was that simple. Chemistry assumed the existence of molecules built from the logically ordered elements of Mendeleev's periodic table. In physics, the smallest particles were initially called atoms (from *atomos*, indivisible), but once the atom had been split there was no end in sight, and reality fractured into quarks and neutrinos, anti-matter and suppositions. The more it seemed to have been clarified, the faster the mystery slipped away or multiplied. That in itself seemed to support the conclusion that the mystery of existence would remain beyond the grasp of the quantitative sciences. Only after I had reached this conclusion did I realise what my most elementary building blocks were: letters and punctuation marks. Sometimes entire words or sentences too, snippets of dialogue or existing motifs. Language.

In my view, every human life consisted of a narrative line with a beginning (birth) and an end (death). Written down or not, the course of such a lifetime always had the essential characteristics of a story. By the same token, one breathed life into an event, real or imaginary, by expressing it in words.

During his stay in paradise, Adam had been charged with naming the cattle, the birds of the air and the beasts of the field: that was a part of the Creation story. To name *was* to create. To re-name was to re-create.

Since I had begun to write, I had developed a great respect for the word. In each sentence I sought words of the right weight and the right sound. I rolled them around on my tongue, sucked on them until they turned the right colour, then strung them together like beads. And although I selected and arranged them myself, the words never did exactly what I had in mind. Once embedded in a sentence, they could suddenly change their lustre or significance, and that was miraculous.

When my daughter began babbling her first words, I listened in awe. As other fathers filmed or photographed their growing child,

I kept track of her forays into language in 'Vera's Big Notebook of Words', in order to get closer to the source of words.

It has been remarked upon billions of times, but I considered it pure magic. First came sounds that resembled 'mama' and 'papa', followed by animal noises like 'moo' and 'woof woof'. Soon things were given names, some of them inexplicable. Vera used them to furnish her gradually expanding universe.

A 'go' was a dummy, 'kapi' a triangular wooden block, and on 26 September 2004 she decided to refer to the saying of grace at my parents' house as 'plate-look'. After the 'amen', she said: 'Gramma, Grampa, 'gain plate-look?'

Vera's world was populated by 'boobies' and 'moo-moos'. She assigned colours to numbers. 'Two is yellow' – that never failed to intrigue.

On 14 January 2005, almost three years old, she said: 'I was thinking that we would bake biscuits this afternoon.'

'What is that, "thinking"?'

'It's talking quietly.'

One year later, when I asked her the same question, she said: 'Uh . . . thinking is just thinking . . . If you don't know what it is, you can't explain it.'

After a holiday abroad, she realised that you could also give things different names. 'Dakook,' she said at the age of three and a bit, 'is Russian for "no". Didn't you know that?'

Not long afterwards I took her to the Star Path, a winding educational route that had been set up in my boyhood beneath the larches in Drenthe province. Within 45 minutes you walked through our solar system, from the pin's head of Pluto all the way to the sun: a yellow-flamed sphere at the edge of the same open field that housed the radio telescopes of the Westerbork Observatory. The Star Path used to be my favourite weekly after-church walk. 'Are we going to the whisper woods?' I would ask, because of the signs everywhere telling you to turn off the engine of your car or moped.

'Look, another planet,' Vera echoed as we passed Neptune and she caught sight of the display case for Uranus at the next bend. She skipped along, from the wooden platforms with weights you could lift ('10 litres of water on the moon', '10 litres of water on Jupiter') to the two 'talking shells' located opposite each other along the path. As in a mirror reflected in a mirror, I saw myself as a young boy, running ahead, my father in tow. The path we followed was built to scale; every metre we walked took us 2.5 million kilometres closer to the sun.

We arrived at the ranks of 14 radio telescopes on the heath. I told her the parabolic antennae were ears, listening for sounds from the stars; to tell whether or not we were alone in the universe. Vera cupped a hand behind her ear and listened too.

She wasn't showing the slightest sign of fatigue, so we walked on to the monument of the broken railway – a buffer with rusty rails curling from the ground – in remembrance of the Westerbork transit camp. A total of 102,000 Jews, including the Kroonenbergs, had been transported from this spot: each Tuesday morning the cattle cars left for Auschwitz, Sobibor, Theresienstadt.

Beside a bouquet of wilted flowers wrapped in foil, a teacher was talking to a group of uncomfortable-looking students.

Vera, in amazement: 'Why are those rails broken?' But I had no words to explain.

My obsession with the word had led me back to the Bible itself. Re-reading it, I was every bit as impressed as before, yet with one difference: now I was reading the Good Book as literature. I had since discovered what John meant by 'the Word became flesh'. The walls of water across the Reed Sea I had come to see as a metaphor for God's omnipotence. There was no need to search for any murky, rational explanation for the flight across the seabed; that only detracted from its miraculous and majestic power.

In reading the story of the Flood, I noticed a hidden symmetry that had so far escaped me. The verses formed a carefully planned framework, like the step gable of an Amsterdam canal house. First, Noah receives the order to build the Ark, followed by the announcement of the impending Flood. Food is brought aboard, then comes the command to enter the Ark, and the waiting starts, for two times seven days. Once Noah and his family and all the animals have entered two by two, God closes the door and the rain pours down for 40 days and 40 nights. The whole earth, including the summit of the highest mountain, disappears under water, and remains so for 150 days.

Then the climax arrives: God *remembers* Noah and the animals.

After this turning point, the film starts running backwards. The water recedes for 150 days, the highest mountaintops emerge, the Ark runs aground 'on the mountains of Ararat'. Noah waits 40 days before opening the hatch. Then he releases the dove and the raven, but it is too early; he must wait another two times seven days before receiving the command to leave the Ark. There is food, and God makes a covenant with mankind. As a reader you're back where you started, yet everything has changed.

Despite the grim moral (the sinfulness of man, God's unreasonable cruelty), I was able to enjoy Genesis 6–9. As a story, I found it powerful *and* credible.

Language was no suitable instrument for laying bare the entrails of mystery – a pen was not a scalpel. With writing, however, you could transcend the breadth of human knowledge, as well as the laws of Newton, with the greatest of ease. You could deepen the mystery, or generate awe for it.

The court scribes of Nineveh made full use of that as they converted the life of the legendary King Gilgamesh into heroic verse. Twenty years ago the Epic of Gilgamesh had stunned me with those few strophes in tablet XI which showed that the Flood story pre-dated the Bible. Now that I picked up the epic again, the power of the narrative drew me in immediately. I read of the superman Gilgamesh, King of Uruk, who ravished one woman after another but nevertheless warded off the explicit advances of the fertility goddess Ishtar ('Come, Gilgamesh, be my lover. Do but grant me thy fruit!'). Gilgamesh, who has befriended the wild man Enkidu, is so inconsolable when his beloved companion falls prey to 'the fate of man' that he goes in search of eternal life to avoid the same fate. In the chroniclers' imagination he ventures to the far shores of the Waters of Death to meet the man and woman who were the sole survivors of the Flood, and who have been granted eternal life. But he is unable to share in their secret.

Gilgamesh remains mortal. He reaches out and grasps the hand of the ferryman who has steered him across the Waters of Death: 'Counsel me, O ferryman Urshanabi! For whom have my arms laboured? / For whom has my heart's blood roiled?'

This story was 27 centuries old, and timeless. Gilgamesh the hero possessed universal human traits, and reappeared again and again in the world's literature, including in the guise of the poet Ka.

The shopkeeper in Kars flipped through his *Langenscheidt* and began formulating his opinion.

'Mr Pamuk is . . .' – he turned the dictionary around to face me and held his finger beside the right word – '*layik.*'

I read: *deserving, worthy.*

'Exactly,' he said. 'He is not worthy of anything.'

My hand reached for the glass of tea, but it was still too hot. Orhan Pamuk, as I was aware, had been the reluctant object of the media's attention all summer, because of his comment about the Kurds ('thirty thousand') and Armenians ('one million') murdered in Turkey. According to his accusers, he had thereby committed the crime of 'insulting the Turkish national identity'. Ironically enough, the charges were based on Turkey's new penal code, reformed to allow the country to join the European Union. Hankering after the West, yet spitting in its face at the same time, this was precisely the Turkish schizophrenia that Pamuk had portrayed so often.

'Kars is a modern city,' the shopkeeper said. He explained that the women of Kars walked bareheaded in public, and could not therefore commit suicide for the sake of their headscarves! At the word 'suicide', he made a lassoing movement over the table, which ended in the tightening of an invisible noose (an abrupt yank in thin air).

'But *Snow* is a novel,' I said.

'Just a moment.' The shopkeeper searched for another word, and ended up with *to abuse.* 'Pamuk has abused us.'

Since conversation was flagging, he phoned his nephew, who spoke fluent English. His nephew, it turned out, was driving across town at that moment, but said he could join us briefly.

I had expected a young person, a student from the local teachers' college perhaps, but the man who came in was heavyset and in his forties, the weightlifter type, smelling of aftershave and trailing a crippled old man in his wake.

'Ali Baba,' the nephew said. He saw no reason to tell me his real name.

'He's the owner,' the shopkeeper explained. The crippled man with the pointed grey beard was not introduced.

I repeated my opening questions and asked the nephew what he thought of the book I had just purchased in his shop.

'Rubbish.'

'You've read it?'

'Of course Ali read it. But even before it was written I knew it would be worthless. This Pamuk is no good.'

'But you do sell his books.'

'I'm a businessman. I'm responsible for my staff. But when I am here in the shop, no one dares to buy a book by Pamuk.'

'Ali is a well-known person here in Kars,' the shopkeeper chimed in.

The nephew crossed his arms and let his car keys clatter a few times against the palm of his hand, like castanets. 'Five years ago Pamuk came here to research that book of his. He took a room at Hotel Karabağ, and he stayed there for three weeks. I wanted to go after him. At some point I was called up to say that he was eating in one of my restaurants. I went over there right away.'

The shopkeeper filled his nephew's glass of tea to the brim.

'I said: "I know you!" He said: "But I don't know you."' Ali leaned back and took his guard like a prizefighter. 'My own waiters had to hold me back. I restrained myself and said to him: "Finish your meal and get out."'

He paused for effect, then, concluding his line of reasoning: 'Pamuk is not a Kemalist.'

When no one else said anything, the shopkeeper explained that a Kemalist was a person whose thinking was 'modern and businesslike'.

In other words, I took it, they blamed Turkey's most famous

writer for all manner of things, but not for his notorious comment concerning the murdered Armenians and Kurds.

'Yeah, that too,' the nephew and the shopkeeper said together. Then Ali took over with a disquisition on the First World War. From what I made out, the Russians, when they realised that they would lose to the Turks in eastern Turkey, began passing out weapons to the Armenians. 'Then the Armenians began killing their Turkish neighbours. That was the genocide. But you people outside Turkey believe in the propaganda about genocide the other way round.'

Ali had, he said in a confidential tone of voice, been married for several years to a British woman from Brighton. So he knew how the West thought: the West saw the Turks as a nation of cleaners and madmen out to avenge their honour. A puppet like Pamuk allowed himself to be used shamelessly to reinforce that image. 'But Kars is a modern city,' he said. 'Everyone here is a Kemalist. In the centre of town you won't see anyone with a head-scarf.'

A quote from *Snow* suddenly came into my mind, the words of a young female Islamic activist who snaps at Ka: 'Here [in Kars], rebellion doesn't mean throwing away your headscarf, but wearing it.' I asked whether political Islam played a role here.

'No,' Ali said. 'Even our imams are Kemalists! Look, this is one of them: this man' – the old man looked up in surprise, as though he had missed something (which in fact he had) – 'is both imam and Kemalist. He prays for our family, our whole family and our business.'

I asked Ali to ask the imam whether he had read *Kar*.

'*Evet!*' said the old man, beaming with approval. 'Good book!'

The shopkeeper and his nephew stepped in. They did their best to bring the imam around. Against all odds, I tried to get a word in edgeways: could they please let him finish? By the time they fell silent at last, the imam had understood what was expected of him. He corrected himself and said: 'It's a good book for Kars.'

Pamuk had put the city on the map. The imam said he had seen the statistics: 10 million tourists visited Turkey each year, but only

174

10,000 of those came to Kars. One tenth of one per cent. But since the publication of *Snow* and the commotion surrounding the writer, there had been more. 'For the first time, in the winter too,' the imam said. 'People like you. And that's important, because Kars is poor as dirt.'

The exterior of the Snow Palace Hotel ('one of those elegant Baltic buildings', wrote Pamuk) had absolutely nothing in common with the brutalist concrete of Hotel Karabağ,. There was no archway leading to a courtyard, 'a hundred and ten years old and high enough for horse-drawn carriages to pass through with ease'. But in the foyer and in the restaurant on the first floor I thought I recognised the setting in which Ka and Ipek had circled each other watchfully.

When I gave my room number to the desk clerk, he handed me both my key and a rolled-up note: 'Tomorrow 8 a.m. Kars–D'-bayazit. In my taxi. 100 lira. Okay? Celil.'

Like a detective in a TV series, I flashed the book I was holding at the receptionist and asked: 'Is it true that Orhan Pamuk stayed at this hotel?'

The man wore a high-collared shirt to cover the acne on his neck. He nodded. 'Yes, he had room 210. Directly beneath yours.' He pointed to a niche containing two armchairs. 'He often sat over there, reading the paper while he waited for someone.'

I took a good long look around the foyer. At shoulder height, against the wainscoting, was a plank full of dusty books, but what I was really looking for was the interior of the Snow Palace Hotel. Noticing nothing very special, I walked to the lifts, past a row of clocks showing the time in Tokyo, Bombay, New York and in Kars.

Buzdağ

ALL THE THINGS that had made an impression on me years ago seemed smaller, less conspicuous. The pear tree on the terrace in Grandpa's knacker's yard, the neighbours' aquarium – upon seeing them again, imagination flew out of the window and these things took on their own true proportions. But Ararat was different. The mountain surpassed the image I already had of her.

Never before had I seen Büyük Ağri Daği, the Great Mountain of Pain, in profile – not even in photographs. From the side it had neither the arresting features of the north face (the Armenian-Christian icon) nor those of the south face (the Turkish-Islamic one). Seen from the west like this, the Mother Mountain concealed her child, the Little Mountain of Pain, from view. But here in the crisp morning air at a petrol station on the high plateau of Doğubayazit, I was nonetheless impressed. While Celil filled the tank, I asked myself why that was: was it me – my mood or expectations? Or was it Ararat?

The total absence of other mountains meant she had the landscape all to herself. Her sprawling shape made her look like a fortune-teller who had settled down on the plain with great aplomb. From her waist hung a threadbare pleated skirt of eroded channels. By way of decoration not a single tree, not even the suggestion of low shrubs. Ararat's flanks were equally bare of human construction; the few villages and clusters of nomads' tents (brown for sheep, white for shepherds) lay at the foot of the mountain, at the very edge of the grazeable plain.

The view was too desolate to provoke a state of rapture. Looking up at Ararat from nearby, most other travellers had almost choked on superlatives. In 1952, for example, Fernand Navarra of Bordeaux had seen before him 'a Japanese pastel' that was 'almost unreal, Olympian!' No other mountain, he felt, 'creates a stronger illusion of climbing so close to heaven'. Two and a half centuries earlier, in 1707, the botanist Joseph Pitton de Tournefort – a Frenchman as well, as it happens – had formed a very different impression: 'Ararat is one of the most dismal and unpleasant places on the face of the earth.'

What one saw depended not only on the angle from which one saw it, but apparently also on the individual and on the moment of seeing; that, I realised, would also apply to the insights and experiences I was hoping to gain. But for now, the question was where to begin. I stood there like a field mouse sniffing a chunk of bread, unable to decide where to sink its teeth in.

I made it to Hotel Isfahan, the Lithuanian climbers' meeting point in Doğubayazit, just in the nick of time. Standing in the lobby, her mobile pressed to one ear, Yildiz watched me struggle with my baggage and the hotel door. It took her a moment to recognise me, but then, without skipping a beat, she held up a finger to express two things at once: 'Glad to see you've arrived' and 'Be with you in a moment.'

The tiled floor of what amounted to the hotel lounge was littered with lengths of rope with metal clamps, ice axes, radios, helmets, pitons, hammers and even a pulley with a harness for lifting someone out of a crevasse. This, unmistakably, was the equipment the Lithuanians had used the week before when scaling 5,671-metre Damavand in Iran. Everything now lay about in readiness for an ascent of Ararat by the north-west face. I hadn't forgotten what Yildiz had said in Istanbul ('We'll be roped-up'), but what were the helmets for? And those hammers? In my mind's eye I saw the Lithuanians having to drag me halfway up the Parrot Glacier.

'And . . . ?' Yildiz asked by way of greeting.

I held up my passport like the ace of diamonds.

'You got it!' Yildiz flipped through to the stamped visa.

Türkiye / Turkey
Giriş Vizesi / Entry Visa
Amaç / Purpose:
SportAğriDaği / MountAra.

Yildiz, a good six inches shorter than me, had on an orange head-band decorated with black mountain goats. She could see that I was having reservations about the difficulty of her expedition. 'Ice is easier than loose stones,' she claimed. 'Especially once you're used to wearing crampons.'

Yildiz had to report to the local *jandarma* that afternoon with the list of expedition members. 'It's up to you,' she said. 'If you want to come with us, I'll need your passport after lunch.'

During the hour I had left, time seemed to become compressed. I checked in, lugged my things up the stairs and splashed water on my face. When I came back down, an athletic-looking fellow got up from one of the couches and walked over to me. I thought he was one of the Lithuanians, but he was Austrian.

'Allow me to introduce myself. My name is Martin Hochhauser.' The tall man with close-cropped hair said he had overheard me talking, and assumed that I was planning to go up Ararat. With the calm of the entirely disinterested, he said there was also another expedition in two days' time; I could join it if I liked.

His offer prompted a torrent of questions.

Who was organising the expedition? A Kurd by the name of Mehmet.

Was he going by the southern route? He was indeed.

Who else was in the party? He himself and a group of Slovenians, he thought.

So that wasn't completely certain then, about the Slovenians? They might be Czechs, Martin said, Mehmet hadn't been clear about that. But we could go and see him; he ran a travel agency just down the street.

Doğubayazit, now that I had time to take a look, seemed to consist of only one street worth mentioning, with outlying districts, barracks, storehouses and *hamams* radiating off it. It had rained and the basalt paving stones gleamed as if polished by the shoeshine boys. Most of the hotels, with names like Urartu, Ararat and Nűh, stood on the main street. In front of the shops and restaurants little petrol-driven generators sputtered to life every time there was a power failure. The city was humming, and in that hum one saw bored soldiers lying drowsily on top of their armoured vehicles.

Mehmet – moist doggy eyes and an ill-fitting suit – wrapped his hands around mine as though I were his son, and had us sit down beneath a poster showing the tropical destinations of Turkish Airlines. 'Tea!' he commanded his assistant, who went to the doorway and snapped his fingers a few times to summon a tea-vendor.

Mehmet turned to me. 'German? Friend of Martin?'

I almost nodded both times, but then said that I came from Holland. I slid forward in my chair to avoid courtesies that might slow us down further. 'I have a visa for Ağri Daği,' I said. 'And I would like to use it.'

The fan of wrinkles at the tips of Mehmet's sideburns contracted into a grin, accentuating the touches of grey in his hair. 'Mehmet doesn't care about Turkish stamps,' he said lightheartedly. 'Your friend doesn't have one either, and I told him the same thing I will tell you: Welcome to Free Kurdistan!'

His hospitality struck me like a punch in the face. Had five months of consular suffering been all for naught? I shoved the thought aside, it could do me no good anyway, and accepted an 'all-in' deal for 270 dollars (less than half what I would have paid Yildiz). This included the use of crampons and a one-person tent, my share in the rental of the donkeys, the services of two guides and also transport in the back of a truck to the village of Eli, where the road stopped and the southern route began. Like the Austrian, I had been added to the expedition of a group of friends from Prague who had yet to arrive in Doğubayazit but were already lumbered with two stowaways.

'This may be the last climb of the season,' Mehmet said as he once again warmed my hands in his.

*   *   *

179

After I had cancelled my reservation with Yildiz, who seemed to accept my decision without disappointment, Martin and I went to a restaurant on the main street for lamb chops.

, We had met barely an hour ago. The neatly groomed man opposite me had a square jaw and a slight tan. He could, for example, just as easily have been a dentist. When he dabbed at his lips with his napkin I noticed that he wore watches on both wrists. I couldn't help but ask why.

'This is an altimeter,' Martin said, taking off one of the two and passing it across the table. We were at 1,590 metres above sea level, I noted. 'Maybe a typical aberration for someone who lives in the Alps,' Martin explained, 'but I always wear an altimeter.'

He was from Innsbruck but spent most of his time abroad. As a relief worker for the Roman Catholic charity CARITAS, he was constantly being sent to disaster areas for short periods of time; he had recently been to Sri Lanka, after the tsunami. After that he had set up a drinking-water project for Chechen refugees in southern Russia. Now that project was finished as well, and – pending the next earthquake or volcanic eruption – he had crossed the Caucasus in his home-built Ford Transit camper van to climb Ararat. Pure coincidence had led him into Hotel Isfahan that morning; he had noticed that the TV in the lobby was tuned to CNN, and had stepped in with a cup of coffee in his hand to watch it.

I told him about Yildiz's prediction: that he wouldn't get far without a visa, that the *jandarma* would haul him off the expedition at the first checkpoint.

Martin shrugged. In his experience there was usually a way around things like that. 'I had to pay Mehmet fifty dollars extra, supposedly to arrange my papers. I'm not really worried.'

Both of us were familiar with the mores in Russia, where a bottle of French cognac could bend laws and regulations in your favour. But soldiers in a NATO country, I imagined, would be stricter, more disciplined. Perhaps I was just prejudiced.

Martin's laconic 'We'll see' put a pleasant end to my mulling over probabilities.

I was curious to know what prompted someone who had grown up in the Alps and who worked for a Catholic organisation to climb Ararat, of all mountains. His reply, once again, was disarmingly matter-of-fact: he always climbed close to where disaster had struck, and he had already done the major peaks of the Caucasus – Mount Elbrus and Mount Kazbek.

His uncomplicated outlook contrasted sharply with the abstractions that had brought me here. Natural disasters, Martin felt, were no *Götterdämmerung*. All you could say about them, he believed, was that they created a need for help.

When he asked what brought me here, I – not to sound too woolly – told him at first only the no-nonsense side of my story. How, as a journalist, I had seen Ararat from Yerevan in 1999 and had been keen to climb it ever since. Now that the moment had arrived, I also had a specific mission involving a difference of opinion between two Armenian geologists: I was going to take photographs for them in the Arguri gorge, a place off limits to those of their nationality. My assignment was to document a stretch of loose rock at the bottom of the valley. One of the experts said it was a lahar, which if true would support his claim that Ararat was an active volcano, every bit as dangerous as Mount St Helens. His opponent believed it was the moraine left behind by a glacier that had melted over the course of a few decades, which would make the expanse of loose rock yet another alarming sign of global warming and rising sea levels. 'Of the coming Deluge,' I added.

The irony was not wasted on Martin. 'Can you get there by car?' he asked.

Unfolding the map on the table, I pointed out the semicircular route we would have to trace around Ararat. It wasn't a given that we could get there: the Arguri gorge lay within a crosshatched 'security zone' where no foreigners were allowed.

Martin wasn't the type to be put off. The next morning, we agreed, he would pick me up at Hotel Isfahan.

*   *   *

The interior of Martin's Ford Transit might have looked suspect to Turkish eyes: it had a built-in kitchen, a table and a folding bed. The outside, however, except for its Austrian number plates, was fairly inconspicuous. Most *dolmuş* connections were serviced by exactly this kind of van: white, with a characteristic black cover over the bonnet. Martin had also had one of those protective covers installed; it was the perfect, albeit unintentional, disguise.

At the checkpoint on the roundabout outside Doğubayazit we were waved straight through. The roadblock close to the garrison town of Karabulak, where all traffic was brought to a halt, was no trouble either. One soldier opened the van's sliding door and rummaged around a bit in the kitchen cupboards, while another examined the car's registration. He jotted down the licence number and checked the picture on the driver's licence against the face in front of him. 'Where will your journey take you?' he asked.

'Austria, ultimately,' Martin said, and that was sufficient: the soldier handed back the papers, and tapped a finger against the brim of his cap in farewell.

The asphalt climbed all the way to the Korhan Plateau, a marshy-looking pastureland and the start of the north-western route. High upon the mountain's flanks I had thought we might catch a glimpse of Yildiz's hired donkeys, trailing a ribbon of Lithuanians. But we didn't see a soul, not even a shepherd. Sooner than expected we reached the Korhan Pass, which the map said was 2,110 metres above sea level (Martin's altimeter said 2,101). We had hoped for vistas stretching far into Armenia, but first we mounted another ridge, this one dotted with bunkers and machine-gun nests. Through Martin's binoculars I could also see armoured vehicles lined up behind U-shaped tank walls. Ararat might have been a holy mountain, but she was also a colossal NATO stronghold.

On the far side of the ridge, Route 975 fell in a tangle of curves down to the River Arax; its fertile valley, shared by Turkey and Armenia, was spread out below us now. From these heights you could read the landscape like a land-use map in an atlas. The dark-green squares were orchards, the light-green patches probably market gardens, and everything in grey and yellow lay outside the irrigation system. The Arax's course divided the greenery like the vein of a leaf.

So lush as the valley looked, so stony and dead were the slopes of Ararat. Despite the femininity ascribed her, she had been known since ancient times for her barrenness. Nowhere did the mountain give up water; inside her, they said, lived 'thirsty dragons with tongues of fire'. As early as the fifth century, the chronicler Movses Chorenatsi, the 'Armenian Herodotus', had recorded local laments about Ararat's harshness: 'If you go hunting upon noble Masis, the spirits will seize you and drag you into the caverns.'

No brooks found their source on Ararat, making her unsuitable for permanent habitation. The only exception was the spring in the Arguri gorge which, until they were killed in the catastrophe of July 1840, had supplied the monks of St Hagob's monastery and the villagers with water. The first scientist who arrived – in 1843 – to investigate the disaster, a mineralogist called Moritz Wagner, attached great significance to the chronic water shortage on Ararat. Everywhere but in the Arguri gorge, all meltwater and rainwater was immediately sucked down into porous rock, causing Wagner to surmise that the mountain contained caverns and underground rivers. Water seeping down must have penetrated the magma chambers of Ararat. Contact between that water and the molten stone (the legendary 'tongues of fire') had caused the volcanic eruption which destroyed Arguri and the monastery.

Two years later, in 1845, Professor Dr Hermann Abich – colleague and friend of the recently deceased Friedrich Parrot – appeared on the scene. As professor at the University at Dorpat he was an authority on Earth sciences. Abich mapped Ararat. In homage to his former rector he named the largest of its glaciers after Parrot, and a smaller one after himself. In the Arguri gorge, he confirmed the existence of caverns exuding sulphurous fumes. His final conclusion, however, was that the monks and villagers of Arguri lay buried beneath a 'normal' landslide, prompted by an earthquake. He spoke of a '*Bergsturz*', a collapse of one of Ararat's slopes; that was the catastrophe, and it had nothing to do with active volcanism. For the next 150 years Abich's explanation held sway, until in 2002 Arkadi Karachanian breathed new life into Wagner's original theory.

In the course of the twentieth century, a Kurdish-Muslim settlement had grown up on the dry layer of packed mud covering the Armenian-Christian village of Arguri. Our map said that that settlement's name was Yenidoğan, and we were on our way there.

We followed the south bank of the Arax through fields of tomato and aubergine. The winding road was busy with tractors pulling trailers full of fruit and vegetables. We had to slalom around them as we passed. Here and there between the poplar hedges a watchtower loomed behind the spiky fence supporting arc lamps every few metres.

It took some getting used to the idea that, not long ago, I had been on the other side. Fifteen kilometres at most from here, yet as unreachable as a different planet, lay the monastery of Echmiadzin. No further than that, in Yerevan's late-Stalinist faculty building, Arkadi was working away at his scientific articles. Between us stood a barrier, trimmed with light-green paint, from which all *dolmuş* or *marshrutki* lines rebounded like a billiard ball. Two worlds ground against each other here, not only on the surface (sealed borders and military muscle) but also deep below it (where the Eurasian and Arabian continental plates scraped together).

Along this route, running parallel to the remaining vestiges of the Iron Curtain, there were more roadblocks than anywhere else. But our van was allowed through, even when we turned on to the gravel road to Yenidoğan just opposite an army base. I looked over my shoulder to see if the *jandarma* might be in pursuit after all, but all I saw was a huge cloud of dust. 'Look at that!' Martin said, pointing ahead. Great Ararat was framed by the windscreen like a portrait. At its centre was the funnel of the Arguri gorge, the only indentation deep enough to cast shadows. All the way up at the top flamed a horizontal transparent plume: a trail of powder snow being whipped along by stormy winds at 5,000 metres.

The Ford Transit growled up the slope, and the higher we went the more exhilarated I became. All my senses sharpened. To the left, above the gorge, I could pick out the triangular outcrop that Ark-seekers called 'Angel Rock'. In the 1980s Jim Irwin had climbed as far as that formation, taking it for the petrified prow of the Ark.

Today, though, I only had to worry about Ararat's geology, not its mythology, and that was a relief. The pictures I would take would contribute to research, and might even appear in the *Journal of Volcanology and Geothermal Research*. Scientific texts, it seemed to me now, were worth perhaps even more than legends; they neither manipulated reality nor tried to skirt it. That is to say: I could suddenly think of nothing else to look for on Ararat – except something as tangible as the origins of a stretch of loose rock at the bottom of a gorge. Lahar or moraine – the morphology of the valley floor could provide an important clue. In an Amsterdam bar before my departure, Salle Kroonenberg had told me what to look for. Pushing together two tables, my former geology professor had traced out several possible cross-sections of the rubble, next to the carafe of wine.

'A lahar,' his private lecture began, 'is by definition volcanic.' The word itself was Malaysian, but only gained currency among volcanologists after Merapi erupted in Indonesia. Lahars were created when water came into contact with magma, resulting in an explosive reaction and the formation of glass particles, which could cause an eruption. Lahars were sometimes glowing hot.

Salle let his reading glasses dangle from the cord around his turtleneck. 'Are there hot springs in the area?'

Not that I knew of.

I needed to find out. He also recommended that I pay attention to the receding snowline, and the speed at which that was happening. You could tell by the abrasion trails left by melting glaciers; he had seen striking examples in the Caucasus, where in recent years an enormous glacier had released the corpses of

Wehrmacht soldiers who had fallen into crevasses there during World War II.

I was surprised to hear him broach the subject. If there was one academic authority who denied that global warming was taking on catastrophic proportions, it was Salle. Professor Kroonenberg publicly proclaimed that the greenhouse effect was not a major problem; in fact, he had put his scientific reputation on the line with that very view. In his lectures and in his book, he sought to demonstrate that the rise in the Earth's average temperature easily fell within the range of natural fluctuations. In the longer term, increased emissions of gases such as carbon dioxide and methane – the human influence, in other words – would prove negligible. Salle had put himself forward as a non-defeatist and repudiator of the prophets of doom. Those who nevertheless went on believing that the Earth was headed for a man-made catastrophe were just short-sighted. In the manuscript he had asked me to read, he had explained that defect thus: 'Man instinctively avoids peering into the abysmal pit of geological time.'

When I read that, I thought: yes, in the same way he recoils from his deepest reflections.

But Salle was talking about something different. He first had his readers take a number of steps backwards, like a painter at work on a huge canvas. Only then could you develop an eye for vast cyclical changes like the coming and going of the ice ages. If you relinquished the human scale and applied nature's own yardstick, you could see that the current rise in sea levels was nothing special. I confronted him with the 'yes but' question that that raised: 'Yes, but what good is that to coming generations?' Salle listened patiently to my objections, then parried them by saying that what he was talking about was precisely *not* the span of a few generations.

His way of looking at things in units of millions of years made, at first glance, one's own existence shrivel into meaninglessness. Man was nothing but a mayfly, and even the collective fury of all humanity couldn't cause a measurable ripple in the cosmic pond. Perhaps, in the face of an impending meteorite impact, mankind would succeed in tucking away the seed of life on earth in cryogenic gene banks far below the surface of Spitsbergen, or aboard a frozen Ark on the moon – the way NASA was considering doing. But to what end?

Maybe humans would actually succeed in destroying all life on earth, but even then: who would mourn for it?

If you expected more from life, you might consider such thoughts shocking or unbearable. Staring into a bottomless, echoless pit did produce a dizzying sense of futility, but it also had something heroic about it: there you stood, in spite of it all – in the face of that overwhelming cosmos. That I could focus my puny thoughts on this, and allow those thoughts to elaborate endlessly, that was my safety net.

The 'stratospheric' perspective was something Salle had turned into his trademark. Peering over the edge of workaday reality, he said, gave us new insights. Into the story of the universal Deluge as well.

In his own fashion (and with his own theory), Salle had waded into the geologists' debate about the Flood which two American oceanographers had resurrected 10 years earlier. In a 1996 BBC documentary, *Noah's Flood*, William Ryan and Walter Pitman had made yet another attempt to bridge the gap between the Bible and natural science, and at precisely the same point – the dogma of the Flood – where geology and theology had parted ways back in the nineteenth century. The basis of their Deluge theory lay in the discovery that the Bosporus must have been formed abruptly around 5600 BC. Close to where modern-day Istanbul lay, a roiling flood of the Sea of Marmara had once cut its way like a dam-burst through the lower-lying hinterland. Ryan and Pitman calculated for their viewers that the saltwater that came pouring in to fill the Black Sea was roughly equal to 200 Niagaras. This deluge, they said, which probably destroyed all settlements around the Black Sea, was the same horrible flood spoken of in the Epic of Gilgamesh, the Bible, the Quran and Ovid's *Metamorphoses*.

NŬH WAS A TURK, crowed Istanbul's *Cumhuriyet*.

'A nice try, but not true,' was Salle Kroonenberg's verdict. He

187

pointed to new studies that debunked the Bosporus theory: the gap had been formed less abruptly, and with less Niagaran violence.

George Smith's explanation, I told him, still seemed the most logical to me: that the Tigris and the Euphrates had burst their banks at the same time, resulting in the legendary Flood. In fact I couldn't imagine looking for the birth of the Flood story anywhere other than in the swamps of southern Iraq, on the Persian Gulf.

But Salle could. In searching for an explanation for the Flood, he felt, one also needed to take a broader view. In doing that you saw that the inhabitants of various continents had Flood legends of their own: the Baltic peoples, the Celts, Indian tribes from Alaska to Tierra del Fuego (when you interpreted the idea more freely, the total was actually in the hundreds), and most of those could not be traced to southern Iraq.

'So you believe in a universal Deluge,' I said.

'Not per se, but there may be a more general, more global explanation for all those Flood stories.' The only credible candidate was this: the melting of the continental ice masses at the end of the last ice age, 10,000 years ago, with the accompanying rise in sea level of more than 100 metres.

I topped up our glasses.

'I admit,' Salle said, 'that there are also problems with this theory. But anyone who goes looking for the answer on Ararat has missed the point completely; they've let themselves be strung along by a missionary's fable.'

It was haymaking time. The final cut of the season had been raked together and was being baled by boys in baggy shirts. Over-full lorries, their cabs barely visible, came weaving in our direction. The heavy scent of grass seed wafted through the windows of the Ford Transit. It was impossible to miss: the fields of Yenidoğan were spread out like a fan at the foot of the gorge, which meant we were now on the fertile layer of mud that had engulfed Arguri and its villagers in July 1840.

Scattered across the fields were boulders, like gravestones in

an abandoned cemetery. I thought about these stones being cata-
pulted out of Ararat's crater ('ballistic ejecta'), realising at the same
time that they could just as well have been brought down by an
avalanche.

Climbing out to take photographs, I noticed a grey thicket of
assorted aerials on the slope above us. Martin pulled his binoculars from the glove compartment and identified the slender metal
saplings as a NATO listening post. 'Our conversation is probably
already on tape,' he said.

This did not feel like the moment for dawdling, so I suggested
we drive on. The children of Yenidoğan came racing up like a pack
of dogs and ran along beside the van for a while. We passed houses
of stone and concrete, some with plastered walls, all of them with
water tanks on their flat roofs. There were eucalyptus trees, and a
stork's nest on a metal rim atop a pole. On a miniature square of
compacted earth stood the village mosque, crowned with a minaret
that resembled a fez.

The highest house in Yenidoğan lay at the point where the funnel
narrowed; from here the road shrank to a set of tracks and climbed
westward, out of the valley, around two or three hairpin bends. We
wanted to go deeper into the Arguri gorge, however, so we parked
the Ford Transit and walked upstream along a burbling irrigation
canal. We had spoken to no one, and no one had stopped us to ask
what we were doing.

For the first 15 minutes we crossed old farming terraces in various
stages of collapse, bordered with rose bushes. Grasshoppers jumped
up at us, sometimes as high as our waists. It felt as though Salle
Kroonenberg was looking over my shoulder at every step. He took
his advisory role in my fieldwork so seriously that when I arrived in
Doğubayazit he was still emailing me images from Google Earth,
which I had printed out between power failures at Mehmet's travel
agency. The satellite image in my pocket showed that the
lahar/moraine came to a point about three kilometres above the
patchwork of fields around Yenidoğan.

The path grew steeper and looser, until at last we reached a large
polished rock blocking the valley. On a strip of grass at its base a

189

few sheep huddled together as though they had something to discuss. A low wall shored up the run-off for the irrigation canal. On the other side of the wet, glistening rock, all agrarian meddling came to an end. It didn't take long to figure out why: the scree-strewn slopes on both sides of the boulder were highly unstable. The tongue of loose rock couldn't be far now, a kilometre at most, but every 60 seconds or so we were startled by a loud rattling noise that came and went in waves. Sometimes we could see the trails of dust that the stones left as they rolled and slid; sometimes we couldn't. Martin's altimeter read 2,446 metres. As an experienced mountaineer, he knew it would be madness to continue along the floor of the gorge; we began zigzagging our way up the western slope. Half an hour later, panting heavily, we were standing on a windy ridge: 2,704 metres.

Behind us (or actually, below us) we could now see the full length of Arguri gorge, and along its floor the stretch of loose rock that ended in a semicircular cone. Further away and higher up we also saw the drab, icy nose of the Abich Glacier. I took a few photos, both with a wide-angle lens for the location and form, and with a 120mm lens for the texture. The lahar/moraine, crumbly as a molehill, looked bare and weathered.

We moved up further along the ridge, looking for a stable slope that would allow us to descend into the gorge again. But wherever we tried, the wall was only loose stone, or else simply too steep. Just after noon, when clouds began gathering along the snowline and hid the Abich Glacier from view, I saw our chances dwindling. I took a few more pictures, realising that this was it: I would not get any closer. The wind whipped at our trouser legs, and, looking down, I thought about the stone altar on which Noah had made his sacrifice – if it existed at all, it was down there with the bulldozed walls of St Hagob's monastery, buried beneath metres of rubble.

Turning away from the Arguri gorge, we took another route back, down a slope crisscrossed by goat trails. From under the awning of cloud rolling from Ararat's summit we looked out across a vast expanse of Armenia, flowing towards the horizon like a mirage. It was like standing on the rafters of a stadium. In the arena below we could make out the sunlight reflecting off Yerevan's tallest buildings. With the naked eye you could make out the split obelisk of the genocide monument, the statue of Mother Armenia on a hillside opposite and the airport's miniature volcano. Further to the west, at the foot of a Mount Aragats now free of snow, I also picked out the four stately cooling towers of Armenia's only nuclear power station.

About to start our final descent, we were at last called to a halt. Two dogs began barking. One looked like a cross between a bulldog and a black Belgian shepherd. The other – a dingy yellow dog, skinnier but more furious – came racing towards us.

Martin picked up a rock. 'Just keep walking,' he said. 'You can always keep a dog at bay, unless it's got rabies.'

I couldn't decide whether that was any comfort. Before we could be submitted to the rabies test, however, a group of shepherd boys appeared, then a man who shouted a command that brought the greyish-yellow dog to a standstill with its head between its paws. We raised our hands in greeting (also interpretable as a sign of surrender). Coming closer we saw a summer encampment of Kurdish shepherd families, tucked away in a green hollow. Without much preamble, we were led to a spot out of the wind, beside a clay oven. The entire family of a man in high boots, who was introduced to us as Süleyman, came out to meet us. Rugs were spread on the ground, the girls and women all went to work preparing food. From a tent supported by a dozen long poles came a steady flow of platters and trays of yogurt, raisins, dried apricots and sweetened tea. The loaves were still warm, fresh from the oven: a drum-shaped hole in the ground with dried cow dung smouldering at the bottom. Two kneeling women were rolling out slabs of dough, which they pressed against the sides of the hole and pulled out again once they were crispy and brown.

'Eat, eat!' The men sat down and began tearing off chunks of bread, which they dipped in the yogurt. The ensuing attempt at communication dealt first with the quality of the meal, then with the children and the animals.

English, German, Turkish – a handful of words in each language, that was all we had.

Someone from the group had spotted a white Ford Transit. We nodded: yes, that was ours.

His coat draped over his shoulders like a cape, Süleyman asked a young man to explain to us that, had we driven further, we would have arrived at his encampment. On a sheet of paper torn from my notebook, someone drew a little map that showed a series of hairpin curves between Yenidoğan and Süleyman's tents. I put an X at the spot where we had parked the camper, and drew a picture of a hairpin. For some strange reason I then embarked on a clumsy explanation of how such bends in the road were called 'hairpins'. To the women's delight I pointed to the pins in the hair of a little girl who was hovering around me. No one had any idea what this was all about until the fellow who had made the map came up with the bright idea of drawing a horseshoe beside my hairpin. Speaking in Kurdish, he said something that could only have meant: 'We call it a horseshoe bend.'

A young woman in a headscarf brought over two cans of Cola Turka and laid them demurely on the rug in front of us. I had the awkward feeling that we needed to offer something in return, but what? My rucksack contained only a camera, a tube of factor 40 sunscreen, a raincoat and a few writing implements. I found my little box of spare pens, twelve in all, exactly enough for each of Süleyman's children. Then I asked the patriarch whether he would mind if I took a few pictures. With a broad sweep of his arms he let me know that I was free to photograph anyone and anything. The result was a tour of the encampment, past the hearth, the sheepfold, the piles of sun-dried cow dung, the animals' watering trough. The shepherds had a tractor, and a water tank on wheels. Surprised at so much modernity, I patted the plastic tank approvingly. The men nodded and gestured enthusiastically, to show that I had understood well indeed: someone had gone to Yenidoğan for water earlier in the day, and on the way back they had passed our van.

The conversation, if one could call it that, turned to water and the lack of it. The stream in the Arguri gorge, we were told, sometimes dried up. But: there had also once been a second source. We were dragged along to where that water had been stored, but maybe we hadn't understood correctly – instead of a reservoir, they showed us a clay shed rather like a silo.

'*Buz*,' someone tried. This was where *buz* was kept. 'Turkish: *buz*.'

'*Eis!*' Martin said. He was the first to realise that this shed was an abandoned icehouse.

Our next question was where the ice came from. Martin pointed up the mountain, but the shepherds pointed downhill, into the Arguri gorge. I pulled out my notebook again and the valley's contours were sketched on a fresh sheet of paper. The same draughtsman who had made the earlier map now drew lines showing the irrigation canal, the run-off below the big rock, and further up, unmistakably, the cone-shaped extremity of the lahar/moraine. '*Buzdağ*,' he wrote next to it. An iceberg!

But what did that mean? Was the lahar/moraine made of ice? All I could think was that the Abich Glacier must have reached all the way down to that point, albeit buried beneath the rubble. The stretch of loose rock would then be neither lahar nor moraine, and both theories would fall to pieces.

The sketch, however, wasn't finished yet; a figure was added, something like those on signs saying 'men at work': a little man chipping away at the cone of rubble. The chunks he produced were shaded in with fast, self-conscious strokes of the pen. '*Buz*. Ice,' was the explanation. The story had taken an unexpected turn; this was clearly not about a solid mass of ice, but about loose chunks. At first I had a hard time believing that the ice was really dug out like this, but there were no two ways about it. The men gave us a detailed report, spreading their arms to indicate blocks of ice the size of a tractor or even bigger. These chunks of glacier had been extracted from an ice quarry. Exit moraine theory, I thought. The Abich Glacier must have been blown to pieces from below by a spectacular act of nature: the violent eruption of Ararat. In 1840, a lahar of mud and volcanic ash, mixed with ice, had been vomited out over a length of four kilometres – that had to be it.

The blocks of ice were split into pieces at the quarry, the men went on, and dragged to the icehouse by horses.

'But not any more?' I concluded, pointing at the water tank. My initial thought had been that progress, in the form of mechanised horsepower, had rendered the ice transports obsolete. But apparently I was wrong: we weren't there yet, we had understood only half the story. The blocks of ice had grown smaller and smaller with each passing year, and had finally melted away altogether. These days you could dig and dig, but the *buzdağ*, the men gestured, was depleted.

I breathed in the dry, pure mountain air like a smoker filling his lungs. In a roundabout way, the lahar also contained a clue to the coming rise in sea levels. Perhaps I had overlooked something, perhaps I was still off the mark, but at that moment, amid the tents of the Kurdish shepherd Süleyman, I thought I had worked out at least one tiny aspect of Ararat's geology.

After returning to the carpets beside the clay oven, to our dismay even more platters arrived: this time heaped high with rice and boiled leg of lamb. Süleyman cut off the fattiest pieces and passed them to us on the tip of his knife.

Questions and comments were directed at us between mouthfuls, insinuating that we were interested in more than just water. We were Ark-seekers ('Nûh' was the key word here); there was no need to pretend.

How could I explain that I was not after the Ark at all, but searching for Ark-seekers? The nuance was too subtle, and even if I had been able to find the right words I feared I would have been tarred with the same brush.

So Ark-seekers was what we were, and hence tragic figures. To his audience's great delight, the mapmaker tried to convince us that we were looking in the wrong place. We shouldn't be here on Ağri Daği, but at Cudi Dağ.

He was about to draw another map, but there was no need; I knew where Cudi was.

Amid loud laughter, the men slapped us on the shoulders. The general drift was: what difference did it make that we were hundreds of kilometres off course? Anyone can make a mistake.

You shall have a son

THE PHRASE LOOKED like it had been chiselled into my baptism certificate. 'And his name shall be on their foreheads.'

The drawer from which my parents had fished it out also contained my and my sister's swimming and road-safety diplomas. I had asked my mother to send it and she had, by registered post.

Carefully, with clean hands, I removed the certificate from its envelope. I couldn't remember ever having seen it before. On the front was a dove with its wings spread, an austere-looking cross and a rolling wave bearing up the fish that symbolised Jesus Christ. The card folded open like a restaurant menu.

> Holy Baptism has been administered to: *Frank Martin*
> *Westerman* [handwritten, in fountain pen]
> On Sunday: *24 January 1965*
> By: *Rev. Dr T. Alkema*
> In the Reformed Church at: *Emmen*
> Bible text: *Isaiah 43:1–2*

My first impression: a relic from an era of which I had experienced only the tail end. No one I knew of my generation had their children baptised.

Still, I didn't want my baptism certificate to remain at my parents' house. My mother would have liked to keep it herself, she was convinced that one day my being baptised would save me, if not in this world then certainly in the next. But she sent off the certificate nonetheless, without a murmur, along with the order of service from that Sunday morning. When I called that evening to thank her, she told me about a farewell service that had been organised for one of the ministers; for the occasion, a gangplank had been built in front of the church door. The congregation of the Advent Church was invited to enter two by two, and the children from the special service came dressed as butterflies, ladybirds and snails, also in pairs.

'Why didn't anyone come as a fish?' the pastor had asked from the pulpit.

All that still went on. But I no longer felt His name on my forehead. Still, I experienced a certain trepidation as I turned to Isaiah 43:1–2.

> I have called thee by thy name; thou art mine.
> When thou passest through the waters, I will be with thee;
> And through the rivers, they shall not overflow thee.

A direct hit. My brain had to work hard to keep me from tumbling head over heels into believing in Providence. That the River Ill had not overflowed me really *was* nothing but a coincidence. My rational mind reassured me that Isaiah 43:1–2 was often used at baptisms. And that not every child so baptised was also saved from a river. Or, looking at it another way, that most of those lost on the *Titanic* had probably been baptised too. As I packed my documents for Ararat, I laid my baptism certificate aside; there was no need to take it with me.

Walking down into Yenidoğan, Martin and I spotted two men sitting on a low wall close to the Ford Transit. Real, authentic Ark-seekers, no mistake about it.

'They've just come down from the gorge too,' I told Martin. Mehmet had mentioned something about a handful of American Ark-seekers and a group of Taiwanese Baptists wandering around on the mountain.

Drawing closer we saw that their hair was not blond, but grey. They didn't look Asian either. These had to be the Americans, iron-willed evangelists who came to Ararat every year to explore it as they saw fit. Fellows with names like Bill and Dick and John, retired schoolteachers; never women.

They welcomed us with a wave and an inarticulate, accent-mangled 'God bless you.'

I knew then that despite their plaid lumberjack shirts, these men could not be Americans. Their accent sounded familiar, so I tried greeting them in Russian. And asked whether they needed a lift.

The older of the two, the one sporting a patriarchal beard, replied in Russian: 'You have been sent by God.'

We had found Ark-seekers who had grown up in the land of scientific atheism. Russians. Ninety years ago their countrymen had taken the lead in searching for the Ark on Ararat, but had been forced to surrender that head-start to the Americans. Now they were back.

'Last night I prayed hard,' said the bearded man, whose name was Igor. 'God heard my prayers.'

Martin made room for the two wiry men in his kitchen, where they had to sit on their rucksacks. It was around five in the evening and the languid heat of the day had gone. Twisted around in my seat, half leaning over the backrest, I acted as interpreter and questioner.

Igor, it turned out, was a monk from the Danilovsky monastery in Moscow. His companion, a pug-faced 60-year-old by the name of Volodya, was his guide and escort. Except for their dirty clothes and blue eyes, they had little in common.

I told him I had lived near Danilovsky for five years.

'Where exactly?' Igor asked.

'Close to Proletarskaya metro station,' I said, 'on the purple line.'

Surrounded by the screeches and cheers of the village children, we turned the van around and headed out of Yenidoğan.

'Our monastery is close to Tulskaya, on the grey line,' the monk said.

To meet like this, I remarked, was quite a coincidence; Igor's eyes flashed as he said, almost reprovingly: 'There is no such thing as coincidence, young man.'

197

My laughter was polite, and perhaps a little pitying. I still couldn't quite believe it: Russians on Ararat. I felt more of an affinity with Russians than with Americans. Nostalgia may have been clouding my judgement. There seemed to be a kind of kinship between us, if only because of the metro stations; these were the beacons by which all Muscovites sought direction.

Volodya, the guide, had been holding a plastic bottle between his knees. Now he handed it to us. 'Take some, this is water from the Arguri gorge.'

'Holy water,' Igor said.

They had tapped it from the only spring on Ararat and were, as it turned out, well informed about the gorge's geography. In a leather pouch around his neck Volodya kept an old Russian map that actually showed the former location of St Hagob's monastery, marked with a cross.

For five days, accepting the danger of an avalanche as part of the bargain, they had camped in what was more or less the windpipe of the Arguri valley. And this was their third consecutive year.

I asked whether they had a *propoosk*, a climbing or perhaps an archaeological visa.

'A visa? Us?' Volodya pointed to the worn toes of their boots, the tattered straps of their rucksacks; no one was interested in a couple of down-and-outs. They had never been arrested, things like that only happened to Americans. 'Last year there was that man with his television camera . . . what was his name again?' he asked, tugging on Igor's sleeve. The monk said he thought it was Ron or Roy or something. According to Volodya, Americans had to empty their pockets each year to buy their way free.

'But not you, of course, Igor,' he said. 'Even the Turks know there's no use fleecing a Russian monk.'

'I pay for this trip with donations from believers,' Igor said solemnly, as if to lend a certain dignity to his apparent mendicancy. 'God will reward their generosity.'

Reaching the main road along the Arax, we turned west. Martin and I flipped down our sunshades at the same time; we were heading

198

directly towards the same spot on the horizon as the low-hanging sun. 'Where do they have to go, anyway?' Martin asked.

The Ark-seekers said they hoped to be at Camp Murat, just outside Doğubayazit, before sunset.

This too at first seemed a one-in-a-million chance: that was where Martin kept his camper van parked. But in fact Murat's apricot orchard, tucked up against the walls of the seventeenth-century palace of Isak Pasha, was the most obvious destination. The level stretch of land served as base camp to most low-budget Ararat expeditions – and Restaurant Murat next door, as Martin had told me, occasionally featured a belly-dancer.

As soon as the loud clatter of the gravel road had died down, I asked Igor whether he had been a believer during the anti-religious Soviet period.

The monk stroked his beard the way a public speaker buttons his jacket, then told us that he had believed in Communism until 1970. As a boy of 13, he too had wept inconsolably at the passing of Comrade Stalin. As soon as he entered vocational school he had signed up with the Komsomol youth brigades. 'I worked as a volunteer in Novokuznetsk, in Siberia,' he told us, clutching the edge of the sink to stay upright around the bends. 'Back then, Novokuznetsk was called Stalinsk. They had already built a steel mill there. We put in a rolling mill right next to it.'

I assumed that he had not been baptised as a child, but I was wrong. In 1942, when Stalin gave free rein to the Russian Orthodox Church during the Great Patriotic War, Igor's mother took him to a cleric around the corner – close to Baumanskaya station. They had never discussed religion at home, Igor said. 'But when I was thirty I went back to that church. I knelt down there for the first time, and that changed my life.'

Precisely how his conversion had happened he didn't say, but Igor had never shaved since that day, and in the mid-1980s he had entered the Danilovsky monastery.

That monastery, I knew, was the seat of the Orthodox patriarchate, and it occurred to me that he might be looking for Noah's Ark as a kind of emissary of the Russian Church. With a slow nod,

Igor confirmed my hunch: he was conducting this work with the blessings of His Holiness.

As a clergyman, he told me, he had immersed himself in those same ancient traditions with which the Bolsheviks had broken so violently in 1917. One was the search for Noah's Ark, which had reached its climax in the summer of that year with the expedition ordained by Czar Nicholas II. A hundred and fifty royal engineers had found the Ark, partially submerged beneath the ice of a crater lake, and had entered it.

'Not all one hundred and fifty of them,' Volodya interrupted.

'Oh, yes . . .'

'A big group like that would never have climbed so high, my friend. They were engineers, they would have set up a base camp. A few of them must have gone on from there.'

But Igor insisted that, 'with God's help', all 150 of them had entered the Ark. The wooden colossus had three decks and was shaped like a box, just as Genesis said. The only thing was that their report never reached St Petersburg. In the months since their departure, the Czar had been deposed and banished with his family to the Urals, pending their execution. The Ark dossier had fallen into the hands of Trotsky, who had destroyed it as counter-revolutionary material.

Volodya nodded, adding that Trotsky also had all the eyewitnesses rounded up and shot.

One day, Igor told us, he had gone to the patriarch with an important question: 'Your Reverence, what is the Church's view on the search for Noah's Ark?'

The patriarch had explained that the Ark was one of Christianity's most important and as yet unrevealed mysteries. He gave his blessing to Igor's search, but also warned him that the moment at which the Ark would be revealed would be chosen not by man, but by God.

I asked Volodya, who was clearly of a worldlier bent than Igor, whether he embraced those same ideals.

'Me? I'm the secretary-general,' he said with more than a touch of theatricality. By way of proof he handed me his business card, which announced that he, Vladimir Shatyev, was secretary-general of the Russian Federation of Alpinists.

'That is a state institution. I'm a civil servant, paid to set mountaineering records.'

As it turned out, he had climbed Everest without oxygen, and
conquered Alaska's icy Mount McKinley on skis. He had scaled
six of the Seven Summits (each one the highest on its continent)
so popular – for want of any other significant challenge – among
alpinists in recent years. The only one missing from his list was
the highest peak in Antarctica, and that would remain missing
'because an expedition down there costs thirty thousand dollars per
person'.

I was curious whether he was still on active duty; in other words,
whether the Russian state was funding this Ark expedition. Volodya
looked glum: his federation hadn't received a single kopek in years,
his only 'sponsor' was sitting beside him. He also said with great
earnestness that he was relieved to have found in Ararat a new challenge. He too had turned his back on the Soviet delusion and joined
the ranks of the 'post-atheists'. One day God would reveal the Ark,
and the scales would fall from the eyes of an unbelieving mankind.
Volodya considered it a fine and humble privilege to be allowed to
do the footwork to that end.

The first stars were appearing in the eastern sky as the two Russians
rolled out their little tent in the orchard at Camp Murat. Martin
and I helped them with the pegs and poles and invited them for a
meal in the neighbouring restaurant, now decked out with lanterns
and disco lights. Half an hour later they appeared at our table, Igor
with his beard combed, Volodya holding a plump bottle of cognac
branded ноев ковчег (Noah's Ark) – Georgian stuff which, the label
indicated, was distilled exclusively for the insatiable Russian alcohol
market.

We toasted our meeting, we toasted Ararat, and when the bald
manager of Camp Murat sat down at our table, we toasted friend-
ship between the world's peoples as well. There could be no mistake
about it: this Hakan was the one running the show. In his jeans
and a bright Hugo Boss shirt unbuttoned almost to the navel, he

made his waiters fairly gallop back and forth between customers. When we came in I had assumed he must be Murat, of Camp-Restaurant Murat; Martin, however, knew that this designer-clotheshorse was in fact a brother of Murat, who was currently in prison for murder. Hakan joined in on two of our toasts, then turned to Martin and me and demanded to know what the hell we had been doing up in the Arguri gorge.

Somehow Hakan knew that we had been in Yenidoğan. He considered it not only an insult but also an act of stupidity that Martin had not told him where he was going that morning. We had walked straight into a military trap. The commander of the army post at Yenidoğan had called him that afternoon to ask – and at this point Hakan acted out the telephone conversation – 'Listen, I've got two foreigners here in a Ford Transit with Austrian plates, do they belong with you?'

Hakan took an olive from the plate. 'What was I supposed to tell him?' he said between chews. 'I told him: "Yeah, they're mine, and they're coming back today because tomorrow they're going up Ararat with me."'

I did my best to follow his train of thought. It seemed rather unlikely that Hakan would be taking a group up Ararat tomorrow. And even if he did, why would he bother to cover for us?

'We have a deal with Mehmet,' I ventured.

'With Mehmet?' The campsite manager pretended to be offended. 'Mehmet is nobody. He takes care of my travel agency in town.'

When Hakan moved off to another table, the Russians shared the final drops of Noah's Ark. 'To the Ark!' Volodya said.

I heard myself joining in the toast.

The cognac was good, but its oily aftertaste called for a water chaser.

Martin poked me. 'So did they say whether they're about to find the Ark?'

Of all the things you could conceivably ask an Ark-seeker, that was the most obvious. There would be no reason to beat around the bush; as soon as someone told you he was looking for Noah's

Ark, all you had to say was 'And?' Yet it simply hadn't occurred to me to ask how the quest was going. At Martin's insistence, however, I did. But instead of listening to their reply, I racked my brains about why I had 'forgotten' this before.

Across the table Igor was waving his hands to show how the clouds had parted late one afternoon to reveal a rectangular white object standing out against the rock.

I didn't want to hear about it; in fact, I couldn't stand to hear him go on about it.

'Until now, everyone has been looking for a black object against a white background, but what we saw was white against black.'

I tried to close my ears, for what was coming next was the standard, inevitable excuse about how they hadn't been able to reach it / how the fog had rolled in again / how the pictures were too blurred. I didn't want to hear Igor say that. Why not? Because I liked him. And Volodya too. I didn't want these two men to make fools of themselves in front of Martin and me.

That was it, for starters. But if I was honest I had to admit that there was something else: a sense of understanding I would have preferred not to feel. Igor and Volodya were Ark-seekers, a group I had begun to regard rather sneeringly. Except that until now I had always placed the emphasis on the prefix 'Ark', something that was impossible to find, that had probably never existed and that stood, as far as I was concerned, for the intangible, a metaphor. All that remained then was the suffix 'seekers'. The fragile world of the Ark-seeker, I realised, existed by virtue of not finding; his goal always had to remain just beyond reach – this was what kept him going and lent purpose to his life. The Ark-seeker owed his singularity not to the Ark, but to the fact that he was seeking. And what, I was doing, I reckoned, came down to exactly that.

Once the main dish of kebabs with bread and yogurt sauces had been served, the fluorescent lights went out and only the disco lamps remained. The revolving mirror ball in the middle of the ceiling sent small fish swimming across the floor and tablecloths. The aquarium of which we were now a part burst into applause when a man in a leather suit appeared, sat down at the keyboard and launched into a number known as 'Habibi', which Volodya told us meant 'beloved' in Arabic. As soon as the first notes had sounded, out on to the floor came a dancer with wavy black locks, real or wiggish, that fell to her hips. Her stage name was 'Dahlia'; waving her arms like tentacles, she shimmied her way amongst the tables.

To use the evangelists' terminology, we found ourselves in an 'antithetical Ark'. No one, not even the monk Igor, was offended. Russians, as I had come to know them, were no ascetics. We revelled in the loose, worldly atmosphere, and a feeling of brotherhood welled up, a sentiment I knew from Moscow drinking bouts where generals or businessmen would fall weeping into each other's arms. We began asking one another about our loved ones. Volodya had a family and grandchildren and everything, Igor was celibate, and Martin turned out to be an *Einzelganger* by choice, a man who felt there was enough suffering in the world without exposing his own progeny to it as well.

When my turn came and I began talking about my wife and daughter, Igor asked: 'How old is your daughter?'

'Three,' I said. 'Three and a half, to be exact.'

'Well then, don't wait too long,' was his advice.

I laughed and said that we weren't *waiting*.

Igor looked concerned, fatherly. 'It's a shame you and your wife don't live in Moscow any more,' he said. 'I know a spring there that could help you.'

That was what I remembered of the evening before the climb. The next morning, with pain in my muscles and a gluey headache I had succeeded in thinning down somewhat with two aspirins, I took a taxi from my hotel to Camp Murat. In the clear light of day I saw that there was also a shed where Murat rented tents, ice axes, goggles and other climbing equipment. None of the one-man tents were complete, so I had to rummage through them all to come up with a set of tent poles that would fit. As I was trying on crampons, I saw Igor walking towards me. He sat down beside me on the low, sunlit wall, the domes and towers of Isak Pasha Palace looming over

our shoulder. From a case he pulled out a small Soviet-made telescope, a Turist-4, that could magnify objects 10 times. I looked
through it at Doğubayazit in the distance below and praised the
clarity of its lens.

'I need forty dollars for the trip back,' Igor said. 'You would be
helping me greatly if you would buy it for that amount.'

In the clumsy attempt at courtesy that followed I tried to give
him fifty dollars, but he refused. Igor was adamant that I should
keep his spyglass, while I insisted that he put my 50-dollar bill in
his wallet with no strings attached. I said: 'But next year you two
will need it again, won't you?' Only when I told him that he should
consider it a donation to his quest from me and my wife did he
finally give in.

Igor folded the crisp new note and tucked it into a little pouch
on the inside of his belt. Then he pulled out a bulging pocket diary
that served as his address book. There were cards of some sort in
it, which he shuffled through as if considering his hand.

At last he found what he was looking for, a card showing a
fourteenth-century icon of St Nicholas the Gift-giver.

He kissed the card and gave it to me with the words: 'You shall
have a son.'

I took the picture of the icon and put it in my passport. Under
any other circumstances I would have laughed.

The Mountain of Pain

SOMEONE WAS JAMMING needles into my Achilles tendons. The day before, in the Arguri gorge, I hadn't noticed it at all, but now I could feel the boots chafing. Not being keen on anything as primitive as self-castigation (and remembering the advice given me), I pulled the roll of sport tape from my pack in order to protect my heels.

Looking after one's bodily needs was calming: it served as a distraction. From the shade of the walnut tree I saw that the Russian lorry, a Kamaz, which would bring us to the start of the southern route was parked a little further ahead. I was ready.

To kill some time, Martin and I scrambled up the steep path to the pasha's palace. Along with the first tourists of the day, we explored the galleries around the courtyard, the mosque that had been in use until the 1980s, and the private quarters (bathrooms and bedrooms) that had once constituted the harem. All that was missing was the huge gate covered in gold leaf; to see that you had to go to the Hermitage.

As we entered the dining hall we heard voices from the campsite below. The Czechs had arrived in their vans, accompanied by Mehmet.

We found them sitting on the ledge outside Restaurant Murat, holding bottles of cola and mineral water: the group of 17 men and one woman had landed at Van the day before and stayed in a hotel overlooking the lake. They were all wearing fire-engine-red sweaters that read 'Ararat 2005'.

Mehmet, still wearing the same baggy suit, took Martin and me by the arm to introduce us to a man in a feathered hunting cap. His name was Tomáš; he was the leader of the climbers from Prague. He spoke a bit of German, in a high-pitched voice and with obvious pleasure, and Russian, albeit grudgingly. I thought I heard some of the others referring to him as 'the doctor'. He decided that Martin and I were welcome to join their expedition.

Tomáš clapped his hands. 'Come on, let's not waste any more time.'

Bald-headed Hakan was nowhere in sight, and Mehmet went back to his travel agency. Gathering our things, we hoisted ourselves and our packs into the back of the Kamaz. I shot off a text message to my wife to say that for the next four days I would be without a signal.

STRT. BLSTRS. OTHRWS OK. XX, FR V 2.

Standing on our rucksacks, we peered like meerkats over the high edge of the steel container. The guides had not materialised; there was only the driver, who ground the Kamaz into bottom gear and rumbled down the rough and windy road to the plateau outside Doğubayazit. From there we followed the E80, the main highway to Teheran. Little Ararat's snowless cone stood out clearly against the blue sky; as the morning wore on, Great Ararat's white cap had already become wreathed in wispy cloud.

Beside the road the billboards grew more numerous, forerunners to the customs complex at the Iranian border that loomed up on the horizon 15 minutes later.

STY IN 1 PIECE OK? KSSES BCK FRM YR GRLS.

Unexpectedly, our driver took the last exit to the right before Iran, away from Ararat. Martin and I were surprised, until Tomáš explained that we were going to stop at the visitors' centre with the fossil imprint of the Ark. For the Czechs, the trip to the boat-shaped formation was not a pilgrimage, merely a sideshow, something added to the programme. 'We only have to hike three hours today anyway,' Tomáš shouted above the engine's roar. 'And it's better to do that after the heat of the day.'

The road climbed again, presenting us with the view of a treeless plain extending far into Iran. After passing a little group of houses and the umpteenth army barracks, we arrived at a hexagonal building: the welcome centre for those who had come to view 'Noah's Ark'.

We were the only visitors, but the elderly caretaker came hobbling out to help us park. The price of a ticket admitted us to a terrace overlooking the silhouette of the Ark. Without being asked, the caretaker gesticulated with his cane and solemnly assured us that the Bible, the Torah and the Koran were in complete agreement on this point: yonder was the mountain which Christians and Jews alike called Ararat, and these were the hills known to Islam as al-Ğūdī; there was only one Ark, and it lay before us.

What we saw was certainly remarkable: a gentle slope, bearing along its length the scar of two upright walls, eroded with age, that arched away from each other before coming to a point (the bow). It looked as though the ship-shaped contour had slid down here in its entirety.

From the thin chains around the terrace hung signs reading KEEP OUT. In exchange for a tip, however, we were allowed to go closer – to convince ourselves, although it wasn't clear of what.

The clay formation felt moist and was bulging with rocks. A few of us walked around to the other side, purportedly to find the hatch where the animals had entered two by two. There was no entrance to be found, and when we climbed over the wall of earth into the Ark the caretaker whistled loudly at us through his teeth. Back inside the visitors' centre we were received with looks of admonishment. I thought it was because of our trespassing, but he directed us with a glance to a display more worthy of our attention. It contained a few seashells, and brown and grey stones with cards captioned: 'Petrified Wood' and 'Fossilised Coral'. Not a word of it in Turkish, but there was a series of clippings in English, ranging from *Life* magazine (September 1960, the aerial photo) up to and including a recent issue of an American evangelist's newsletter with the headline: 'Government confirms: "This is Noah's Ark".'

On a stand beside the photograph of Atatürk was an open book, a religious volume I assumed at first, but it was the guest book. I added my name and the date to it, but couldn't muster any apt comment. To me, this imprint of the Ark was like the photograph taken by Viking I of face-like shadows on Mars. Odd, but nothing more than that.

Flipping back through the guest book, however, I discovered that the majority of visitors felt differently.

Evidence that demands a confession. I say 'yes', I'm a believer.
Scott & Jean Michael, Maine, USA

Verily, God has left proof that He exists.
Andes Poh, Singapore

These and other professions were written in a firm hand, proud and frank. Others, in sloppier handwriting, had committed jokes to paper. Someone from Haifa had drawn two giraffes in the outlines of the Ark, and a citizen of San Francisco had written in magic marker: 'And God spoke unto Noah: Thou shalt make of the Ark a tourist trap.' I noticed that all the professions of faith were signed, while the mockers remained anonymous.

After an hour's stop, the Kamaz took us on to Ararat. We crossed the E80 and drove – unhindered by roadblocks – up the southern slopes. We saw the farmyards of the hamlet of Eli roll past, and a dilapidated mosque with a tin roof. Rattling its every bolt, the truck continued uphill, out of the village, all the way to a bulldozed pull-off that marked the end of the road. As soon as the tailgate was lowered, we hopped out like fleas, to be welcomed by two brothers, Ferhat and Avdel. A group of about 10 donkeys, their ears held flat against their necks, stood waiting motionless.

Martin's altimeter read 2,435 metres.

As long as I didn't think about my feet, things were looking good; the road between me and the summit of Ararat seemed wide open.

Lunch was waiting, spread out on the bonnet of a white four-wheel-drive with CAMP MURAT painted on the doors. There were wafer-thin loaves of bread (*lavash*), tomato slices, white Persian cheese (*brinza*) and little buckets of honey. While we were dribbling honey on the cheese and tomatoes and rolling it up in bread, the brothers lashed our bags on to the donkeys. Ferhat, a Lucky Strike wedged in the corner of his mouth, tightened the straps. He was wearing a baseball cap, an oversized fleece and a pair of tracksuit bottoms; his brother Avdel wore trodden-down, low-cut shoes.

For a group thrown together like this, we didn't talk much. The silences were long and frequent, precipitated perhaps by the grandeur of the mountain above us. Figuratively, we were sitting on our baggage: the way Russians do to make room for thoughts and emotions before a long journey. It was a way of pausing and allowing the parting to sink in, or of reflecting on the obstacles to come. Stopping and thinking about it made the road ahead seem less endless. Today all we had to do was to follow a series of goat trails to the base camp at 3,200 metres. Tomorrow (Day 2) would be the climb to the approach camp at 4,100 metres, where we would spend Day 3 acclimatising. In the early-morning hours of Day 4 we would push on to the summit. Our arrival, at 5,165 metres, was planned for sunrise. I had painkillers and anti-inflammatories with me, as well as the blister pack of glaucoma medicine that would let me go on for another 12 hours in the event of an oncoming headache, nausea and loss of appetite (the symptoms of altitude sickness). My physical condition was up to snuff; I was well prepared.

When I noticed that my mobile phone still had coverage, I sent a message home. I told them there was a foal going along with us, but that the foal didn't have to carry anything. The reply, which came almost immediately, sounded cheerful: my wife was pleased that we were still in contact, and Vera was beside herself about the foal; she wanted to know what its name was and whether it still drank milk.

The hike to the base camp was not particularly demanding. I could easily have done the whole thing in sandals, but instead I was wearing 'Category D' boots with rigid soles and uppers that had not yet moulded to my feet. While Avdel drove his donkeys out in front, I felt the skin on my heels and ankles grow soft and begin to tear. We had spread out in a long, loose ribbon: one by one, the Czechs began putting on warmer clothes over their sweaters, causing the fire-engine red to change into a growing number of colours as we climbed. Chin up, I told myself, and swore that I would keep it up as well.

We made our first camp on a flat stretch of ground at the foot of a mass of congealed rock. Tents were springing up here and there around me, but I first rolled out my sleeping mat in order to see to my feet. There was no need to puncture the blisters; they were already open. I dissolved two aspirins in the tea Avdel poured from a sooty kettle, and put up my silver dome tent. Only after I had helped myself to a plate of rice and mutton outside Avdel's mess tent and sat down on a boulder beside Tomáš and Ferhat did I notice the sparrows. They were hopscotching back and forth on the withered grass.

There was no wind. The evening was illuminated by an orange globe with just enough voltage to turn Little Ararat a reddish brown. The slopes below us were pocked with miniature volcanic cones; their craters, already in the shadow, looked like the lids of cooking pots.

When I said something about the sparrows, Ferhat told me that this was his twenty-first season as a guide on Ararat; the birds knew by now precisely when and where they might get a grain of rice from him. His grey hair was close-cropped, and he looked as skinny as the cows we had seen grazing around Eli. As soon as his plate was empty he pulled out his cigarettes. Tomáš and I said no thanks, and Ferhat lit one up. Leaning back on his elbows he told us that, back before he became a guide, he climbed this mountain every summer as well – to bring his sheep to pasture. The only difference – and here his grin revealed a set of black and yellow teeth – was that he and Avdel no longer took a flock with them, but a gaggle of climbers.

'And you also go higher these days,' Tomáš added.

'These days we go higher,' Ferhat echoed.

His parents and grandparents had never gone a step beyond 3,200 metres, for that was where the grass stopped.

I asked whether he ever worked for Ark-seekers.

'You bet! For Bob, Dave, Bill . . .' Most of them, he said, were loaded with money. Bob, for example, would spend 15,000 dollars

211

a week without batting an eyelid, but he was also demanding to the point of tyranny. 'Bob wants everything right now, and exactly the way he wants it. If I tell him: "There's a danger of avalanches that way", he says: "So what?"'

Ferhat spoke English in the American manner, forcefully but not rudely, a way of speaking which he had adopted from his clients and now used to take their measure. He told us about an Ark veteran, John McIntosh, who had fallen badly two weeks ago on the east face. Crucially, this American weighed more than 100 kilos; he broke his ankle and could no longer stand. 'An army helicopter had to come and take him away.'

But what did he think of their quest?

'What do you mean?'

'The Ark . . .' I said.

'Come on, they don't care about that.'

Now it was me who felt like asking 'What do you mean?', but Ferhat needed no prompting. He had been guiding them long enough to see that the story about the Ark was merely pretence. In plain view to our left was Iran, Armenia was behind us: the mountain we were on was a strategic bulwark in a geopolitical game. The tip of Ferhat's Lucky Strike glowed brightly as he spoke of the 1980s, when everyone was still worried about the Soviet Union. It was no coincidence that the moonwalker Jim Irwin had been so obsessed with Angel Rock, above the Arguri gorge: that position offered the best views of the Iron Curtain. But as soon as the Soviet Union collapsed, the Ark-seekers stopped coming to the Armenian side. 'Most of them didn't come back for years.'

'They wanted to, but they couldn't,' I said. 'Ararat was closed from 1990 to 1999.'

According to Ferhat, though, that did nothing to undermine his argument. 'Since the attack on the Twin Towers, most expeditions get a visa.' That seemed only logical to him: the American war on terror had turned the border zone around Ararat into strategic terrain once more. The Americans had entered Afghanistan, then Iraq, and it wouldn't be long before it was Iran's turn. 'Once they have a little more time on their hands they'll use that business about nuclear energy to invade Iran too, you'll see.'

Tomáš asked how he could be so sure.

'I told you, didn't I? It's just a matter of keeping an eye on what these Ark-seekers are after.' Ferhat observed evangelists the way a farmer observes flights of swallows. From their manoeuvres he believed he could tell exactly what was going on. Lately, for example, all the Ark-seekers wanted to go to the east face, and preferably to Little Ararat by way of the Iranian border – supposedly because no one had ever looked there before. Last year, one of them, Robert Cornuke, even announced that he wanted to search *inside* Iran. That came as no surprise to Ferhat, having seen a similar shift of focus when Saddam Hussein was chasing the Kurds out of northern Iraq. In the rain and fog, tens of thousands of Kurds had crossed the mountains into Turkey. At the peak of that crisis the Ark-seekers had suddenly decided they needed to be on Mount Cudi, in the thick of where it was happening.

'So you're saying that all Ark-seekers are spies?' I asked.

'Take John, that fat guy who fell a couple of weeks ago. Do you really think that if I broke my ankle, an army helicopter would come to pick me up?'

Ferhat threw away his cigarette butt; the sparrows hopped over to it. Our shadows, and those of the rocks around us, stretched long and thin across the tents.

It wasn't that our guide had anything against Americans per se. 'The only thing a lot of my friends can say is "Yankee go home",' he said. 'They refuse to understand that the Americans are the Kurds' allies.'

The Americans, and nobody else, would see to a free Kurdistan – as a buffer against the Arabs.

Ferhat opened his penknife and used the blade to sketch the impending incursion in the dirt. Future Kurdistan, we saw, would include not only south-eastern Turkey but also parts of what were now Iraq and Iran. 'All we have to do is be patient. Nelson Mandela spent almost thirty years in jail before he became president, and that's the way it will go with Abdullah Öcalan, too.'

When Ferhat talked about the PKK leader who had been held since 1999 as a martyr to the Kurdish cause on a prison island in the Sea of Marmara, he didn't speak in a muted voice, but loudly and clearly. Why did we think our Western governments protested so vehemently against his possible execution? Out of humanitarian concern? Or was it opportunism? 'Someday they're going to need Öcalan,' Ferhat said. 'So you tell me.'

Maybe he was right, maybe he was wrong. Whatever the case, I was fascinated to see that any rusty old point of view could be twisted 90 degrees to make the world seem a very different place indeed. Mehmet's unabashed 'Welcome to Free Kurdistan' had set my mental wheels in motion, and they hadn't stopped since. 'We'll have to surrender Ararat to the Armenians,' Ferhat concluded in a tone that suggested the decision was up to him.

Talk of Armenia and the inevitable Armenian question called for another cigarette. Ferhat spoke of 'crimes' that put the Turks to shame. 'Did you notice the bulldozing equipment along the road to Isak Pasha Palace?' he asked.

We had: the Kamaz had been forced to wait repeatedly for men in fluorescent orange vests. While widening the road, our guide told us, the workmen had stumbled upon an unmarked grave, probably from 1915. He said it was an open secret that the remains were those of Armenians, but that you couldn't talk about that in Turkey.

Now Ferhat lowered his voice at last. The authorities, he said, had ordered them to simply lay asphalt over the grave. That's how it happened in Turkey. But as soon as the borders were redrawn, super-powers like France and America, which had absorbed the largest part of the diaspora, would provide compensation for Armenia. In Ferhat's view, if you added it all up there was only one possible outcome: an independent Kurdistan for the Kurds, Ararat for the Armenians and a Turkey that remained intact from head to torso, from Ankara to Istanbul.

Tomáš remarked that there would then be no more work for him as a guide on Ararat.

Ferhat grinned. 'I've already thought about that. I'll go and work on Mount Cudi,' he said.

*   *   *

The chill rising from Ararat's stony soil drove us into our tents. I brushed my teeth and nestled into 800 grams of eiderdown. Before falling asleep, I switched on my headtorch and jotted down what I had just heard. I headed it 'Ferhat's Sermon on the Mount'.

Instead of putting away my notebook, I read back through what I'd written in the last few days. I had carefully recorded the facts, such as the geology of the Arguri gorge, but not a word of what had affected me personally. That came as something of a shock, and I forced myself to think about what exactly I had come to do on Ararat. Why was I so intent on reaching the summit? What was I trying to prove?

Leaning on one elbow, the headtorch still in place, it dawned on me that I had set out on my journey with the wrong idea. I was not an unbeliever climbing a holy mountain in his fortieth year to establish whether there was anything true or valuable about the faith of his childhood. It was different: by conquering Ararat I was testing myself to see whether I could leave that legacy behind. And whether I wanted to. I was inclined to rely on knowledge and science – things that existed undeniably. Beyond the veil of the tabernacle there was nothing, and along Ararat's snowline were no angels with swords of fire. With my passage to the summit I would convince myself that, when push came to shove, I put my faith in reason: I would not stumble over a chunk of gopher-wood.

Day 2 began with a dazzling sunrise. Ararat's icecap stood out against a cloudless sky. Through the binoculars you could make out a little outcrop of rock in the distance, just below the snowline: the spot where we would set up our attack camp.

As we climbed that morning, wisps of mist rose from the valley, moving quickly and light-footedly along the scree slopes; at the same time, I had the less-than-glorious feeling that the pain in my heels was rising as well, pounding and piling up in my sinuses. An ascent of almost a full kilometre took its toll on one's knees, thighs, spleen and lungs – and caused static in the perceptual antennae. Sweetened tea helped. I knew I should eat something, but couldn't for the life of me.

Clouds moved in and the temperature dropped. The mountaineer's rule of thumb is that it grows one degree colder for every 100 metres climbed, and by the time we reached 4,100 metres, nothing remained of the season's heat. The air was not quite freezing, but almost. Everyone had put on gloves and ski hats, except for Avdel, who was stoically heating a pan of rice on the gas burner.

The area around base camp had been wide enough for a game of football, but at the high camp space was at a premium. Spread out over a hillock in the shape of an emaciated shoulder, about 15 pitches had been levelled, each just big enough for a tent. Amid the rocks, a few steps away from a precipice, I found a place for my Pole Star. Rolling down to the left and right were endless slopes of rugged pumice and basalt. Above us the snowfields protruded from under the hem of cloud like dull, tattered rags. Everything looked grey and black; we had entered the realm of nature from which all colour is drained. Words like 'pretty' or 'beautiful' no longer applied; you could taste nature's hostility in the dryness of the wind that formed crusts on your lips.

Avdel's rice didn't appeal to me. To get something into my stomach, I took a piece of bread and some grainy brinza. The honey I tried to pour over it had coagulated.

It was still only around four in the afternoon, but the guides themselves barely took the time to eat. Ferhat urged everyone to have their fill and go to bed with a full stomach. 'Eat and sleep' was the motto. Why all the hurry, I wondered, if we were going to stay here for 24 hours? When I asked Tomáš, it turned out that he and Ferhat had devised a different plan. He repeated to me what he had already told his countrymen in Czech: a storm front was on its way across the Caspian. In order to beat the weather, we were going to skip our day of acclimatisation. The take-it-easy plan, intended to improve our chances of success, had been exchanged for a plan of attack. We would start for the summit at two in the morning: five hours to the top, four of them in darkness, ten minutes on the peak, then two hours back.

'You do have a headtorch, don't you?'

'Yes,' I said. 'But what worries me is altitude sickness.'

'Oh, but you can beat that too,' Tomáš said with what was meant to be an encouraging wink. To calm my fears he told me that he was a doctor, a specialist at an impecunious state hospital, true enough, but a doctor first and foremost. 'It always takes a few hours for an organism to develop altitude sickness. Who knows, maybe by that time we'll already be making our descent.'

As I crawled into my tent around 4.30 p.m., I thought: right, here we go. The easy part was behind us, tonight would be the real thing.

Inside my dome I plastered my heels with the soluble bandages called 'second skin', then taped them again. After that, because I'd heard that Ferhat had called to receive the latest weather report, I checked my phone. One of the five little green stripes was still bouncing up and down on the screen; I was at the very limit of mobile phone coverage. Purely because I could, I punched out a message, letter by letter.

CAMP 2 4100 M. NRBY SNW & CLDS. NO TRBL W/ALT SCKNES. TMRRW SMMIT. XX F.

The little contraption tried to establish a connection, but told me: FAILED/SAVED IN UNSENT MESSAGES. I pressed the button again and again but it didn't help. I kept trying doggedly, until, half an hour later, MESSAGE SENT suddenly appeared on the screen.

Just as tensely, I waited for a reply, but instead it began hailing.

The rattle on the tent cloth sounded at first like distant applause, but soon grew to the roar of a lorry emptying a load of gravel. This was not normal, and it was only getting louder. I lay flat on my back to better register the slightest changes in pitch and intensity. I noticed that you could detect a change in the size of the hailstones, or in the angle at which the gusts sent them whipping down. There was a rumble of thunder, followed by the vague growl of a storm cloud knocking about on the slopes. I was expecting flashes of lightning, but none came. When the strongest gusts hit the tent I tensed, bracing myself for that one faster-than-the-eye movement that would rip the nylon from over my head. But my tent did not rip, nor did it crash to the ground. After a while (15 minutes? an hour?), darkness settled in, and I resigned myself to the situation.

Pushing a button to light up my phone's display, I saw that the bouncing green bar had dozed off to a static dot. Okay, I told myself, it's only a hailstorm.

The irritating thing was that I hadn't counted on getting through to my wife and daughter. But now that there was a reply from them floating around out there, I was determined to receive it. This was absurd: here I was, lying under a dome in a cloud at 4,100 metres, clutching a dead telephone.

I began fantasising about the questions Vera might have asked in her text message.

'Are clouds hard or soft?' (Clouds are soft as velvet, but the hail that falls from them is hard as rock.)

'Where's the little foal sleeping?' (Good question.)

Three and a half years ago I had cut her umbilical cord. From that moment on she had steadily explored and expanded the world around her, in the last few months with questions that drilled deeper and deeper into bedrock. One evening when she had been unable to sleep, I had sat down beside her with a little jar of sleeping cream. 'Close your eyes and put your arms straight down on both sides,' I said, 'and now breathe slowly.'

'Papa,' she said after a while, her eyes still closed, 'the person who was born first, whose belly did he come from?'

What, I asked myself, was the half-life of purity? Was it possible to recreate it on laboratory scale, and, if so, how long would it remain stable?

That the hail had made way for snow I noticed only when the canvas began bulging in at the sides, and I had to knock it back into shape.

Sleep was out of the question. My bladder was slowly filling with tea, but going outside to pee would be too much of an ordeal. The mere thought of it kept me awake, and so the circuits in my head ran round and round. An eternity later, at one in the morning, I heard Ferhat's voice. We had 45 minutes to be ready, and those minutes went by very quickly. Pulling on climbing gear within such tight confines was hard work. Just from the neck up I wore a ski hat, a hood, a pair of goggles and a miner's lamp on a terry-cloth headband. Dangling close to my lips was the nozzle of my 'camel bag'; its tea-filled reservoir was on my back, between the muesli and chocolate bars. Drinking was more important than eating now, and it also helped to ward off altitude sickness.

I slid out of the tent feet-first. It was dark, but there was light reflecting off the snowy ground. The fog was so thick that a second grey dome appeared to have been lowered over my tent. The snow was still falling; I was a tiny figurine in a glass paperweight that had just been shaken.

The freezing cold closed over my nose and mouth like a dust cap. Climbing to Ferhat and Avdel's tent I saw that other bundles of light had gathered there as well. No one said a word until Ferhat announced that our departure would be delayed by one hour because of the fog. Then the beams that had been cast hither and thither over the rocks and snow went tramping off in all directions and disappeared into scattered tents. I walked back towards mine, but found myself standing at the edge of a cliff. With no one else in sight, all I could do was retrace my steps. 30, 50 metres at most. This time, without having seen a tent anywhere, I arrived at another steep drop. I felt flushed, and began talking to myself. I thought about shouting for help, but what would I say – that I had lost my way, 10 paces from my own tent? If necessary, I reasoned, I could wait outside for an hour. That was an option. Picking out another set of footprints, I stumbled upon a small tunnel tent that had been immediately above my Pole Star. I slid down over a rock and found myself at the awning of my own igloo.

Once inside, still fully dressed and shivering, I lay listening to the sound of my own breathing, until at three o'clock a voice echoed through the camp: departure postponed till five.

I must have fallen asleep, for at a certain point daylight woke me. It was a quarter to eight, Monday morning, 5 September 2005. There were no voices, and my first thought was: they've left without me. I wrestled my way out of the tent and, to my relief, glimpsed a shape just as it disappeared into the fog.

It had stopped snowing; the layer that had fallen last night creaked beneath my boots. Further up on the shoulder of rock I found Ferhat and Tomáš holding steaming mugs of tea. They were talking about the weather; in summer, the layer of cloud around Ararat was supposed to disperse at night. Normally the sky cleared before midnight, and remained clear until around eight in the morning. Last night had been the exception. Apparently the storm front had already reached Ararat and the upshot was that we would indeed wait here for 24 hours.

'So we're going to get to acclimatise after all,' Tomáš said.

Nothing was lost this way, it simply meant we were reverting to Plan A. But how often could you rev yourself up for a test of strength?

Back in my tent I took off my mittens and peeled away my coat, windbreaker and down vest. My feet were getting a day off. I ate and drank from my climbing provisions and fell asleep again, only to awaken with a start two hours later at the sound of shouting, this time in Czech. I recognised Tomáš's high-pitched voice. He was clapping his gloved hands and shouting words that sounded like vague echoes of the Russian for 'we're going' and 'twenty minutes'.

It was 10.45 in the morning when we made our belated early start. Luck had it that the fog had lifted suddenly, allowing us to see for hundreds of metres across the white slopes. Besides Martin and myself, 14 of the 18 Czechs were going for the summit. Four were staying behind; they had headaches and were feeling nauseous. Ferhat took the lead, Avdel would bring up the rear.

There was no path, no tracks to follow either; the group cut its way through the snow. We walked straight into another cloud, which enveloped us with cold. It began snowing again, lightly at first. By taking regular steps I could establish a rhythm that numbed the pain in my heels. I didn't notice when two of the Czechs turned around and went back half an hour later. Avdel led them to the high camp, then caught up with us again.

From a distance, a mountaineering expedition might look like an exercise in collective will, but that's only an illusion. None of us had anyone to rely on but ourselves. The trick was to match your

220

movements to your breathing. Every disturbance (a slip of the foot, a rock to be scrambled over) taxed your strength. If you paused to mutter an oath too, your body lost just a little extra energy into the bargain.

The whole problem was one of thin air, of the oxygen debt that only grew worse the higher you climbed.

Our human chain clambered up through a tunnel of drabness, a chute through which the snowflakes blew into your face like debris from a building site. The first time we stopped to drink I saw that Tomáš's ring-shaped moustache and beard were covered in frost. The cold was only noticeable when we stood still, and had it been up to me we would have pushed on to the top in one go. I was finding it increasingly difficult to get back into the rhythm of the climb. Counting helped. I started reciting multiplication tables and doing sums, which after a while made way for images and thoughts. Fernand Navarra came to mind, the Frenchman who had begun to see before him the Stations of the Cross in the cathedral at Padua as he approached the 5,000-metre level. He had compared Ararat with Golgotha – and himself with Jesus. Other climbers had seen Noah before them the whole way, and spoke of the incredible sensation of following in his footsteps. With suitable deference, even down-to-earth Friedrich Parrot had claimed to be the first man to conquer Ararat *since Noah*. But of all my illustrious predecessors one in particular stood out: the British diplomat Sir James Bryce. In 1876, he had stumbled upon a weathered piece of wood in a crevasse high above the treeline. It was 1.2 metres long, and clearly fashioned by human hands; stunned, Bryce fell to his knees – beside the walking stick that Parrot had left as part of his cross on top of Ararat half a century earlier.

And what about me – what was I experiencing? No glorious emotions or sublime insights; I needed every ounce of energy I had just to climb on.

Close to an overhanging rock on which someone had painted the words 4,810 M – MONT BLANC, we took a five-minute break. I sucked on the mouthpiece of my camel bag, but to no avail. The tube was blocked with frozen tea. The Czechs were carrying flasks; I had to pull my professional drinking bag out of my backpack and unscrew the top. As soon as I removed my mittens, I felt my fingers stiffen. What was more important: getting some warm tea into my stomach, or protecting my fingers against the chill at $-15°$? In my haste I dropped a mitten, which immediately slid a few metres down the snowy slope. Cursing the camel bag, I hopped down to fetch the mitten, and as I picked it up I remembered the advice of the saleswoman at the mountaineering shop: tie them together with a length of cord and run that through the sleeves of your coat, the way they do at nursery school. 'At five thousand metres, losing a mitten can be fatal,' she had said.

There's no sense panicking over something you haven't even lost, I told myself. The crucial thing was to restore the equilibrium in my head. We had one more hour and two difficult sections to go. The first was what they called 'the Ox's Hole' – a ravine we would have to circle carefully, one foot in front of the other. The second was a steep, at some spots almost vertical barrier of ice (in fact, a side wall of the Parrot Glacier) just below 5,100 metres. Past those, you found yourself on the slanted plateau beneath the summit, and all your troubles were over.

We surmounted Mont Blanc. Besides the mental and physical difficulty of getting underway, the maddening oxygen shortage now began taking its toll. I panted more deeply, bent over further as I walked, and began to feel a ringing sensation in my head. To keep moving I began reciting prime numbers, and calculating π to as many decimal places as I could. That helped me get back into the groove; my thoughts began fluttering off again in all directions, then circling around my daughter. I remembered how she used the term 'counting-letters' for numbers, and thought about how she had handed language to me anew. Vera helped me to savour new words, dipped in the primal soup from which they arose. Counting-letters, a beautiful word like that from her own lips, *that* for me was the miracle made flesh before which I would willingly fall to my knees. She had conjured it up, out of the void. Now it existed and had taken on real significance, for it uplifted me.

This, as far as I was concerned, belonged to the realm beyond comprehension. There were some things off which the concept of 'explanation' only ricocheted, things that were immune to unravelling or to clarification. It's that simple, I told myself. It pleased me to be able to acknowledge that. Religion provided set forms for what might be hidden within the sphere of the unknowable, I realised, but the forms themselves were arbitrary. I preferred to rely on my own imagination.

Beside the Ox's Hole at 4,950 metres, Ferhat was waiting for us. The hole turned out to be a chute that slid off almost vertically into the void. We had to skirt it one by one. As long as you kept your eyes ahead and didn't look down, there was no reason to lose your balance. Ferhat led the way in order to stamp down the snow. Martin followed, then Tomáš, then two of the Czechs. Avdel nodded that it was my turn. As soon as I started the traverse I knew that, despite my fear of heights, I would look down into the Ox's Hole anyway. It didn't make me falter – 50 metres down, the rollercoaster slope ended in a fogbank that looked soft as a safety net.

Once past the Hole, I was overtaken by a euphoria that erased the pain in my head and heels. The gradient grew steeper, our steps smaller. We headed out on to the ice but had no need for crampons; the fresh snow was firm enough footing, and more of it was falling all the time. I noticed that I had gone back to simply counting. No more mathematical series, no more calculations, just 1,2,3,4 . . .

The wall of the Parrot Glacier was less steep than I had imagined. We didn't have to climb straight up it either, but were able to traverse along a kind of rough stairway of ice, the steps of which Ferhat chopped out with his ice axe. It was slow going; after each step I rested my hands on my knees, drew in three deep gulps of air, then took the next. About three-quarters of the way up that sloping ladder I suddenly grew confused. First, out of the corner of my eye, I saw that four or five climbers had remained behind, then I heard screaming from up above. With only a couple of metres to go, I saw that the men already on the plateau were bending over strangely. Or, more accurately: they were doubled over and waiting.

The moment my head poked above the edge of the ice, I had the breath knocked out of me. Snow was whipping into my face, and I had to shinny up on to Ararat's roof. When I tried to get to my feet, the gale-force wind knocked me back again. This was like my old, recurring nightmare about finding myself alone on the top deck of the tower block on Speenkruidstraat, 11 storeys up and being blown closer and closer to the edge by the approaching storm.

I saw Ferhat waving as though signalling a plane to stop on the runway. 'This is the end,' his arms waved. 'We're going back.'

But the Czechs were having none of it. The rolling plateau started at just under 5,100 metres, its apex was a good church steeple's height above that. I saw them put their heads together, then turn to the guide. They had no intention of giving up, and neither did I. Hands pointed: over there the field of ice swept up a little higher, that was where we needed to be. Despite the fog, the piercing cold and the horizontal onslaught of snow, none of us even dreamed of turning back. We were going for the summit, and that was at 5,165 metres.

Ferhat gave in; shoulders hunched, he began carving out a new path, away from the icy ridge. The gently sloping fields of white looked like snow dunes; first we climbed a little, then went down the other side. It was impossible to fix a course. No one had brought a compass. The wind, now slicing at an angle from in front of us, was the only thing indicating a direction.

Fifteen minutes later, Ferhat turned around. His face was smothered almost completely by his lined hood. Leaning back into the wind like a helmsman, he shouted again: 'This is it!'

Our guide wanted to start the descent right away, but Martin held up his altimeter for us to see: 5,105 metres. This was not it, not yet.

The summit lay 60 metres higher, and within reach. The Czechs protested again. Look, the field of white went a little higher over there! But Ferhat refused to go on. He pointed to the tracks we'd made; in half an hour there would be nothing left of those knee-deep holes, and we might go on wandering up here for eternity.

I saw Tomáš doing his best to persuade his countrymen, and realised it was all over, for me too.

Turning away, I stared for a minute or more at the sight of fresh snow erasing my footprints. The holes were filling with white powder at a furious pace, swept smooth with the field of ice all around.

Acknowledgements

W<small>HILE WORKING ON</small> this book, I came to see the Flood story as a vast carpet still stretched upon its loom. The epic poets of Mesopotamia started it, once upon a time, and gave it many variegated motifs of their own. Centuries later, the monotheistic priests picked up the thread and added the black bands of human sinfulness. They reduced the plethora of gods to that One, lone God.

Since then, both literature and the visual arts have embroidered endlessly upon these themes; that, in the end, is what I have also tried to do, to take part in the weaving of something that will last longer than I will.

The sources I consulted in doing so have been mentioned only briefly in the main text, often without information concerning their origins. Hence the following.

An indispensable reference work and primary source was the Bible, in the edition published by the Nederlandsch Bijbelgenootschap (Amsterdam, 1975), and for the purposes of the English translation, the King James Version.

The quotes from the Epic of Gilgamesh were taken from the translation by Maureen Kovacs (Stanford University Press, Palo Alto, 1989). In the same breath I would like to mention *Assyrian Discoveries*, by the man who unearthed the Epic, George Smith (London, 1875). A discussion of Smith's archaeological finds can be found in two publications from the British Museum: *The Babylonian Story of the Deluge and the Epic of Gilgamesh* (London, 1929) and *The Babylonian Legend of the Flood* (London, 1961). The

Flood story as told by Ovid can be found in Book 1 of his *Metamorphoses*.

Among the works on the Flood important to me were: *Noah's Ark and the Ziusudra epic* by Robert M. Best (Enlil Press, Fort Myers, 1999), *Noah, the Person and the Story in History and Tradition* by Lloyd R. Bailey (University of South Carolina Press, Columbia, 1989), *Noah's Flood, the Genesis Story in Western Thought* by Norman Cohn (Yale University Press, New Haven, 1996) and *When the Great Abyss Opened, Classic and Contemporary Readings of Noah's Flood* by J. David Pleins (Oxford University Press, New York, 2003).

Of the novels in which the Flood theme plays a role and which inspired me, most directly in formulating the experience expressed in the first paragraph of page 176, special mention must go to Julian Barnes' *A History of the World in 10½ Chapters* (London,1990) and Yann Martel's *Life of Pi* (Edinburgh, 2004). The autobiographical *Passage to Ararat* by Michael J. Arlen (New York, 1975) also fascinated me and provided food for thought. The comment in the chapter entitled 'Buzdağ' about Man recoiling from his deepest reflections was inspired by Jan Willem Otten's *Specht en zoon* (Van Oorschot, Amsterdam, 2004).

The book by Salomon Kroonenberg spoken of here as a manuscript, with the working title *Yesterday, Today was Tomorrow*, is now creating a public furore under the title *De menselijke maat, de aarde over tienduized jaar* (Atlas, Amsterdam, 2006). I also consulted the collection of Kroonenberg's columns and essays published as *Stop de continenten!* (Lingua Terrae, Amsterdam, 1996).

The two editions of Friedrich Parrot's travel accounts compared and commented upon are *Reise zum Ararat* (Brockhaus, Leipzig, 1985) and a facsimile edition of *Journey to Ararat* (New York, 1885). Biographical information about Friedrich Parrot was taken from Marianne and Werner Stams' epilogue to *Reise zum Ararat,* and from *Der Dorpater Professor Georg Friedrich Parrot und Kaiser Alexander I* by Friedrich Bienemann (Reval, 1902). Concerning Parrot's contemporary, Hermann Abich, I found biographical details in the article entitled 'Hermann Wilhelm Abich im Kaukasus: Zum zweihundertsten Geburtstag' by Ilse and Eugen Seibold, as published in *International Journal of Earth Sciences* (2006, pp.1087–1100).

Among the twentieth-century travel accounts of particular use to me were: *Journey to Armenia* by Osip Mandelstam (with a fore-word by Bruce Chatwin, London, 1980), *The Red Flag at Ararat* by A.Y. Yeghenian (New York, 1932) and *Kapoot, the Narrative of a Journey from Leningrad to Mount Ararat in Search of Noah's Ark* by Carveth Wells (New York, 1933). Fernand Navarra's books from the 1950s deal exclusively with his attempts to find the Ark; I had recourse to the English translation, *The Forbidden Mountain* (London, 1956; original title: *L'Expédition au Mont Ararat*), and the German, *Ich fand die Arche Noah, mit Weib und Kind zum Ararat* (Darmstadt, 1957; original title: *J'ai trouvé l'Arche de Noé*).

Other works by Ark-seekers, or about the search for the Ark in general, were: *The Quest for Noah's Ark* by John Warwick Montgomery (Minneapolis, 1972), *The Lost Ship of Noah* by Charles Berlitz (New York, 1987), *The Explorers of Ararat*, compiled by B.J. Corbin (Long Beach, 1999) and *The Ark, a Reality?* (New York, 1984) and *Quest for Discovery* (Green Forest, 2001), both by Richard C. Bright.

The inner world of Ark-seeker and moonwalker Jim Irwin is explored in the following works: *To Rule the Night, the discovery voyage of astronaut Jim Irwin*, written with ghostwriter William E. Emerson (Philadelphia, 1973), *More than Earthlings, an astronaut's thoughts on Christ-centered living*, published under Irwin's own name (Nashville, 1983) and *More than an Ark on Ararat*, written with another ghostwriter, Monte Unger (Nashville, 1985). The autobiography of his wife Mary Irwin, as told to Madelene Harris, bears the title *The Moon is not Enough, an astronaut's wife finds peace with God and herself* (Grand Rapids, 1978).

The book mentioned in the text as *The Flood: In the Light of the Bible, Geology and Archaeology* by Alfred Rehwinkel was published in Dutch as *De zondvloed, in het licht van de Bijbel, geologie en de archeologie* (Buijten & Schipperheijn, in cooperation with the Reformed Books Publishing Foundation, Amsterdam, 1971). Recent collections dealing with 'intelligent design' were *En God beschikte een worm: over schepping en evolutie* (Ten Have, Kampen, 2006), and an earlier work, *Schitterend ongeluk of sporen van een ontwerp?*

Over toeval en doelgerichtheid in de evolutie (Ten Have, Kampen, 2005), both compiled and edited by Cees Dekker et al.

The Bosporus theory discussed here is described in *Noah's Flood, the New Scientific Discoveries about the Event that Changed History* by William Ryan and Walter Pitman (New York, 1988). One of the critical counter-studies undermining Ryan and Pitman's theory was published as 'Statistical analysis and re-interpretation of the early Holocene Noah's Flood hypothesis' by Ali Aksu et al., in the *Review of Paleobotany and Palynology* (Elsevier, volume 128, 2004).

The scientific dispute between Arkadi Karachanian's team and their opponents led by Rouben Haroutiunian was dealt with in 2006 in the *Journal of Volcanology and Geothermal Research* (Elsevier, volume 155, 2006) under the title 'Historical Volcanoes of Armenia and adjacent areas revisited'. Among earlier publications by Arkadi Karachanian used by the author were 'Volcanic hazards in the region of the Armenian Nuclear Power Plant', in the *Journal of Volcanology and Geothermal Research* (Elsevier, volume 126, 2003) and 'Active faulting and natural hazards in Armenia, eastern Turkey and north-west Iran', in *Tectonophysics* (Elsevier, volume 380, 2004). An important but less recent source concerning Ararat's geology was 'Die gegenwärtige Vergletscherung des Ararat' by N.A. van Arkel in *Zeitschrift für Gletscherkunde und Glazialgeologie* (Salzburg, 1973).

The thesis by my former mathematics teacher Wolter Knol is entitled *Generalizations of Two Relations in Bessel Function Theory* (Groningen, 1970).

General background information about Ararat's surroundings was taken from, among other sources, Neil Ascherson's *Black Sea, the Birthplace of Civilisation and Barbarism* (London, 1995), *Imperium* by Ryszard Kapuscinski (London, 1995) and *Ararat* by Sen Hovhannisyan (Yerevan, 2004). August Thiry and his book *Mechelen aan de Tigris* (Mechelen, 2001) drew my attention to the former Noah celebrations held on Mount Cudi in south-east Turkey, as described by the British archaeologist Gertrude Bell in *Amurath to Amurath* (London, 1911).

With regard to the history of the Armenians, I learned a great deal from *The Crossing Place, A Journey among the Armenians* by Philip Marsden (London, 1994); *Armenia* by Gevorg Oganesian, a propaganda publication from the series *Socialist Republics of the Soviet Union* (Moscow, 1987); *Armenië*, from the country series published by the Netherlands Royal Institute for the Tropics, written by Stan Termeer and Elmira Zeynalian (Amsterdam, 2000), and *Met vallen en opstaan, de Armeense gemeenschap in Nederland; wat daaraan voorafging* by Beatrice Demirdjian (Amsterdam, 1983). The quote from Movses Chorenatsi, 'the Armenian Herodotus', was taken from *History of the Armenians*, translated by and with commentary from Robert W. Thomson (London, 1978). The speech quoted from in the text was delivered in 1903 in Berlin by the philosopher Georges Brandes (born under the name Morris Cohen in Copenhagen in 1842), and republished in the 2 July 2005 edition of the *Frankfurther Allgemeine Zeitung*. I consulted many sources concerning the 'Armenian question', including the Dutch *De marteling der Armeniers in Turkije, naar berichten van ooggetuigen* (Haarlem, 1918).

In addition to these historical reference works, I discovered insights and facts about Turkey in novels such as *Portrait of a Turkish Family* by Irfan Orga (London, 2002) and *The Legend of Ararat* by Yashar Kemal (London, 1975). The books of Orhan Pamuk were, for me, experiences of another order. I revelled in *The New Life* (New York, 1997), *My Name is Red* (New York, 2001), *Snow* (London, 2004) and *Istanbul: Memories & The City* (London, 2005).

Among the books that served to whet my thinking on the phenomenon of religion, pride of place goes to *Het krediet van het credo; godsdienst, ongeloof, katholicisme* by Ger Groot (Sun, Amsterdam, 2006) and *The Twilight of Atheism; the Rise and Fall of Disbelief in the Modern World* by Alister McGrath (London, 2004). *Walking the Bible* by Bruce Feiler (London, 2005) also provided a welcome overview.

A glorious exploration of the spiritual world of the mountaineer is found in Robert MacFarlane's *Mountains of the Mind* (London, 2003). The same applies, albeit in a very different way, to *Into the*

Wild by Jon Krakauer (New York, 1997). The 'climbing guide' I used on Ararat bears the title *Mount Ararat Region, Guide and Map* (Reading, 2004).

The mountaineer who provided me with advice and assistance is Rozemarijn Janssen. About her ascents of peaks including Aconcagua and Mount McKinley she wrote *Stappen tellen naar de top* (Kosmos, Utrecht, 2003). I found interesting background information about mudwalking ('horizontal mountain climbing') in the book *Wadlopen*, compiled by Jan Niemeijer (Triangel, Haren, 1973).

In addition to Rozemarijn Janssen, who was always ready with suggestions and encouragements on the subject of mountain-climbing, I would like to thank the many others who provided me with behind-the-scenes support: Jan Abrahamse and Ties Hazenberg, who introduced me to the history of mudwalking; Kees Bronsveld, the water polo player who described to me the tragic circumstances of the fatal hike with Third World students in 1980; Yade Kara, author of the award-winning debut *Selam Berlin* (Zurich, 2003), for her insights into and anecdotes about Turkish traditions related to the Flood; Artush Mkrtsyan and Tatevik Tovasian from Gyumri, who guided me along the Armenian–Turkish border; Pieter Waterdrinker, Moscow-based writer, who showed me things during my 1999 trip to Armenia that would otherwise have escaped my notice; Robert Brinkman, who loaned me his personal 'Deluge archive'; Patricia Kaersenhout, who sent me a passage about the Flood story among the Masai taken from *Zonen van Cham* by Paul Julien (Scheltens & Giltay, Amsterdam, 1950); the Russian Ark-seekers Vladimir Shatayev and Igor Yakovlev, who granted me access to the unpublished account of their travels; the Dutch Ark-seeker Gerrit Aalten, who spoke to me at some length at the foot of Ararat, and has since sent me a great deal of material; Tomáš Petrák for generously offering to include me in the 2005 Ararat expedition he had organised; and Antheunis Janse, headmaster of the Christelijke Schoolgemeenschap Vincent van Gogh in Assen, who succeeded in unearthing for me the 1961 directive for teachers on the subject of 'controversial issues'.

My sincere thanks also go to those others who are mentioned in this book. The names of a few of them have been changed – at their own request, and for reasons of privacy and, in some cases, their own safety. I deeply appreciate their help, suggestions and direct contributions. In addition I would like to thank those to whom I could always turn with questions and doubts, and who finally gave their critical and insightful comments on the manuscript: Hans Bleumink, Salle Kroonenberg, Emile Brugman and especially Suzanna Jansen. I am very grateful for the role played by my parents, Piet and Riet Westerman, and my sister Moniek Westerman, who – without asking for it – were involved in this book directly and from my own idiosyncratic point of view: not casually, but in such a way that they have become a part of it.

Interwoven with this book like no others, to my great joy, are Suzanna Jansen and Vera Adinde Westerman.

Amsterdam, 4 January 2007